# HOUSE OF ELISE

## ONCE UPON A DJ...

# HOUSE OF ELISE

## ONCE UPON A DJ...

# NIKKI ELISE

# FOREWORD

I've worked with Nikki a lot over the years, be it interviews or on DJ line-ups together. I'm proud to know her as a fellow strong female in the industry and I'm really looking forward to this book being launched. I know it will help others who are embarking on their own musical journey.

Amber D

# PREFACE

For fifteen years I was one of the most successful and high-profile presenter DJs based across the East of England, but reaching Wales and the Southwest, and Ibiza as well as playing a stack of venues in between and in London.

I was an average young woman working through life's big question: what should I do with my entire future? When I finally gathered up the courage to chase my true ambition, I turned all my focus sharply onto my dream career in presenting. Nothing else would do.

Now, drag your mind back (if you are old enough) to a time before the internet existed, with very few avenues into this occupation throughout all four surrounding counties. This was a major challenge from where I lived in the middle of straw-covered fields. Some had pigs or potatoes, although I'm impartial on planting!

If you want to present today, right now at this very minute, you can simply pick up your phone, place it in your hand and upload almost any video onto a multitude of global platforms whilst eating your bagel! But in the late 1990s the internet had not yet splattered across the world or hit your office desk. Big dreams like mine were far from the reach of ordinary people outside of big city life.

From an early teenage obsession discovering rave cassettes tapes and playing The Prodigy CDs on repeat, astonishingly, I turned it all into a massive career! That was a surprise even to me! From 1999 spanning right through the decade of dance, we were the UK's 'house music generation'.

Driven by determination and passion, I became a renowned and respected music icon based in the East but working with international DJs and labels. Every single record label that put out great tracks was on board with my show, *House of Elise*, and that was just the evening show! There were many more.

With sweat dripping from the ceiling, I lived, breathed and delivered endless DJ sets and radio shows as well as skipping back and forth to work and party in Ibiza as much as physically possible.

At the same time my other skill set is property. I bought, managed, renovated and even built a house! House and houses, presenting and property. That's me! It was all going meticulously to plan until I was so rudely interrupted by total disaster. When the door slams firmly in your face, what are you going to do? Ultimately, you must evolve.

It's my ever-changing lifetime of opposites, including deciding to stop and become a parent, which turned out to be the hardest job of them all, except no one tells you that.

Why were there no warnings? Perhaps like road traffic signs or a high vis jacket… anything really! It's vital to me that we can laugh together, otherwise I couldn't see the point of writing the book!

During my media time working for Vibe FM and KISS FM, the question people asked the most and still ask me to this very day is, how did you get into that? So, this is my story in my own words of before, during and what comes after your club days are over. Once it's all gone, your dreams shatter and you hang up your headphones for good, what would you do?

It's the road I walked through rejection, challenges and change with enormous highs and hideous burnout lows, all neatly packed within these little pages.

Join me on my wild ride, won't you?

Nikki Elise x

# CONTENTS

# PROLOGUE

It's Friday 15 June 2007 and after my radio show I'm driving 275 miles (ish) to Wales. A day or so before this, I realised this road trip was going to be long and lonely. I decided to take action and called for back-up. After searching my friend bank of who might actually rock up with me and be away for most of the weekend, I called Dave.

'Hi, Dave. Do you want to come to Wales with me this weekend for Escape into the Park?'

'Yes,' said Dave.

He's a great friend. Everyone should have a mate called Dave! He works with me on my specialist evening show, compiling the music news and sometimes puts in a guest DJ mix. I have known him for ten years or so as he was around in my clubbing days. I think our first real meeting was at Gatecrasher's Summer Sound System, their outdoor event in sprawling fields under the sun with about 10,000 other people.

On Friday morning I'd arrived at the studio as usual around 9.30 a.m. to plan, write and broadcast my show for 12 to 3 p.m. It was KISS 105-108 in the East of England but mine was the only networked show, meaning lunchtimes were simultaneously transmitted on our other sister station KISS 101, Wales and the Southwest. So, both east and west sides are my transmission areas for presenting and including events. London's KISS 100 (KISS FM) runs independent programming, hosting their own separate shows.

I presented my show and then afterwards I walked across a mighty divide, two metres of carpet, into the spare studio. I recorded some voice drops and audio bits to be ready on the system for on-air weekend promotions. So, along with all the other presenters, I can be heard on other shows, so a bit of me seeps into your subconscious when I'm not even there. It's cross promotion. I had no time to hang around today as I had to get home to meet Dave, eat, grab my packed bags, kiss my cats goodbye and drive across to Swansea.

Being part of my newly expanded broadcasting patch, I've got my first gig at one of the largest festivals on the southwest coast: Escape into the Park. It's huge. We drive for around four hours or more. Dave is easy company, which is great as it's quite a trek. We arrive late into the night and check into the Marriott Hotel booked by the events team as it's only a few minutes away from tomorrow's gig. Dave has booked his own room and I arrange his VIP guest pass.

We arrive at the bar at around 10 or 11 p.m. I crazily order a tomato juice, chill for half an hour then go to bed. I do not sleep well, meaning I sleep shit! Waking every couple of hours over and over, it's a bad night even by my standards.

Not sleeping is a regular thing in my life and a real pain in the arse when I have to constantly deliver live shows and a massive DJ set the next day.

In the morning, we meet around 9 a.m. for breakfast with a few producers and other colleagues. We discuss the day's agenda briefly, how shit I slept and then it's straight to work for the team debrief in the press area inside our KISS tent. It's the first time I've met in person some of the crew from 101 and they strike me as friendly and professional.

The event site is beautiful. It's set in the gentle turns and sprawling slopes with enormous trees, lush thick green grass and clear blue sky. There is a vast main stage and dotted about between the trees and kind of hidden are the biggest marquees they build. There are about five I think, although you can't see them all at once.

Calvin Harris is headlining along with Erick Morillo, Armin van Buuren, David Guetta, Eddie Halliwell and The Shapeshifters. It's impossible to hide my excitement at being part of such a magnificent event in a truly stunning setting. Although I've played this size before, it's still thrilling, every time. My face and cheeks will physically ache later from smiling so much. I find this a regular occurrence in my line of work. My cheeks quiver, a bit shaky from over-smiling muscles. You can feel it most when trying to hold the smile for photos.

I'm playing the Polysexual Arena with Tidy Boys, Lisa Lashes, Rob Tissera, Amber D, Hixxy & MC Storm, Alex

Kidd, Andy Whitby and Cally & Juice. Quite a few I've met previously and played with at other gigs. Loads of them have been interviewed or guest mixed on my show *House of Elise* on KISS 105-108 East of England. It's kind of like meeting up with your colleagues and friends at work except that it happens to be an enormous 25,000 people party and some of the best experiences of your life will be shared on that day.

We spend a couple of hours working backstage on interviews, audio and video. We vox pop and grab samples from mostly teenagers and twenty-somethings. We also go for a walk about to check out all the arenas across the whole site. I notice how incredibly buff a lot of the Welsh lads are! They look like they've been in the gym since birth with bulging biceps and it isn't just one or two. It's entire groups of lads, totally ripped. I've never seen that before. It's the noughties (which never really caught on much as it sounds a bit stupid). In the 2000s.

I make my way up through the trees with Dave and round the back of the stage. I'm nervous with the same anticipation for my performance as I am for any live DJ set. I'm human. I feel some nerves but not massively. It's well planned and just part of the excitement. There is a lot riding on this, as it's the biggest marquee I've ever played, although I've worked some very large crowds of 5,000, 10,000, sometimes 25,000.

One of the best things with an event of this size is standard equipment! It's top of the range standard and therefore excellent. You don't always get this in clubs and it can be a right pain in the arse trying to play live from old, different, weird or crap decks and mixers.

This is top-end Pioneer across the board with the industry standard of two CD decks and mixers, two Technics vinyl decks (there's three in some arenas) mics and monitors. Jesus, they are the biggest monitors and speakers I've ever seen and I'm about to find out why. I unfold, build and deliver my set. I hold nothing back. You should know I've never really delivered warm-ups… I'm the main kind of DJ! That's no disrespect to any warm-ups and I've done loads and worked with loads. There is a time and a place for it all. It's just more how I play music: all or nothing.

After years of tireless practice and dedication to my craft, house and dance of all kinds, you transcend the technical delivery and structured performance and somehow launch yourself into the mindset of the people going crazy and the crowd will willingly follow you anywhere you take them.

Like always, I have a pile of Red Bull and water and I start from empty. There are like ten people on the grass below my stage. I'm new to this place so I'm the first up this year and it's zero to so crammed full that no one else can fit in. It's my usual style within twenty to thirty minutes. I don't warm up really. I smash it, deliver and cane it like hell!

I learnt how to read a crowd long ago. I can tell you how they feel by how they move, when they are tired, bored, happy… it's all in the face. Each and every one gives me feedback that I use to my advantage. I know what they want and I direct them where they need to go. Euphoric highs, spanking beats, ridiculous base lines… it's like being the conductor of an orchestra all by myself. I do my thing and they follow on, devoted to the DJ. We are in perfect harmony getting higher and higher. It's a flow from me to them and them to me. This energy rotates through us all together, around and around. If you've ever been to a big gig or large festival you know what I mean.

Dave has been off checking out everywhere doing a recce to assess the whole place. He's very professional and thorough as he is one of Norfolk's finest hard house promoters. He pops back up later on stage behind me and says mid-set, 'There's no one outside, Nikki. The other tents are all empty. Every single person that's come though that gate so far has come in here with you.'

I'm catching all available and I hold them with an invisible power, a circular energy force, and everyone wants a piece of my set.

It takes hours and hours to get the total amount of festivalgoers through security and all who've made it in the gates are now in my arena! Sweet! Usually, they will spread out into all the other areas and spaces but not this time. In front of me I guess at about 5,000 or 6,000. It's wall to wall people in less than thirty minutes back to back with no space anywhere. I know I've totally smashed it but don't forget you can always screw up. It's live and it's an altogether new level of loud in the marquee but I never did mess up, not by that point in my career. I don't remember any mistakes in general. Sure, I've made little ones in the past, but that's how you learn.

It's an out of this world feeling delivering that moment to the crowd. They stand together tightly packed, dancing full on and loyal to the DJ, sweating and screaming in front of you, united in dance. Right then, nothing else matters in the world. You have just been through the most intense hour or so together.

We all know it is the best moment on the planet right at that moment and everyone feels the same. It's the most incredible exchange of energy you can ever feel.

Dave says to me, 'That was the best warm-up set I've ever seen.'

It isn't flattery. He's been to hundreds of gigs and seen the best play. He's just giving his honest review of the set. It's a nice compliment from a fellow DJ.

At around 1 p.m. I have signed, sealed and delivered my signature Nikki Elise hard house style. The most intense and complex part of my job is done for the day. Now I need to prepare for my afternoon's work, tracking down and gathering interviews with the superstar DJ line-up.

I have to DJ with my headphones up louder than ever before trying to cope working through the arena noise and synchronised screaming crowds. My ears are ringing the loudest noise I've ever felt and it takes some time to adjust my entire body back down to earth. You pump yourself up to an enormous performance level giving all your energy out, then you gotta get right back down to work. I can't really hear normally for a good couple of hours due to the insane volume I have just worked with up on stage, so I try hard not to shout during my interviews.

I am critical of my own sets but I can say, hand on heart, I pulled that off pretty well. A spectacular set. I'm very happy.

# EARLY LITTLE ME: LIFE IN THE 80S AND 90S

## LIFE IN THE 80S

Born in 1978, I am a child of the gloriously simple eighties. The last of the old generations following thousands of years before us by not being indoors. Most of my childhood is spent playing freely outside unless it is utterly pouring with rain. All this fresh air time with dozens of friends exploring the woods or very occasionally all alone if no one was coming out to play. The last time before we evolve into a world of computers, health and safety, globalisation and buying any toy you want from China. Almost anything goes as long as you arrive home before dark.

I grew up in various tiny villages around the very flat Suffolk and Norfolk borders and I am a girl outside of the rigid 1980s standard mould! I have short hair, make a lot of noise and dress like a boy. Emerging as a skateboarding teenager in the 1990s, I discover boys, grow my hair, play rave cassette tapes and ride my motorbike a lot.

The eighties are full of risk and in the nineties, even more so! Delightful, dangerous risk! No child has any concept of what might happen next and that's why we try everything. (Even now I can look back and go wow! I did well to survive some of it.) Swinging on a rope over a red-hot bonfire, for instance. The look on my poor mum's horrified face when she walks around the corner and sees both her children doing that. We're like, 'What?' Tunnelling into haystacks, that's a no-no. I learn from Dad's level of anger which is a first. Riding pillion on a Yamaha YZ 100 motocross 'backwards' at sixty miles per hour across a muddy field. Probably lucky no one saw!

It may be sensible to add the key TV phrase around at the time: 'Don't try this at home.' Please do not repeat my developing brain's foolishness!

I can only apologise from the bottom of my heart for clingfilming the high school art block toilets. Again, no idea of afterwards. Everything we try is new. We have no TV or videos to reference, no one to copy, even I'm surprised at the results… flooding. Big flooding. It's April Fool's but I'll never ever do it again. I learn what guilt and anguish feel like. Not good. Remorse too.

## GAMES

I play swing ball in the garden learning to smash it so hard we often break the clumpy plastic rackets. I learn to play tennis alone against the barn wall next to my house. This vacant slightly falling down clay lump barn contains a pony in the small stable and doubles as a giant climbing frame. With a vast high clay-tiled roof, it is very satisfying to walk up to and right along the high ridge and often at dusk. A bit older, I jump off the side of this single-storey roof with a giant umbrella to see if it will act as a parachute! And I do mean your standard beer garden pub sunshade. It's a rather ambitious project that I'd been thinking about for at least a couple of hours. It did work as you feel its mushroom-like shape grab the air underneath it and then you crash down fast onto the grass! Perfect for a soft toy perhaps… I like science.

In another afternoon of material experiments, I learn that you can position carefully and break the clay roof tiles on top of your head quite easily. Adding some more force, I apply our own house concrete roof tiles to the very centre of my head. These do not break well at all; it is very painful. (I recently told Dad about this experiment and he looked at me and said, 'That explains a lot.' I did not go on to tell him that I also tested out his office stapler by applying it directly to my left thumb. I can confirm it hurts like hell. I realised that immediately, shouting out in pain. I will not try that again.)

The empty land to the side of the barn is just another natural play area. It doubles as an extension of our garden. We use walkies-talkies and hide in the long grass after dark. If someone gets too close to finding you, you have to switch it off for the feedback noise. But when my brother realises I've switched off, he knows I'm very close by and he discovers me hiding in the weeds. There has always been something more exciting about games at dusk or into the evening. It's more intense, right? Like hide and seek under the cold moon and starry sky. (We actually did that as adults quite a lot, seeking out the creepiest locations. Why not?)

Opposite the road and on the left side of my house, there is a large overflow ditch which is mainly empty. When there are sufficient friends to play with, at least six or more, we play 'bog marsh'. Bog marsh involves two teams standing on opposing sides of the ten-metre-long section of ditch. The defending side has the higher ground by a metre or two and the attacking team has to go across the ditch, up the steep bank and try to break past the defence who throw you back down into the grass ditch. If you get past them you are victorious but in a team game you need everyone up together which is quite tricky. If there is a small amount of water in the bottom, you get wet feet, or worse, or partially covered in mud. We play forty forty too like most kids but bog marsh is a homegrown team sport.

## TOYS

As soon as I'm old enough to play in the garage with my dad and brother, probably about six, then that's where you'll find me. Look at all the stuff in Dad's garage. It's like an Aladdin's cave of tools and creative fun. You can drill bits and cut wood up on the giant bench saw. We solder circuit boards and make mini light sets. The three of us do a glass melting experiment one day. Very dangerous and not advisable to copy but it's great fun. We melt some glass where it drips in molten liquid then spits at such force that it shoots across the garage and leaves a cooled tiny fine string of solid glass behind it a few metres long.

I also set fire to my jumper playing, or rather cutting, with the angle grinder. I don't even notice until I take my safety goggles off and look down to see myself burning. My quick-thinking big brother fills a glass milk bottle and throws water over me. Thanks. We note that some jumpers, i.e. sports sweaters, are particularly flammable. Science! I'm not injured although it does burn a tiny hole in my T-shirt too.

When we are very young, Dad builds a wooden go-kart made with big fat wheelbarrow tyres. We modify it in an instant, cutting the rope off and using the steering control by the wooden wheel shaft at our feet. Sometime after that, I may have been about ten, he arrives home triumphantly with a red metal petrol engine ex-racing go-kart, which can easy reach thirty to forty miles per hour. We ride it mainly up the woods on several miles of dirt lanes. I'm a good driver as I'm small and light and that means fast. We have secondhand bikes like BMXs but cheaper, covered in stunt nuts and Spokey Dokeys with the endless coloured beads clattering around both wheels.

I have my first and bad accident around here. We forgot to look at my breaks in the garage, shooting off and round the top of the garden and stopping (or not) at the top of the metre-high patio steps. I can't stop and fall headfirst, faceplanting onto the concrete below and putting my teeth through my top lip. (I still have the scars. I have many, many scars. It's like a lifetime's collection of stories stamped on me.) I run to Mum crying and get one whole day off school. (Now, you have to fill in a form at school to account for the drama but in the eighties you just turned up at school with a massive hole in the front of your face.)

With practice I kit myself out like the gadget kid from *The Goonies*. Everything I can fit in my coat pockets to take to the woods for a day. Hammer, nails, string, penknife and useful stuff. I'm so small I can literally bang in nails upwards in a diagonal line and climb up like a ladder to reach the lower branches. Separately, there are two huge oak trees which need nothing except yourself to climb. One is so huge it's like a vast tree castle. We take bits of board and sheets and add to it, and build wooden step ladders or use ropes sometimes to help us get up. Or take an axe and cut any smaller or fallen trees into bridge ladders and angle them up the side. We aren't the first generation of kids to climb these giant oaks as partial remains of older tree houses existed.

Certain types of trees and branches are really flexible and excellent materials for making bows and arrows with string and a penknife, if you happen to have these tools on you! My brother builds a mighty longbow one day at home and it is epic. On his first trial from the far side of our garden he shoots it straight though the neighbour's wooden fence. We are amazed at the power. Dad takes this away as it is clearly too good. As a kid, his own brother accidently shot him in the eye with an arrow and he came close to losing his sight. I guess he is rightly cautious with this potentially lethal freshly built toy.

## DREAMS

As a small child I desperately want a drum kit. Mum comes up the ladder into our house's mainly empty loft. With our chipboard floor, we have a vast play area covered in pen car tracks.

She says, 'I've got you a drum,' and hands me a little white metal drum.

Toys are not as easy to find and cool things like a real drum kit are incredibly expensive and well out of any normal family's budget. Drum kits I guess will always be a dream. I'm a bit disappointed although grateful she has tried her best and as I hadn't specified an entire drum kit, one had not arrived. I take it with thanks assuming she's done her best with little money and working all day. The need of drums remains with me for a long time.

My iconic dream toy (that I never got) is a peddle bike in the Argos catalogue that looks like a motorbike. The only thing like it anywhere that I've ever seen, just this one, and it's £99.99. (In today's money that's more than a PlayStation, massive monitor, headphones plus gaming chair and I was under ten years old. I never wavered; I always wanted that toy. I didn't get one.)

I try to pick up a secondhand Etch A Sketch one day at a school swap shop sale. I see it and manoeuvre round the packed tables and stools but sadly I move too slowly through the crowded classroom. It is gone seconds before I can reach the table. If things go, you don't get them as you can't afford to buy them so that's that. No etching for me. No drum kit, no pretend motorbike. No one minds, not even me. That's just how things are.

We also spend a lot of time up Snetterton racetrack watching cars and bikes at the weekend particularly with my cool mum. We have monster truck videos on VHS and I have racing bike posters on my wall; the red Ducati is the only one I remember. The need for the motorbike remains with me.

At the weekend, as we get older, we start loading our ZX Spectrums rustled up with pocket money from Banham car boot sales. Some games are great and you can put your cassette in, sometimes overnight, and they may well load by the morning! Mostly they bleep and screech away for five minutes or so, sounding like they are in pain thinking about loading the game. It really depends what mood it's in on that day.

## PRIMARY SCHOOL: OUTSIDE

In a way we are the last outdoor generation that are truly free. Even education isn't a priority (not that I noticed), you just turn up.

We have a lovely sports guy arrive who takes us for more specialised PE lessons called tumbling. Tumbling is a very popular sport and at my peak, probably by the age of ten, I can confidently jump at least eleven kids all lying quietly and tightly packed, side by side on the grass. I run fast, leap right over all their bodies and end with a somersault landing on an old double mattress. The day I try to jump twelve practising on the school playing field I nearly snap my neck. It hurts quite a lot. We may not have even had a mattress that day! We like to practise. Risk does not exist!

Some kids naturally crash hopelessly on top of the piles of floor kids but that doesn't happen often. If you are the kid who lies on the end of the floor line, you get stepped on countless times. Imagine the full weight of a running kid and one foot pinching on your arm or side of your chest before they fly over you into the air and hopefully roll neatly onto the mattress. You can hear the squealing of the occasional stomped-on kid if it goes wrong if you are lying at the other end. But in general, we practise hard like any other sport and we are really good at it.

It is a kind of makeshift gymnastics floor and aerial display with virtually no money and no equipment, except the old mattress driven over in the back of his car or perhaps his trailer. We love the eighties! At the end of the summer there is a sports day and we all line up, with around twenty, maybe thirty, of us spread out on four opposing corners behind the mattress in the middle of the playing field.

With cleverly rehearsed choreography, four teams on each side can weave in and out of each other running, spinning head over heels, landing neatly and jumping off back into formation. All to a rapturous round of applause from our proudly spectating parents. All this is the grand finale to our sports day that always features some running, trying to run (tripping over in a sack) and a joyful egg and spoon race. I never win any of these tricky races. I don't think I ever won a race actually!

## CROSS COUNTRY

Then there is normal PE: the cross country running. At this young age, almost all kids love it mainly because it means escaping the classroom. (Not that dreaded freezing winter blizzard kind that high school would force moody teenagers to run in and other dreadful weather conditions like daylight!) So, primary school running is great fun and I'm good at it and I'm fast. I'm usually always girl number two at the finish. I always look at the back of the same girl who is just ahead of me, but I can never catch her.

The guidelines for safety are one or possibly two teachers standing at the school gate entrance to greet the arrivals back at school and that's it… Really, that's it. Nothing else is required! We run from the school along a one-mile footpath next to a field, across a tiny back road and on into the woods. Then we run down the tree-enclosed lane on the side of the woods, then actually a good half a mile down a dead-end road and back to the school. Yes, all with absolutely no teachers present whatsoever. This circuit must have been around one to two miles. About three kilometres if you don't know what a mile is. I must assume there is no teacher at the front as I never see one. We are not all together, just all spread out. Perhaps there was a teacher once… somewhere?

An entire class of children all aged ten or eleven and totally loose in the woods. Incredible, isn't it? Just the freedom that no one bats an eyelid and all the kids return to school safely. One time I ask to do another lap and start running the wrong way as last week we'd run in a different direction. A teacher sees me at the last minute and gets me going round the right course. I was so far ahead of the other kids I have time to happily do it all again.

Now I have no idea if it is this time or indeed another time, but no one is behind me so I think I'm at the back as I'm on my second lap round, but I have some disastrous issues with my lungs. Pretty sharpish I collapse completely unable to breathe on the dead-end road. I lie totally alone as a small frightened child barely breathing. After some time spent in utter panic, wheezing and spluttering for air and my life, and completely alone, I keep thinking someone may walk out of a thatched cottage and see me but no one does. It's pretty scary as my lungs shut down so much that I can't stand and I fall to the floor. After a while I manage to get up off the cold tarmac and get back to the school more than half a mile away. I must have been taken to the doctor at some point and this turns out to be the start of my turbulent relationship with my wanker mate: asthma.

## PRIMARY SCHOOL: INSIDE

My brother is one of the last kids to get the cane for being difficult and, well, basically a pain in the arse. I'm not in his class but I hear many tales about it. He has a gift for being repeatedly and incredibly annoying, and every single day if he feels like it. Only there is no cane so the teacher, probably at his wit's end, takes him out into the corridor and hits him across the bum snapping the only thing he has, a long wooden ruler, which makes everyone laugh even more hysterically adding to the teacher's immense frustration. He can't control him or punish him either only adding to the kids' classroom highs and the lows of a tortured teacher. Satisfying playground news like this spreads very quickly.

Classroom 3 has the only male teacher who is easy to wind up till smoke comes out. The same one who got fed up with my brother. This class is terrible. It is so dull and a lot of maths. I wonder whether if I'm always away ill missing the whole subject entirely, probably with tonsilitis, or just crap at learning maths. The other kids seem to learn their times tables somewhere, but I never do. I have nailed two, five, ten and bit of six! Go me!

I spend many lessons aimlessly looking out the window at the playground imagining some alternative universe lives in that big empty space. I wait for the teacher to tell me to pay attention but he never does, so I regularly stare out of the window, thinking how that empty space could be amazing but not in this instant. There is nothing there other than the reality of now or breaktime in five minutes. That space exists differently only through time... I'm about nine.

Then it's up onto the top, classroom 4, as there are only four different rooms, with the headmistress. My last couple of years to ride out till I can join my older and best friend again. Lou and also Nic P have all gone to the gravitational pull of big school. I'm just waiting for my turn to join them again.

We do some more interesting experimental projects now at least. We also do practical science experiments with water trays (probably like today's sink or float), and this is a break from the norm. Also, there are now coloured maths boxes. Oh crap! It seems obvious after a while that no one is really checking my work at all. When all the other kids go up to green from yellow, I'm still halfway through yellow. After feeling very behind I just start on the next box with them. I remember the maths test (that was probably on a Friday). I repeatedly get consistently low marks, often eleven or twelve out of twenty. It is quite disappointing to be repeatedly low on the dreaded weekly test but no one questions it or helps me so I don't worry too much. I'm not into maths.

We have a clear green plastic tortoise that can hold a pen and be programmed to draw lines and patterns. In a world before computers, this is way cooler, the height of cutting-edge technology, the school's pride and joy, a state of the art, computerised digital drawing aid. It's tortoise-ology! No one on earth has ever seen anything like this bad boy before. If you damage the robot or lose its pen, you will be kicked out of school. Fact.

## DRAMA... NO DRAMA

The primary school Christmas nativity play is a focal point for all. I never understand why I never got the lead role in the Christmas play. Each year for maybe five hopeful years, I think it must be my turn. Surely this year the teacher will call my name. This time I can sparkle in front of the audience! No, not once, not ever. I'm always cast as someone on the fringes of the play usually with a tea towel on my head, maybe the innkeeper or the innkeeper's mother or something very sidestepped!

I fully get this now. It's called 'favouritism'. Each year the head picks her favourite (and realistically much prettier) girly girls and boys to be Mary and Joseph. More or less, you can bet and consistently win money on the same kids. Almost all kids would like to be cast as the lead in a play just once. We call this inclusivity. It is very definitely *exclusive* at my school. Dressing mostly like a boy in the eighties is not acceptable for landing a lead role although I will never know this. How can I have known? I just miss out. I'm excluded year after year like many other kids. This is the start of my never *yet* (remember those three letters) started relationship I want to have with drama but teachers always refuse me. Thanks for the zero help… never mind.

## THE 90S: GOOD GOD, THEY ARE INCREDIBLE

I can honestly say I was born for this generation; its hallmark is music heaven. Nowadays I doubt if it's even possible that in a world drowned in social media, apps and technology most people will ever feel truly free again. The more we have, the more trapped by it we become and mostly we don't even realise it's happening. My mate told me the other day I was out of touch as I don't have TikTok. I'm just independent of the need... I don't like to conform and I won't renounce my life or time to social media. Only for business, advertising and work purposes is where I will get involved. I've had Pinterest for a number of years (I tell myself it's a magazine). Anyway, I don't think it's possible to have more fun and excitement than I lived through in my teenage years. Although not all my friends were lucky to experience life the way I did.

It's hard to summarise how epic it was to unknowingly join the house music generation. I never knew music would become my entire life!

As a little girl, I guess around eight to ten, I had my first vision in my grandmother's kitchen. I don't think I told anyone, but equally I may have said something to my grandma in that moment. Perhaps I just imagined it? From nowhere I saw myself on stage but I was all alone. It was just me standing there.

That image always stayed with me especially as everything I knew about a stage involved lots of people, like a play or a band. I didn't even realise what I'd seen for decades. I clearly see it now. It was me; I saw my future. I just thought it was my imagination which was a bit odd with Grandma Nora, a beaker of squash and a Rich Tea biscuit.

## AT HIGH SCHOOL I HAVE TO WEAR A SKIRT

This is a massive disaster and a merciless ordeal. Some sort of teenage punishment that only I appear to suffer on the first day of school, like the stress isn't enough already because I haven't worn a dress thing since I was five. It feels about as cruel as putting a boy in a skirt on his first day. Tossers. The school that is, not my parents. My neon white unshaved legs look all gangly and uncomfortable and what the fuck are they on my feet? Proper shoes? Jesus! I don't think I've ever owned a pair. I remember a state of near desolation looking for them in Bury St Edmunds with Mum. She must have dreaded taking me shopping.

'Mum,' I beg, 'Why don't they make any shoes in white? They would look less obvious.' *More like my trainers*, I think.

Mum explains sadly they don't make school shoes in white. I really feel my life force draining from me.

Poor Mum. I'm utterly incapable of clothes shopping. It's like my most dreaded form of torture being dragged around shops for things I hate to my bones. It makes me feel a little unwell. The shoe searching makes me feel powerlessly uncomfortable, freakishly sad and forced beyond my coping ability and all for what? Stupid high school. Finally, we buy shoes and go home.

Lou's my best friend at two years older, and her younger sister is in my form. She is very supportive even though we are not close friends. She confidently tells me my skirt looks good. Her kind words on that day help me. It is nice of her as she knows how much I'm struggling with it.

Some weeks or month later I collapse in tears at Mum's house demanding the hideous hair be gone from my legs. 'Mum, all the other girls shave their legs. God help me, look at mine.'

Mum looks briefly and quietly explains that, if I want to, I can simply shave it all off now in the shower with her razor tonight! What, really? I thought I would die of shame looking so bad. Cool… I built this into a massive issue and I was utterly clueless as how to salvage my horrendous life. With some minor squirting red streams of blood down my shins, it is all fixed in about five minutes. How kind life is.

## BOYS ;-)

In my first year of high school, I'm on it! I share chewing gum with one the year before but I don't kiss him, so it doesn't count, right? I bag my first one pretty much before a lot of people are thinking about guys. I know exactly what I want: him. I meet 'my type'.

I proudly put in my rave cassette tape on Mum's car stereo as we drive back to mine. He is sporting a seriously cool clothing statement, one that I've never seen before. He has one trouser leg rolled up tucked into his sock and one down as he is just so rad! He takes out his Walkman and puts his headphones on for the journey. I ask what it is as I've never heard of it before.

'It's hip-hop,' he says.

He is very quiet in our car, probably a bit nervous. I'm quite grateful for him choosing his own tunes at that moment as I'm about to make an epic unforgettable fuck-up!

I've forgotten that before in my bedroom playing with my cassette tape recorder I realised I could record my voice! But record what? I'd done a very new trial of talking or MCing of sorts and clearly run out of things to say which turned into swearing my head off trying to sound cool, I think (I really don't know what I was thinking). Just a one-off adlib that I forgot I recorded, all blasting out of Mum's car's speakers in front of the newly bagged first boyfriend! I almost died. Fortunately, Mum doesn't realise it's me (or does and still says nothing), just tutting and switching it off quickly! What a major cock-up and I get away with it and don't even get told off by Mum. It's very embarrassing and yet somehow no one says anything on my first date. I'm very lucky as I slowly sink down on the back seat of the car.

After a while we have his moped dropped over to our house. I think I had mine age ten or eleven. I'd been driving Dad's van on a private drive, along dusty tracks. I learnt to drive somewhere around eight onwards as soon as I could reach the peddles sitting on the very front of the seat. From then on, I was driving on any land, friends' fields, dusty lanes or wherever was open.

My brother has a 90cc scooter and I have a 70cc scooter. Both old fashioned. I've put big knobbly tyres on mine. We spend hours cutting down all the mud guards to make them look like dirt bikes. No one has money and everything is modified. It's the norm. My boyfriend's bike is a 50cc and that sleeps in the garage, neatly lined up with ours. It's a shame we break up. He has to come to collect his bike and take it away from the others. It feels sad. The break-up is sad. The poor bikes!

## CLOTHES SHOPPING

The best I can do on (what is now called) non-uniform day is to go to Norwich with Mum a month earlier and buy one Sweater Shop jumper. Everyone has one so that's all you need with jeans for those six months to a year. So, there I am realising I'll never really be on trend as I basically have no interest in clothes. They do not achieve anything practical unlike the massive chop saw in Dad's garage. It's quite a bit of kit! And spare petrol (for our bikes) hiding in Dad's generator.

Anyway, it turns out when I'm older I do actually like clothes shopping (a little bit) but it's such a ball ache trying to plan an entire afternoon, driving an hour into the city, endlessly wandering around shops and not finding anything you like. I have rather marked shopping out for me as a nope. For me and clothes.

I do quite a few shopping trips mostly to Chapelfield or Topshop in the city but me and clothes are not good friends. One day, upstairs rifling through girls' clothes, I hear something magical. It plays in the store over and over and over and it never seems to change and it never ends. The more it goes on, the more I'm like, 'Woah, what is this? I'm absorbing into the groove.'

Curiosity boils over and I have to ask the staff. It turns out to be Primal Scream's 'Come Together' from *Screamadelica*, so somewhere around 1991. The endless song is over ten minutes long hence it really catches my attention that day in a rhymical never-ending mellow man. It's one of the first albums I ever buy based right there on that experience. Not something I usually do. On the track 'Loaded' it says, 'And we wanna get loaded, and we wanna have a good time. Away, baby, let's go.' That becomes a power phrase later on with my all-new influx of friends.

As time goes by, I bin the school skirt in favour of black trousers and deep red Doc Martins! Peace is restored!

## FIRST (ONLY) MUSIC EVENT

One summer, Mum's friend Lin (my second mum) takes us and her two girls Kate and little Nic to Great Yarmouth for the Radio 1 Roadshow.

I must have been quite young as I don't remember much except there was a radio sticker! Kate thinks maybe it was Steve Wright as she listened to his show. According to a random website list, on 22 July 1991 Steve was there but between us we can't recall who we saw. I know it was a man. Basically, females in radio did not feature much then. I'd never heard one.

## SPORT

At school I get myself onto the hocky team a year early as girls are banned from playing football.

Seams unreal, doesn't it? My kids are so shocked by this asking, 'Why can't girls play, Mum?' I always tell them how lucky there are to have football training, to have the choice. Think of the countries that are still banning women from the freedom of choice, even now in 2024.

I proudly run out onto the sports pitch for the first time. Can you even imagine the excitement of seeing a real big pitch? I run fast and alone towards a huge white metal football goal.

The teacher says, 'Where are you going?'

'To play football,' I shout back.

She waves me back. 'Girls don't play football. We're over here on the hockey pitch.' And that is that.

I honestly think I would have made a good footballer. I have lightning reactions, great balance and, as a child, a good strike. I'll never know.

Starting hockey nearly as a teenager is a totally new skill that I have to learn. I'd been kicking a ball since, what, age four.

So, not having a choice, it's hockey as there is no tennis or basketball team. Which sucks as I'm good at tennis. Nearly everyone loves basketball and you really see all the girls' characters come alive on the indoor court. I'm often team captain and select my girls. I don't like how with me picking kids out, some get left at the end unpicked till last. And every single time just out of friendship preference. I really try hard to rotate my selection each time to include everyone. As I'm often captain, I don't stand in line much but I would happily have stood there last a few times but imagine if that happened week after week? How would they feel? Demoralised, I think, even knowing it's coming again. I try to remove that from the selection process and rotate people. Inclusivity, I presume (this word wasn't really a thing in the nineties). No one taught me, I just want this to happen. I will add I'm not perfect in school but as I grow, I become a better person.

There may be a netball team but it's just not for me although I have friends who love playing it. Getting the ball and giving it away? Nope… it just doesn't add up in my Neanderthal brain. That ball is mine and I'm gonna whack it into the net or slam it through the hoop! That's my aim.

I'm on the hockey team early by year 4. Miche from my village also joins the team. She's also fast and agile with good skills. She later moves in with me briefly after a turbulent and deeply painful family life. I offer her a chance to get out and seek a normal life. She bravely took this choice so young, aged only seventeen, and is now one of the most well-balanced, happy people I've ever met. I just wanted to help any way I could. I found myself a bit of a rescuer as time went on. It's good to help people.

## NO DRAMA

During the last years of school our attention is turned to choices and what you may do with the rest of your actual life. Now I want to take history and drama, but both are denied to me as maybe I've already chosen too much arty stuff. And let's not forget I do *not* look like the girly type who can gracefully pretend to be a tree for half an hour. I am excluded from drama again!

I do get art, sport, design technology and… GEOGRAPHY! What the hell? I like history! I am disappointed with no drama but happy with the rest. Alongside this you have double science which I'm actually good at, English where I turn up and maths where I suck. So badly in fact that after the initial few years, I'm moved to the bottom class where I wander in one day like the lone maths ranger. Lucky for me I have a couple of girl pals in there who I get on well with so we can all just suck at maths together. There is basically no point in us partaking as we can't do it no matter how hard we all try. Once accepted that we are all equal at the bottom, it's really cool as there is no pressure to achieve. None at all… it's great!

## BUILD A SOCIAL LIFE!

It becomes apparent that I need a new group of friends as I don't really fit anywhere. Lou, my childhood best friend, is all grown up and we don't spend much time together and none at school. I endlessly roam the corridors at lunchtime a bit like a lost dog who keeps escaping and checking in on the same neighbours. I am friends with loads of people, girls and lads from school, but still I feel unfulfilled. I decide to act, to bring about change. I think about how to branch out from my own life. I need to move on and try a new strategy to bring about change.

I actively spend a lot of time with my only friend Kate from my very first school in Hopton. Our parents have been friends for years. Now Kate is cool and embraces being a hippie or grunge as I will come to know it. She goes to another school in Suffolk. WAY COOLER! Her friends are totally awesome, funny, clever and laidback. That's me; I've finally found my crew. There are also older guys from her village in the pub who will all become my friends, boyfriends or whatever for the entire teenage years of my life. Everything becomes firsts at this point. First drink, first smoke, you name it, it happens right about here. Endless cider-fuelled party weekends away from home. An epic transformation of my life is under way. I have deliberately sought out a big drastic change by branching out, seeking new pastures and it works. Satisfying.

Our clique is cool and to me they don't seem all that interested in fashion either and listen to weird music. That's ok with me. As if fashion itself is not interesting enough, they have deliberately chosen a different route. It turns out they are into fashion but I don't get grunge (so I just don't realise).

I'm heavily into rave music and have no idea how I discovered it really, but boy, am I into it. There is a lot of pirate rave stuff around on cassette and there are rave generation albums and stuff you can buy like *Rave 92*.

Here are a few harder but chart ones: Blue Pearl's '(Can You) Feel the Passion', Urban Hype's 'A Trip to Trumpton', Praga Khan's 'Injected with a Poison', and Liquid's 'Sweet Harmony'. Don't tell me you can't hear the pianos of 'Sweet Harmony' right now. Play it. The opening is so raw it brings goosebumps every time. So pure, so rave, so me. It's my new whole world. That track captures what the scene feels like. You can't just plain listen to it. You actually feel it surge through you. Incredible. The dark, the silence, the break beats, the piano. I'm also listening to more raw stuff like pirate radio tapes and Radio 1.

## AT FOURTEEN I BECOME A WOMAN

I'm very independent in my early teens and by choice I'm doing my own laundry and mostly cooking my own food. Mum does cook for me if I stay at hers a few nights. Dad pays for food and gives me a weekly allowance to manage myself. I buy all my own items for school and clothes or whatever I need. I learn to budget. I'm all grown up in every way. Except one.

By the time I'm fourteen I literally know everything and I do mean *everything*. I have arrived fully at me. Not arrogant but just completely sure of who the fuck adult me is… Nick!

All the details in life I know. I'm an adult. I take care of anything I need myself and I gain curves! I have boobs, boys and develop an awesome group of friends. Together we have an amazing and outrageous Diamond White cider-fuelled, pub gig, music-based social life. Kate, Inny and Anna and a big bunch of others are into this grunge thing. Often we come in packages of two friends; I don't know why, it's just how it goes down. So, there is Kate and me then always Inny and Anna. Pretty often Jane and Abby too, plus less often Rachel and Sarah.

At the start of the night, we inquire as to who is gracing us with their presence this weekend. Which of the twos will be joining us for this momentous two-day time in our lives. A massive lovely bunch of wicked friends, our crew, the group.

They rock. It truly changes my entire way of life. I'm a wanted, appreciated, fully integrated integral part of the group now. Nick and they are all of that to me. It is something I have never felt before. Let's call it a bond.

They introduce me to moshing, although being a little raver I never get it! I'm like, 'What's all that about?'

I stay well clear at the back of what looks like really weird dancing (thrashing about) and throwing cider in the air in front of various stages and bands. Still, I love the buzz of being out in the dark for the night. We go to loads of gigs all over the place but I mainly remember gigs in the Rose and Crown in Stanton with live bands and sometimes we'd all camp in Inny's mum's field.

Inny's mum's friend has an airplane hangar in the field right next door to his house. This is where I spend most of the next four years partying. They are very liberal parents and it has such a relaxed atmosphere. This is where I'm introduced to *The Rocky Horror Picture Show* on VHS. The most far-out movie I've seen so far is Val Kilmer in *The Doors*. They listen to really different music to me but I appreciate something new and a different genre to enrich our shared world. There are many house parties, and once a caravan party, in between gigs and village hall weekends. Often Rage Against the Machine is at full blast screaming, 'Fuck you, I won't do what you tell me.' Unapologetically angry noise and it is all very new to my excited ears.

Anna and I became pen pals to bridge the gap in between the next weekend out. We write regularly, a couple of times a month sometimes. Our signature is drawing little sheep pics at the bottom that say, 'Bah.' I've no idea why but mainly sheep and other various amusing silly pictures it is. A sheep on a treadmill springs to mind as sort of a cartoonish caption ending. Why just write words when you can also draw idiotic pictures? A sort of sign-off caption footer.

The other thing is the clothes. They don't seem at all interested in following fashion. Now nor do I have to. With barely any fashion sense as a young teenager I go up Snetterton Market, see a mustard brown knitted jumper and think, *That will fit in nicely!* Put on my Doc Martins and a pair of jeans and I'll be done. Nice one. (Anna still takes the piss out of me to this day about that jumper. A crying with laughter emoji would sit nicely right here.) I don't think I have any other clothes that kind of work, or really any other clothes. The others naturally have way more style than me.

I have this new crew and my all-new music life is exploding. My brother is taxiing me about from weekend sleepovers, parties and gigs. We see live bands at least once a month and I'm seeing friends from faraway lands (across the Norfolk/Suffolk border)! My life is all far-out, independent and very, *very* cool. I'm seeing guys… not all at once… I'm going to leave that there!

## LEAVING HIGH SCHOOL

I'm truly gutted with a D for PE. I don't have the memory for the science part of the exam but the bigger problem here is the essential three: maths D, English D and science BB. A C grade is good for GCSEs, but a D is less than good.

Common sense tells me I need to retake one and with maths I was genuinely surprised I didn't score lower, so it can only be English. I go onto Diss sixth form studying leisure and tourism (as it sounds interesting) and retake English.

With that all sorted, school is finally over and it feels so liberating. Right, now priorities. It's time to get wasted with my mates! Bring on the parties! The summer of 1994, leaving school, is the best summer ever. It's greater than I ever dreamt it would be. It's an all-encompassing feeling, an everlasting euphoria, a real coming of age and I never have to do school again!

I'm totally free in every way, a feeling I've craved for so long. We party hard as usual in the summer sun for months and months on end with not a care in the world. Except for this one thing that happens towards the end of the summer.

I'm sixteen and suddenly Mum is paralysed overnight. What has gone so wrong literally overnight? I get a call and find her in hospital later that morning with no use of her entire right-hand side, neck down. It is devastating. No one knows what to say.

In that week, I grow up the rest immediately.

She is in hospital for nearly a month. I'm at Lin's a lot of the time, with Kate, and she becomes like a back-up mum, a mum number two, as mine is temporarily missing. She listens. At times I know I need to cry but it never comes. It stops altogether. Mum will never see me cry about her situation. I figure it is the only thing I can do to help, not let the severity of the situation show in me. I will not make it harder for her. I will handle it.

She does go on to walk again in time. It takes months and months of effort, using wheelchairs on and off. She is never able to work again. I become a partial career at times when it's needed but most of the time I can still live my life.

## WORK!

Like most teens I work through quite a few various jobs. Waitressing at big functions is my first loved long-term job. I do it for several years from fourteen onwards. It's exciting, fast paced and demanding, under the pressure of kitchen service and working with a team to deliver successful nights. I stick at being a sports assistant at Center Parcs for a year or so whilst working my way through life's big question: what to do with my entire future?

After quitting leisure and tourism at sixth form as it is just too much study and, well, boring, I go into what I know, our family business of building, and start working with my dad as a labourer. Very few women did these jobs back then. It would be fifteen years before I would see other female tradespeople although there must have been some around. Dad used to build houses but following the recession he has gone into smaller building jobs, extensions, repairs and maintenance.

It gives me the freedom of being free from further education and living and earning my own money as an adult. It's interesting, dusty and sweaty work but a welcome change in life. I am wise though and by staying on at sixth form one day a week I can retake English and get my grade C. I know I will need this later. I stay the year, meeting sharp and witty Helen who introduces me to Suzie, six feet tall and hilariously funny. We click immediately following our first lunchtime trip to the corner shop.

One thing is becoming clear to me. I'll be at work for, what, half of my whole life! Just think about this new reality of adulthood. If I'm required to work eight hours a day for five days a week *forever* then it needs to be bloody good for me too! Think of all that time at work. My more than brilliant life spent working. It needs to be satisfying for me, not just necessary.

My dream ambition has been growing in my mind. Since I was a teenager, I've been heavily inspired by French and Saunders and their hilarious comedy sketches. When *Absolutely Fabulous* arrives, I'm close to addicted. I VHS-tape every single one! As well as my love of the then cutting edge shows like *The Big Breakfast*, there is *TFI Friday* and *The Girlie Show*. Channel 4 is on to something big.

I watch *The Big Breakfast* TV comedy genius and presenter perfection with Chris Evans and Gaby Roslin although I more remember Jonny Vaughan, Denise van Outen and Paula Yates. This is ground-breaking TV. It's fun and fresh and, after waking up with that, I pack up only peanut toast sandwiches and crisps every day, a bottle of squash and a flask of tea and go to work with Dad in the van.

We repair roofs and fascias in Diss where I rip off a split wooden barge board like a maniac. It spins round and punches a rusty nail into my wrist. Luckily right in between the middle of two veins. It's my almost invisible scar. With blood streaming down my arm and not too bothered, I carry on after wasting a couple of minutes on a plaster to stem the flow dripping all over the place. I also drive the van and trailer to collect all the materials from Jewson's ready for the next day. I'm popular at the builders' merchants.

Dad has to try to harness my energy and turn it into serious focus. I'm all muscle and not much skill at the start with little forethought for the bigger picture. As I settle into the job, I learn multiple building skills, as being a labourer means you need to know a little about everything to feed all the other tradespeople. I work several days a week, so not quite full time, around English at sixth form.

We build shuttering, mix and pour concrete pads, repair fences and carry out maintenance at the local pig farm which was also a large slaughterhouse. I often eat my lunch in the van looking at a giant industrial steel bin full of discarded pig heads. The smell around there is pungent. (I can still tell the difference between pig shit and chicken shit after all these years! Life skills!)

We get up on the scaffolding for roofing. We strip it all off and replace it with felt and batten then retile the whole lot. I do all the labouring so it is my job to carry everything up the ladder and stack out hundreds of tiles. When we're bricklaying, the lorries drop off the pallets and I stack thousands of bricks ready for the next day with red metal brick clamps swinging from each hand. For small jobs, I mix the cement in a wheelbarrow and for bigger projects, use the cement mixer so I'm fit, really fit.

Doing a bit of carpentry one day Dad asks me what I want to do.

I say, for only the second time ever, 'I want to be a presenter.'

He laughs a little and suggests I become a plumber. He thinks I'll make a good one.

I do not want to become a plumber. Dad's suggestion is based on good knowledge and is reasonably accurate but about fifteen years out. Timing perhaps. You must realise this is the nineties, I live in a field, I'm never going to make university. My dream is not really an option.

## ANYWAY... FOLLOW THE DREAM

I leave sixth form just before I start building. I'm jobless for about six weeks and trying to collect some money for the first time.

The woman asks me what job I want and I say, 'I want to be a presenter.'

I can still remember her clearly. Her eyes open wide when she tries to stop them from rolling into the back of her head and helpfully says nothing. Her face says, 'Dream on.'

Sometime later I meet a careers advisor. I don't know what one is. I've never heard of it. I have a meeting in Thetford aged eighteen where I'm asked, 'What do you want to do for a living?'

No one was interested before, so I stay silent for a few years, but this guy actually wants to help me. To my surprise he is quite happy with my reply. I'm expecting another polite, 'Talk to the hand!'

The careers advisor trip is very enlightening. It's the first time anyone from school onwards has ever listened to me and then on top offers me any help with this idea. In my high school careers questionnaire assessment, it had come up as option number two: 'presenter'. But being from the countryside in the nineties it's about as stupid as choosing an astronaut for NASA!

I still remember the man saying I could study a two-year college course in media.

Media? What's that when it's at home? I've never heard of it before. Someone is listening, interested in me and can point me in the right freaking direction.

I have been searching for that for a long time and I'm on the edge of a new dawn, a doorway into presenting. At eighteen I go back to college and start over again. This is where I'm meant to be and it's incredible.

# CHAPTER 2

# CLUBBING, RAVES AND MEDIA ROCKS!

**DESK**

By eighteen I'm mostly living at Mum's new house and we are great flat mates. Before she retires through illness, she has some glamourous roles for big corporate companies. She has high fashion suits, fast cars, showrooms and an office! Mum is so cool that she is the person a lot of my friends look up to and Lou sees her like an idol. At five-foot-nine tall she is quite a striking woman, warm and gentle underneath and matched with fun and good humour. Often at the weekend she takes all three of us to Snetterton racetrack to watch the cars and bikes fly round the circuit.

Mum loves playing tapes of Chris Rea, Pet Shop Boys, Tina Turner and *The Phantom of the Opera* full blast in the car which makes all car trips quite exciting as young kids. She declines to make us attend Sunday school where a lot of the village kids go. She is not interested even though my grandmother is a church person and runs the plays and amateur dramatics for Sunday school.

She is given a red Renault Turbo for a couple of months before she gets her own car working for Alfred McAlpine. It's just so fast as the average working person doesn't have Turbos. She also has a one down from the top of the range Vauxhall (we can't remember what type). At Cala Homes she has more company cars, but I only remember one of the earlier Mondeos. It's an exciting world filled with new cars all the time in her sales role, selling new homes for Cala at £600,000. Now they would be worth two to three million.

I walk through these decadent showrooms in various locations based all over East Anglia although her final site is down in Bishop's Stortford. These homes are painted and laid out in such luxury and filled with designer objects and furniture. It's like nothing I've ever seen before. No one has homes like these where I live in the nineties. When the sales homes are wrapped up, they don't keep the small items and she brings home things we can keep. I remember ceramic wall art faces and my giant four-foot white plastic watch hung as my bedroom clock. Mum gets a dining room table and a rather nice large wardrobe in her bedroom.

At Bishop's Stortford one day I'm sitting at her desk waiting for her to return and finish work. Her office is typically a not yet sold double garage on the housing estate. It's at this exact moment I decide *I* NEED A DESK! This is more than looking at a desk. It's a point where I realise a new life can occur from a desk.

I had seen a desk before, surely, you must be thinking. Well, yeah. Dad has a desk in the spare room, but I never registered it to be important as you can't see it. It looks like he's been burgled with everything tipped out in panic covering the full-length worktop and the carpet. This is an important working condition decision that accrued to me in that instant.

A desk matters.

## SEX SHOPS

Late one night in my bedroom, I discover the raw power of the Chemical Brothers playing a long set on Radio 1. I've never knowingly heard them much before and my ears find this intoxicating sound extraordinary.

The novelty, the exciting by-chance discovery and the sensation of fresh sounds are incredible things for a mind to experience. Music makes you feel things in an instant, feelings that aren't there less than a minute before and feelings with such depth and intensity. It's pure escapism and for me, it's especially like that with dance music; it's the power that stems from the breaks and the builds, creating those highs. It creates euphoria for free in your mind and body. You don't have to do anything to feel it. Just listen.

Inny, Anna and the other girls have departed for university so that group has dissolved. Fortunately, Suzie and I are back together after being separated by difficult circumstances. Hurrah, for we are an awesome twosome! And we will be an effective team shopping for outfits in sex shops in Norwich. My shopping has evolved!

That's where the best PVC gear can be found for our club life adventures. Suzie has her six-foot tallness and a black cat suit and I have opted for almost the same but in silver with separate shorts and top. Wow, we are impressive looking together, smouldering hot or just thoroughly sticky with sweat as that is what really happens when wearing the most practically rubbish material for dancing but definitely mastering the look we wanted.

We are some badass PVC-clad club bitches (hilariously silly and funny) always laughing at ourselves. I've always hated pubs where just nothing ever happens. Nothing except more alcohol. I don't get the point of being at the pub to sit and do nothing. Why do people do that? A good old rural village pub with largely the same few people in it year after year. Most people around here seem to really enjoy the pub, some going weekly, monthly or to special nights and whatever is on. Sometimes I do go as there is nothing else to do in a village at night and it's likely that sporadically some people you know may be there, maybe catch up with some of the lads.

I'm speaking of several different pubs as I have friends from many different areas now. If it has a pool table, I can cope much better. As a kid we have a large pool table at home so Lou and I are pool sharks from an early age. (Just last month Lou won herself £70 in a game of killer against strangers! Nice one, Lou.)

## CLUBBING!

Not to say all pub nights are dull, but when I enter the club scene it's like socially everything I've ever wanted from a night out. Everything I've been missing with pubs since I was a teenager, all wrapped up in a nightclub. This is perfection. Music is underpinning all our new adventures.

We discover the legendary Pam's House in Ipswich the very moment we both turn eighteen. (It may well be the first nightclub I ever went to.) Pam's House is incredible. It's the next level of clubbing and there is nothing else like it around here at the time. Clubbing is our all focus, our main hobby, and we go sometimes twice a month driving up early and arriving home in the small hours in the dark. We can be in heaven all night long for about ten quid! Amazing, I know!

We go early to get in cheap and hang our coats, swapping for (and often losing) the coat ticket. We buy a bottle of water, then refill from the sinks in the bathroom. That's how you do it for ten quid. It's at Club UK in Ipswich and later it becomes Kink but mostly for us it's just Pam's.

The venue itself is spectacular. The Maltings with its vast size has wooden beams and hosts a small cosy back room and then the main room with double height ceilings and a large dancefloor with a separate low ceiling dancefloor to one side. Upstairs, the bar area is also large, and it has a balcony viewing all the action on the main floor below. It is pure heaven and is also the largest venue I've ever set foot in. It's our home for two years and for Suzie a decade or so alongside various other promoters' nights. We are so new to it all that we just go along without a care as to who will play. We just know it will be great every time. We're looking for a music hit and it delivers every time. It never fails.

Like clockwork it is always the two of us and often other girlfriends join us there. It's as though we are destined to be together. We have not always been friends. A very young Suzie was at my high school, but I didn't really notice her. She left due to severe bullying around thirteen but at the time no one knew why she left. When she came back to sixth form, life gave us another chance to be friends.

It is our alternative world, our nighttime home. It's like walking into another realm where all your troubles melt away. There is no past, no future, only right here, right now. Music is the bedrock of our new life, and we begin to follow promoters and the big names who come to play the never-ending thumping, pounding beat of our new life: hard house music.

Pam's have their own DJs and homegrown talent. I particularly love Bongo Ted when he drops his live percussion on stage. They also bring in superstars like Danny Rampling and other big names.

I can never say for sure who I saw in the early days. Maybe I saw Brandon Block somewhere, maybe I didn't. I'm *relatively* confident I saw Lisa Lashes there. It was the first time I'd seen a female DJ, and she was up on the main stage commanding the audience with spanking good tunes. I can't say a hundred percent for sure but I'm reasonably confident it was her. We never had any flyers as we were too far out in the countryside. It was only as we became regulars and we got deeper into the scene that we knew who was coming up prior to the event.

All the dancers find and make their own incredible outfits, and it's mostly inspired by visits to Ibiza. It's a freakish fun music fetish where you can indulge your entire being all night long. It's my full colour and very loud life and now I know exactly why pubs have never hit the spot. We have hit the next level of lifestyle. Clubbing.

There is hardly ever any trouble unless some twat grabs Suzie's arse then he's in for it. I saw her grab a six-foot bloke by his ponytail and shout in his face. Brave and stupidly risky I thought. When pubs shut their doors at 11 p.m. people go on to the club. Except us. We just skip the pub! We are there at first opening, dancing for hours and hours till the end, which was always 2 a.m. as is the universal licence for clubs. Occasionally they pull an all-nighter by getting permission to stay open till probably 4 a.m. (It was crazy late back then! Hence called an all-nighter but not actually as that would have clearly been at least 6 a.m.)

We lived for dance music in all forms. We were the UK's house music generation. Granted it started out from Chicago in the late 1970s and 1980s and spread rapidly across the US but honestly, we knew nothing of that... Nothing at all. I'd never heard of any of that. I only knew many years later when Dad bought me a new book: *Last Night a DJ Saved My Life*.

That was hard house and all new in the 1990s. I don't recall any specific tracks as they were largely lyricless except first hearing Kadoc's 'The Nighttrain' whilst dancing in the intimately crowded little backroom. It thundered its beats rolling beautifully out of the dark. It was quite a moment. Tunes like 'Bang to the Beat of the Drum'... 'Bang, bang, to the beat of the drum, bang!' Stuff like that but mostly underground tunes that you would only hear there. Play that now... I can't type properly for desk dancing! That rhythm, man, that little break beat... it's almost so simple, it's spectacular.

We named one tune 'Bacon Slice' just to identify it whenever Pam's played it, but never found out what it was. There was no bacon in the lyrics whatsoever. We'd all jump up if we were at the bar getting drinks. 'Come on, girls, it's "Bacon Slice"! Away, baby let's go.'

'Turn Me Out' by Praxis featuring Kathy Brown is one of my all-time greatest tunes. Just throwing that out for you now.

## RAVES: LEGAL OR ILLEGAL? NO ONE KNOWS

East Anglia is firmly on the UK's music map for having an enormous underground rave scene in the 1990s. With its far-reaching high energy raves in big venues and warehouses playing drum and bass with live MCs, or usually smaller dance parties in barns or tents with a more hedonistic vibe from house or psytrance. Make no mistake it's very much alive, and we are firmly embedded in the house scene and that's where I spend my youth. I have no concept that we are riding the music wave of history. I just party hard like everyone else.

In conjunction with all the nightclubs (that I could only attend at eighteen) I go to mini raves. There are endless legal and illegal tent parties happening all over Suffolk and Norfolk. A few are ticketed but for most you can just turn up. It's amazing how this network of parties can be planned, conducted and found by all of us in the middle of muddy fields under the cover of darkness. Sometimes we drive deep into the countryside for hours to locate them.

There still aren't many mobile phones around, just a few. I buy one as I drive a lot late at night. This way of life is largely conducted by word of mouth or maybe the odd call if someone's car gets near to it. You always know when you're getting close to your target as there will be loads of cars pulled up on the grass verge at the side of the road in the middle of nowhere.

The government works hard to bring in new laws and try to ban noise-driven outdoor gatherings with loud repetitive beats. People well know the risks they are taking and still they go ahead. It may reduce the size or sheer quantity of outdoor parties, but it by no means erodes the unstoppable undercurrent of our generation's weekend way of life.

Along with Kate and some pub friends, if you aren't into nightclubs, you are into tent parties! Lou and I had hooked back up now after many years with far less communication during school. It turned out we'd both been going to these countryside raves and so our lifestyle and whole group of friends are aligned once again.

Sometimes you'd just be somewhere out and about and a party would literally spring up near you. You could hear the beats for miles and miles in the stillness of night. If you followed the music across muddy fields, through brambles and ditches, you'd reach a pop-up party.

I'd been attending tent parties and field parties, this underground culture, since I was about sixteen. Usually around 100 to occasionally maybe 300 people would arrive at the scene. Illegal parties can always be hit and miss if the music is not good. Often blokes will be up on the decks banging out psytrance stuff at those type of events and it is not always inspiring to dance much although everyone will be dancing slowly, just not always having it large! They have atmosphere though, I'll say that. It's always incredible, very much a tribal gathering of likeminded free happy spirits. A couple of big names are Mr Whippy and Mr Pitts putting on the best parties along with many other local promoters in marquees and tents sometimes even giant indoor events like one I went to once in Norwich. No idea what it was but it was very big.

I go to a rave in a field where there are two coppers quietly standing on the grass in between two pitched music tents. It's so far into the field and hidden in a bit of a dip that although they discovered it, there is nothing they can do about it. They just stand there sometimes talking to people, being nice and not hassling anyone as the tent parties are always chilled out. I assume the party is illegal as the police are there, but they can't stop it due to the obscure deep countryside location.

I go to a big party in some sort of hanger somewhere near Snetterton racetrack one day. The bigger ones all have luminescent sheets hanging with spirals and tribal designs to light up the side walls. I never saw a single fight, not ever, at any one of these events, and no one ever came along to stop these parties. Maybe they had permission; it was obvious some of the big ones did. You just couldn't tell. There was never any trouble, or we wouldn't have been involved. I never even saw a bottle being thrown. All the partygoers were peaceful people who just wanted to dance.

Another huge party in a tent comes one night out of the blue in the field opposite Knettishall Heath. They have a couple of platforms and two good dancers on podiums. This is more thought out than most events. Classy stuff. (I don't remember exactly but I think about 200 to 500 people were there.) It is massive. One of the dancers on a podium may be my sister-in-law's friend; her boyfriend is a DJ. There are never usually platforms for dancing. It is a very big marquee. I go to dozens of these events as every month or so there is something going on in the darkness.

## MEDIA ROCKS!

Whilst studying I go through a break-up; many things are changing. I wouldn't have ever been seen outside of my house without makeup on (not ever) but I just can't do it. I can't put it on for a whole month. Tough times! Anyway, six months later another relationship begins that I stay in for a while… a couple of decades.

During my West Suffolk College time the course is brilliant. At last, I have found my further education home fully submerged in lovely media. I'm set on becoming a presenter right from day one (or two years prior really) whereas most of the others don't seem to know what they want. We shoot and edit film and start to use a mixture of analogue and digital editing gear. You can splice audio on black tape by cutting with a knife on an eight-track in a sound booth, which is already seriously dated. (I never really knew why it was there. What the hell was it for? History perhaps.)

We sit about watching films (learning), dissecting and writing scripts, and making posters. On the computers I design a CD cover using lots of the little Cream superclub logos flying about in space. I write and present a car video, of course! My brother has converted an Astra himself into a four-by-four, a very impressive feat, and I take out Martin the tech support teacher who helps me film it. And to be fair to him, he does some (ok, quite a lot) of the editing. I have not yet fully worked out the slightly odd college digital editing desk kit. It is quite confusing to me.

We shoot and make a music video to Lou Reed's 'Perfect Day' as it is the specified track. I use my cat dreaming of fish in the fish tank. Well, it seemed like a good idea at the time. Two of the lads are making very funny comedy sketches with them just being odd characters. They are very good. (If YouTube or TikTok had been invented then, they would have been global superstars, but sadly it wasn't at that time.) There are no platforms to showcase anything and boost you overnight. It's all planning, dedication and long, long commitment. There is no immediate, no matter how hard you try.

I take whatever work experience I can find. This is my strategy: learning on the job. There is no way I'm going to uni or study any further as I want to get a job in presenting. Did I mention that? A lot of the others are still at a loss for what to do afterwards but not me. I'm on it with my plan.

I buy a short presenting course over a few days in London which gives me some useful tips and we interview making vox pops and perform pieces to camera to go on my VHS showreel.

I do go for a couple of TV auditions. At one there are about forty of us, all sitting in chairs, who are called up one by one to say a few words. Nope, I don't get that job either, but it really doesn't feel like it suits me anyway. I don't fit the TV mould but I don't know that yet. It just seems like a lazy way to interview to me. Just say one line? Is that it? They are looking for a type of person. Definitely not me.

I go off to SGR FM in Ipswich for my week or two of work experience. Some of the studios still have *carts*! I've never seen them before. They are just so prehistoric and they love their sung jingles. Sung jingles on practically every ad break. 'Suuuung jiingggllle' all the way. However, it's great! They let me open the post and that's so cool as it is full of new shiny music CD singles, the most exciting kind of post. I really enjoy my week shadowing there.

We visit lecturer Phil's voiceover studios, his other line of work, but it isn't for me I think. I set about applying for jobs soon by trawling the phone books and looking for television companies to send my letters and showreels to. It takes a long time to get all the info and write so many letters. I send thirty or forty letters nationwide and every single one I receive back with a crushing, 'No, thanks.' (These were the days when people actually replied by post.) Lucky for me, I don't really see the pile upon pile of rejection 'no jobs here' letters. All I see is the many bits that say, 'Get some experience.' So that is my next plan. Thank you for the information.

Inny and Anna return on summer breaks where we take holidays in Newquay that roll out in the summer of '96 and '97. We even go to a nightclub or two which for them is unusual. We also get near drowned out of our tents one year as it never, ever stops raining. The mud in front of the tent is so deep that half of us, including me, quit the camp site and bugger off to a nice warm and dry youth hostel. The toughest girls remain and stick it out in the mud, but it doesn't cause any friction. Everyone is happy.

With more blissful teenage holidays imminent, Suzie has decided we are going to Ibiza for the first time.

## IBIZA: THE FIRST OF MANY

In Ibiza with the girls for the very first time! HOLY COW, THIS TRIP IS EPIC! There are four of us: me, Suz and two of her friends. We stay in San Antonio Bay on the further side where you catch the little ferry across the water to get into town at night. It is pure magic. We party in Eden some nights. Other times we go in Es Paradis complete with sunburn diving into our first ever foam party.

An old friend Kellie and her girls are there at the same time, so we meet up sometimes with monster nights out on our own bar crawl. It is also one of the worst alcohol poisonings I've ever managed to give myself. That night after all the San An bars, I literally crawl on my hands and knees along the floor. On reaching our fourth level, or somewhere around there, is finally our room. Some lads we'd seen out in the town manage to get in our room. I'm in bed when this lad opens my bedroom door and starts talking to me! What the hell? Nothing to worry about though as our six-foot security Suz quickly chucks those chancers out. She's like our hired door woman.

'Out!' she says with her very angry face. She looks and sounds like she means business. In general, most people don't fuck with her.

Another eventful night is being stunned by the sheer scale and brilliance of Manumission. It's probably the world's greatest freakiest club night on planet Earth. It's hosted in the world's largest nightclub Privilege. It's so vast it has a swimming pool in the middle. A massive pool right in the middle. It is just mind blowing. Ten thousand people together in total euphoria in love with house music and the ultimate club show. I think the theme is good ship Manumission.

Perhaps not surprisingly I have a bit of a thing for sailors after that. It leaves quite an impression!

Upstairs in the open-air bit, there is a metal wire-like structure that looks like a giant golf ball. I stare out to the stars feeling the warm night breeze on my skin wondering how I'm so lucky in life to arrive at this moment in time. This place, here… Just then Suzie's platform shoe snaps. Total freaking disaster! How is this happening to us? Why? The flight, the tickets, the bus ride taking ages to arrive… it's in the middle of nowhere. The money, the clubber's dream, the club… It's Manu-fucking-mission!

The dancers are out of this world scattered on many podiums. There are performers descending from the ceiling on satin ropes and sailors (of sorts) on stage. The creme de la creme of clubbing in Ibiza, maybe the whole world, and her freaking shoe breaks! It isn't just any shoe, like a four-inch-high platform boot heel. The heel snaps off. Timing. Not only can't she walk on the floors, which are basically just broken glass, she can barely stand with one working shoe. Suzie says she's leaving as her feet are impossible to manage. We have to leave and it's agony for us all. The highs and lows of a teenage life right there. That's what I recall anyway.

Suzie's memory of the exact same evening in September '97 is she had already broken her white platform boots previously on a night out so now she was down to the last black pair. She broke them basically en route to the club on the bus, of which we all had a group discussion about what the hell to do next. The result was she would carry on and just look for some sort of shop in the superclub that might have flip flops or something. The bouncers said there were no shops and glass everywhere. It was not like home. At Pam's we could have just found a space to dance with a clean bit of wooden floor. We walked around and it became apparent, like the bouncers had said, it was a sea of broken glass shattered everywhere. It was utterly hopeless and quite dangerous, so we had to admit defeat, devastating defeat, and retreat home. Our overriding memory is the agony of having to leave. We weren't there long at all.

## READ A BOOK

Princess Diana had died just before we left and I spend my minute's silence out on the hotel's balcony, as it is such a loss felt by the whole world. I had been reading a book in the quiet moments of the holiday. Sometimes it is so graphic I have to take a break and put the paperback down.

Another trip of a lifetime regarding that book will soon prevail for me: Beijing. Somehow someone high up in the college has arranged a sort of student swap. Some of their students will come here and some of our media students will go there for seventeen days. It cost around £400. It is far cheaper than a holiday as it is mostly just the flights but also very expensive out of the blue and I have no money as a student. We have to pitch in a letter as to why we think we deserve to go, as there are only eight or ten places and around twenty students in my class.

Fortunately for me I get accepted. I'm so hellbent on presenting I think I can transfer into words why a trip to China Central Television is essential for my current study and future career. Dad has one condition. If I am to go to China, I have to read his book so I can understand some of the country's history.

Read a book, go to China? Deal!

## CHINA

The book I was reading out in Ibiza was *Wild Swans* by Jung Chang. Three generations of Chinese women undergoing hardship and suffering like I've never heard before. It's the first book I've ever had to put down and take a break due to the horrific descriptions of the violence they endured and the atrocious foot binding. Armed with my paperback's brief history lesson, we fly out from Heathrow and onto China.

It's a long flight whereby we chat and, somehow, I sleep in a seat as I'm so thin. There's Phil, our teacher, and a bunch of sixteen- to twenty-year-old students (I'm quite old at nineteen). We stay at a student base somewhere about a thirty- to forty-minute drive from Beijing. I think it's a university. (Yep, my memory is sketchy, you'll get used to it. I have.)

I notice they have bars on all the windows and the rooms are quite basic but clean and good enough. The food is amazing and I try so many different things that I have no idea what they are. We eat breakfast and dinner there like a full feast every time. I've never seen anything like it. I'd only eaten my first Indian meal at a restaurant aged seventeen. It's a full-on cultural experience in every way.

There's a bit of a language barrier and no mobile phones there. We get to call home once or twice in the whole time due to the time zone difference, so calls are incredibly difficult. We are very well looked after, but quite alone on the far side of the world. I do not miss anything really except some English food and him (my boyfriend). I miss him so badly I feel sick to my stomach each morning on my car ride into work at China Central Television Studios. The only way to deal with this physical hurt is to block him out as I can't fully function for twelve hours feeling that way. Once I establish the total mental block strategy, the hurt in my stomach ends instantly. It's weird. It feels new to me, but this strategy works.

The first week's weather is clear blue sky but as the wind lessens the smoke pollution just chokes everywhere. Our driver brings us into the city each morning as we travel through a dull-coloured toxic cloud blanket. Looking ahead through the thick grey air, you can hardly see anything in the distance. The weather seems very constant. Once it's thick with pollution, it never clears; it just stays the same every day we are there. On our tiny island of England, the weather changes by the hour. Here it only seems to change after an entire week. Laura has an asthma attack one evening after the long ride home; we have to sit her on the campus steps to help calm her.

Once through the gates at China Central Television, our working days are set out to us. We study and shadow various areas with pretty much unlimited access. In the evenings after work, around 5 or 6 p.m., we sit in groups and exchange conversation with some of the staff. Teaching spoken English for an hour a night is part of our working terms. I explain that I live in a four-bedroomed house in the countryside and how Dad had built it. They have never heard of such a big house with so many rooms and ask lots of questions. A lot of people say, wherever we go, 'Princess Diana'. They know and seem to feel our nation's loss. Teaching in small groups of maybe seven or eight, we really bond in this brief hour. It's great.

I make a new pen pal for some years to come. One of the girls we are teaching is very fluent at speaking English, smartly dressed and chatty. Her dream is to own a passport to travel to the USA. We realise they learn American English and it is hard for them to obtain a passport. So much so that no one has one. Not a single person I speak to there owns one, but they know sometimes someone can get one but usually only for work purposes. They have hope.

Every day, boxes of lunch are sent to wherever you are working that day. It is always the same thing: a whole fish in a box with plain white rice. I'm grateful for lunch, but I've never seen a whole fish on a plate before. We struggle a bit with the food differences. A lot of the time we end up piling into the new and very upmarket McDonalds down the road as it is the only thing around that we recognise.

I lose a good half a stone by the time I arrive home; I think we all lose some weight plus we are walking miles and miles each day. But honestly the evening food and restaurants we go to are out of this world. We eat all kinds of things like snake but with the language problems we often have no idea what else is being consumed. It's amazing to sit at the table with course after course brought out with so much diversity. They are very kind hosts. One night a rat runs across the floor, but it's no problem. He's minding his own business!

China have DVD. (At the time this was totally unheard of in the West for years to come. Maybe a decade? I can't remember exactly when it arrived to the masses. I know it was a long time. We were being sold more VHS recorders for years so then we all had to buy again when DVD showed up.) They are also using digital pens and drawing boards to create images on screen. And they have the layered graphics that you tend to see on every single Netflix show intro now. They are so far ahead it is unreal with breathtaking equipment and special effects.

We can also see how regulated it is and all running to a completely different agenda to us. It appears that almost everything is made for the government or state and how they want it to be seen. Our TV is run by companies like ITV, Channel 4 and the BBC. Nothing to do with politics really. Here, everyone does as they are told. There doesn't appear to be much creative freedom. If you present the news in the wrong tone or words, you can get sacked and then you might not work in news again. This is a serious place with serious consequences. In any country you must follow the rules, and we are here to teach English, learn and observe media production, so that's what we do respectfully: our job.

One day after a lot of signed documents, we get permission to film on Tiananmen Square. It can be a dangerous place to film as you must do the right thing with the right people with the exact permissions. With that in mind and guards walking about, Phil has to take some time out in silence. He can well remember the recent history of Tiananmen Square and its tanks. Although as a student I don't really feel it at that age. I don't have enough life experience. It resonates deeply with Phil though.

I set about presenting my work piece to camera. 'I'm nineteen years old, I'm halfway round the world and I'm on Tiananmen Square.'

I do that about ten times trying to work out what I can say on my first try and without getting arrested. Travel is still more a luxury and this is far-out travel of a different kind. We are allowed to use the editing suites afterwards and keep our video tapes. All sorted and cleared as ok to keep. At the end we receive a certificate of study and training from China Central TV.

We are usually out for twelve hours a day to and from Beijing. On our nights off back at the university campus we wander through the windy dark concrete streets to reach a bar to unwind. One night there are some Japanese students hanging out in there and we strike up a good rapport. The Chinese are very quiet and money is scarce, but these kids are as loud as we are, fashionable and fun loving. (I still have the photos.) It is a great refreshing night of laughs much like any other pub night with students.

Every night I wake around 3 a.m. and look over at my roomie Laura sleeping peacefully and I wonder why she never wakes up. I always did every night.

We visit many places and spend hours and hours travelling around to see the tourist sites at the weekends. We travel hundreds of miles on a minibus to so many places including the exquisite Summer Palace, which I love, and we walk on the Great Wall of China. (We visited more places perhaps even the Terracotta Army but that's how long ago it feels to me now, that I'm not sure.) It is site after site of amazing places.

We watch the Peking Opera somewhere downtown in Beijing. It is quite spectacular although not all the teenage students enjoy it. They are a little overwhelmed with the very different culture, drastic food changes, struggling with the length and pace of the trip and basically homesick. Once, we go into a very big nightclub.

The Forbidden City is incredible. There is an area full of wind-up clocks, I presume, collected from all over the world. That is the furthest I think I've ever walked; it literally never ends. We visit an art gallery and I buy a three-foot Chinese hand scroll of a colour hand-painted tiger. (The full scroll didn't survive too well, but I have the tiger part in a glass frame now. It reminds me of the whole experience.) After an eternity and a surreal new working life we fly back home, exhausted but successful and thoroughly cultured!

I found a photo ID stamped 'China' and the certificate that states I completed a study of professional TV production techniques on 8 November 1997. The newspaper article appeared in the local *Mercury* on 5 December 1997 complete with a picture of us students, teacher and our chunky film cameras on the Great Wall.

Back home and fresh from my faraway culture and thinner from eating rice (due to not being able to eat the fish for lunch by day three), a new radio station appears on my Sony car stereo with the name scrolling across the digital display and it's called Vibe FM, rhythm driven on 106.4 FM.

Nothing cool has ever happened in Norfolk. Nothing, period. So, what's happening now? Nothing new has ever appeared on the FM radio dial, so much so that I didn't know it could happen! Radio 1 is for our age group and that's it. That's all we have. How have they done that? Who's done that? An entire new organisation to tune into proudly saying every twenty minutes, 'We've put a dancefloor on your dial.' It's the perfect strapline, an iconic summary. In fact, it's so big it's got four separate frequencies and they keep repeating, 'Vibe 105-108 FM.'

I listen and boy, it's just so cool, so new, young, fresh and dynamic and they are having so much fun. I remember saying, 'Right, I'll be going there soon.' I call and book an appointment and rock up a few days later still jetlagged from my flight back into Heathrow.

Showbiz timing and jetlag… I know that will work in my favour.

# CHAPTER 3

# ENTER VIBE FM AND BECOMING A PRESENTER DJ

By day I'm working on building sites and by night at the weekend I'm dancing in clubs. I assume someone had invented gyms, but no one goes to the gym, not a single person I know. Dad plays squash at the sports centre and people are just ordinary at this time. (No enormous buffness like on YouTube today. Just normal looking people!)

I love a bit of sport, but I can never get into the gym. It feels to me like being trapped inside. It's like a workout factory and if it works for you, it works. I try a few times but it never floats my boat. I'd rather be outside where possible but if the weather's off, some indoor time is necessary. I buy some typically nineties *enormous* gold plastic, presumably concrete-filled, dumbbells. That's just about my time with weights the few years I put in aged sixteen.

I have some now, but often I just look at them and make sure they are lined up correctly on the floor! Job done! I've tried to combine weights with yoga afterwards as I'm more likely to bother to pick them up this way. It took a full twenty years for me to reach yoga on my to do list (there's been quite a lot on my list), so back on weights could be next, you never know. In fact, I've worked out that if I lift the weights, I can lie on the floor gasping for breath doing a spot of recovery yoga in between reps. It's working out well currently.

I also have my new rowing machine as I like to rotate my sports a bit. The rowing machine is still current as I don't have to do any thinking. I just switch off and row watching Jake the Treasure Hunter on YouTube. It's quiet too, which is good for my duff ears under the ear defenders, which soften the sound of the piston working away, and the squeaking, which is probably me.

As a teenager I have a full-length red and black punch bag that hangs in the middle of Mum's garage. When I take it over and walk into the kitchen fully covered in gift wrapped black bin bags, it looks a lot like I'm carrying a corpse over my shoulder. Lucky the neighbours don't see. I think I would have had to say something to appease the situation.

## REGIONAL RADIO

I confidently pick up the phone and book my appointment at Vibe FM. Oh yeah! I meet the programme controller Baz Jones. (He may have had a different title then but either way Baz was the boss.) He comes across as professional but approachable and gives me a brief tour around the place. The new built brick offices take up the whole of the ground-floor level with managers' offices, a meeting room and two large luxurious studios with one small production room in between. Oh my gosh, this is something else. It's so lush. I try to manage my excitement and look professional.

They have brand-new custom built twin soundproof studios in the middle of the light orange offices with matching blinds, the station's brand colour. Each studio is fitted out with the same mirror image. I'm told they cost a million pounds to build, and it looks like it. We have a good chat and I impress them with all my many work experience placements. I casually throw in that I still feel jetlagged from recently flying back in from China. (At that time China Central TV was the world's biggest broadcaster and teenagers didn't say that every day.) Baz says I should come back sometime. Whoop, whoop!

## I VOLUNTEER

Towards the end of college we are put forward for some real work projects. I film and edit a wedding video with a lad from the course. We get paid well and do a reasonable job in a couple of days. After some time passes, I firmly get my foot into Vibe's door and never look back. I pay attention to everything and everyone I possibly can. I start with opening the post and making tea for everyone, lots of tea. Refreshments are a very important social aspect of work. It's more than just a drink, isn't it? It's bothering to take the time to give the extra bit. I don't have to make tea, but I do often out of choice and frequently people make tea for you in return. Tea's not in the manual. It's not essential to fulfil your job, it's more of a social bond. Or coffee if that's your thing. In fact, I'll revise that statement a little! If you've got a 2 a.m. radio shift, or any work shift, I'm going to upgrade tea to essential. In fact, it's almost survival at that hour, isn't it? If you make shit tea, you're not going to get far, are you?

I volunteer all my time and little by little learn all the different aspects of the radio industry, mainly in programming. It is helpful to have some understanding of what the sales team are doing, so I listen to understand them. I firmly imbed myself into the orange fabric which adorns the office walls, and I learn fast. There is production studio software and on-air studio broadcast output mixing desks and software with several monitors, with jingles, idents music, adverts and so on. Then there is music programming software, music editing, travel bulletins, film reviews, RAJAR, target audience demographics, content, planning the station branding and so on.

You name it, I have my nose in it all and it is bliss. This team of people is the coolest team I've ever met. I learn from the grassroots up everything about my new passion: radio.

## TV

Glen White and I get on so well. He's like working with a big brother, and I learn so much from him. I shadow him at almost everything in the station. Whatever he is doing, I'm close behind. He is a presenter DJ and the head of music. He gets himself a TV slot in Cambridge and asks me to join him presenting it.

On 15 May 1998 I feature in a few newspapers including the *Diss Express*. 'An interview slot has brought media student Nikki Elise closer to fulfilling her dream as a TV presenter.'

Cable is a new thing in England and Glen gets us a slot on Red TV. I recruit Alex from college as our cameraman and we go out and pre-film bits on the streets in advance. I co-write and co-present our weekly youth music magazine style show called *Mix It Up*.

Our show is a mix of music videos, sketches, callers and chat. It has a similar format to *The Big Breakfast*. It's a youth magazine style show where we play music videos around the content. At the time, *Big Brother* is new and interesting on the television. I write our comedy sketch as a spin-off called 'Small Sister'. It's good fun with lots of silly humour. It features Nina, who is our main morning Vibe FM news reader, but based in

Norwich. Glen and I pre-produce our own comedy opening titles with us behaving like children chasing each other round a park with water pistols and silly sunglasses.

We work from two different studios and produce two different seasons over a couple of years. (When we needed a new camera operator, Charlie Bird came on board. When filming she went by the name of Charlie Cam.) I don't think many people were watching. Maybe six, ha-ha! I've no idea… could have been hundreds or thousands. It makes no difference how many are watching when you do live shows as your focus is only the job. Delivering content in the shows to get the flow perfect.

There is a lot of advance prep and we work late into the night. It is such a laugh and a good learning process. I make presenter showreels and mail them out to dozens and dozens of companies getting absolutely nowhere. I have received a lot of nos in my time, so many I can fill a bucket full with all the letters.

## RADIO

Aged twenty I leave college in July of 1998 with my BTEC National Diploma (with maybe a Merit, maybe a Distinction, or perhaps a bit of both). Even to me my certificate is not that clear. Anyway no one ever asks me for it, not once. I then fully commit myself daily 9–5 p.m. for about a year for free. I virtually move into the building. I'm very happy and quite skint but that doesn't matter as I'd have sacrificed anything to be there. I love the team, and they love me. It is so exciting to be involved with such a powerful but cool brand.

One of my first paid jobs is a TO (technical operator). I drive a pre-recorded weekend show, two hours work, £20. Sometimes the DJ calls me up in the studio if, on occasion, I make a mistake on-air whilst transmitting his show. I used to think, *What a geek listening to his own show!* Sometimes I go to the bathroom, and I come back and the song has run out. A radio nightmare! If the pee break breaks transmission, this is not acceptable! If the music ever stops, the broadcasting has failed and it does not fail by itself. Mostly it's human error. People start running from all directions and it's major panic stations! Unless it's late at night and you're the only one there. (However, some years later when it would be my show on-air, I'd be doing exactly that, listening in late at night and insisting on precision and very high standards. Although I had the decency to wait until the working week to discuss it professionally and there was a high chance I'd have been pissed on a Friday night.)

I work on Breakfast production promos and producing film reviews. I love the film press packs and CD sound bites so much. They are a delight to work with. A little CD audio surprise package and working out what I can construct from this delight today. I produce the radio advert for *Hill House*, a 1999 fantasy horror. Trouble is I produce it a bit too well and it's at nighttime, playing out on-air after dark. With creaking doors and screams, I have pumped them up to the max on the editing software. Excellent work, but a bit too scary for daytime radio. I'm asked to tone it down a bit for our younger audience. This is me getting creative! It scares the shit out of people.

## VOICE COACHING: I CAN'T SPEAK PROPERLY

Nothing is ever straightforward for me and there are some other barriers in my way. Baz has politely flagged up my voice and diction. I cannot go on air reading a travel bulletin saying, 'A four'een.' Oh crap! I need to be able to say, for example, 'A four-teen' nice and neatly in the Queen's English. Pronunciation matters.

Regional dialect is unpopular with mainstream media and some accents aren't accepted in the trade. I hadn't realised that my newly acquired street accent is now a big problem. It could have been broad Suffolk, which I'd never spoken before, but if it didn't fit, it didn't get on. Ironically my neutral voice of two years prior probably would have been just about ok. Baz is helping me with suggestions and guidance. These options include elocution lessons (that I've never heard of) and singing lessons that are good to strengthen the voice… Oh, ok… Singing, me? That must be a joke!

Upon learning what elocution lessons are, I find a basically archaic lady who is extremely posh, living in the heart of Cambridge. I pay her as my voice coach to teach me to speak 'properly'. I remember reading *Pickwick on Ice*. What the actual fuck is that? But I do all that is required of me for months on end trotting into central Cambs and back home again. Information is power and Baz had given me the info. I begin to understand the voice as a tool. It is an instrument and therefore it can be worked with, practised, modified, tuned and pitched. I get quite a rapid transformation under way.

I also take up singing lessons with my wonderful, much younger than my voice coach and quite posh teacher. She teaches me to strengthen my diaphragm (I didn't know I had one). We get on well and we laugh a great deal; she has a naughty twinkle in her eye. She starts playing the piano, giggling and then we both burst into fits of laughing. On reconciling ourselves that we have to get the work done, she composes herself and we start again, telling me to sing watching myself in the mirror. Unknown to me previously, I find this utter torture. It's then that we realise I have real issue with looking at myself in the mirror. It makes me feel so uncomfortable, my eyes skirt around the room trying to avoid eye contact with myself. It's worse than buying a new bra! When you get yourself half-naked squashed against a Marks & Spencer's three-sided, florescent-lit mirror, that always ranks highly for me at the top end of discontentment.

We sing 'Somewhere Over the Rainbow' and a whole bunch of other badass shit. Maybe a theme from James Bond. I practise and practise, and she thinks I'm doing really well. The results of my efforts are obvious and I become strong voiced at last. (Note that I would do my breathing and vocal warm-up exercises most working days during my morning car ride for the rest of my career. Commitment to detail and warm-up my voice, daily.)

I have all my notes written on sheets of paper to study at home. I script, record and produce myself a warm-up voice CD to practise repeatedly until I sound professional. I don't know if anyone else did this, but I did. I use it to warm up almost every day in the car CD player on my drive to work, for years and years, until I could do it from memory.

Even when I know it off by heart, it is still useful to repeat the words and phrases, particularly if I've been partying my ass off and am absolutely knackered on Monday mornings. I want to reiterate that I take breathing and vocals very seriously. I buy a book on breathing and speech for goodness sake. I read the whole thing to understand sounds and letter formation. (It was doubly useful as an adult when my autistic toddler son would be struggling with areas of speech. I could break it all down for him easily as I knew what parts of the mouth formed what parts of the words and why some sounds and letters were physically hard to make. It was useful knowledge that served me well. Effort: one hundred percent.)

## FIRST SHOW, SMALL CO-PRESENTER

When I start out, Becky Jago is on Breakfast with Baz: The Baz and Bex Breakfast Show. She is a lovely girl at the time. Well, she's in her early twenties, she is clearly a woman. A lovely person, warm, genuine and funny and we get on so well. I get my trial runs covering her sometimes with the travel news and we have been given a new slot. The new show is created to push full Breakfast back till 7 a.m. to help Baz, who is a DJ in the clubs, presenter for the Breakfast show and responsible for all programming. We are *The Girl Power Hour*. It must have been in late '98 or '99, weekday morning 6–7 a.m. I now earn £70 a week and am having a blast. We have so much free reign in creativity to write and deliver almost whatever we want; it's so much fun. That's our role: to create fun!

I part-time co-present pre-Breakfast with Bex driving the desk for about a year. Personally, and professionally, we write or produce bits with scripts and content however we like (within the brand settings) and just mess about on air for an hour each morning. (In all my years at Vibe, I smiled almost every single day and all day long.) I'm also working as the Breakfast show content producer. I produce all their Breakfast audio sound bites, jingles and promos. Momo, the station's producer, makes all the Breakfast's bigger sound packages and competition audios. He makes everything else. He's in charge of the sound of the station.

I've run out of money to live on, and I need to make more to pay for the running costs of my burgundy red three-door Vauxhall Astra. At my request my brother has welded on twin tail pipes and I fitted a custom-built base box in the boot, a subwoofer, of course. Sadly, I have to leave my adored full-time, but still mostly unpaid, job and go back to the building site again.

I keep the part-time work and having been in the glamour of media for a year I return to the building site feeling a bit deflated. But I'm not afraid of hard work so I get on with the two jobs for some time to come, getting up around 4.30 a.m. each morning to start around 5.30 a.m. prepping the show. Sometimes I get in by the skin of my teeth at about 5.50 a.m. in a whirlwind panic. Ad break is at 5.55 a.m. Jesus, I'm on-air in ten seconds! We've all done it.

Later that day, covered in brick dust, I evaluate what I have, whilst shovelling sand and cement in the yellow concrete mixer. I gain a huge wealth of knowledge and skills. I purposely carve out a starting point into presenting in regional radio, with a huge audience and a powerful brand. A small door is open, and I will never give up on my dream. I stop for a flask of tea and cold toasted peanut sandwich. Nick is on the building site; Nikki is back on air tomorrow at 6 a.m.

## BIG SHOW, BREAKFAST CO-PRESENTER

Becky (known on air as Bex) also has dreams and lands the role presenting the weather at Anglia TV. We say our goodbyes and off she goes. After Bex leaves I take the lead host, writing and co-presenting roles, driving *The Girl Power Hour* with Gemma. I earn my promotion from the ground up.

Aged twenty-two, around the year 2000, I land my first big show, the biggest of all in radio. I'm given co-presenter on Breakfast with roughly 30,000 plus people turning in every morning, maybe more. (It feels almost odd now, as without it being written down here, I literally had forgotten that I did this number of shows. The journey was so varied; I'd forgotten the early days.)

Breakfast is awesome and the flagship show for all radio stations. Baz is a clever, warm and funny guy, but he can come in grumpy. So carefully I make his cup of tea or coffee and wait until he speaks. It's usually tea but if he asks for a coffee, beware, the morning is gonna be a tough one! The cup of choice can foretell the level of tiredness and therefore how to proceed. It is early getting up at 5 a.m. and it is painful for anyone. (I was exactly the same after a few more years working insane club land shifts. Many years later Stu Grant even politely pointed out Nikki's grumpy in the mornings. I tried to make more of an effort after that tip. I was mainly staying quiet saving energy for the show… and knackered.)

I wave goodbye to building sites. Finally, I'm a full-time presenter plus producing all the Breakfast trailers and promos. Sitting eagerly in the spare on-air studio which is mainly the production studio, I sift through listening for all the best bits to montage. I develop my own style as I can do your regular show best bit or bits, but I look for bits of noise that just sound funny. Us squeaking, umming or erring, or whatever is unusual. Then I cut it all together so it is just a quick-fire montage of ridiculous sounds. Fresh ideas that sound quirky, and we can say, 'Look at us. We don't take ourselves too seriously.' Life is about having fun and Vibe FM is all about fun. I create different sounding promos throughout the week, from ridiculous to informative to encompass a range of promo styles that sound a little different. I loved audio cassette stories as a kid and now I get paid to make my own little audio adventures. Can you even imagine how much fun I'm having?

Baz, Jane (our new events manager) and I pop to Barcelona for a few days on a recce of some sort. Reconnaissance work for radio events includes links, i.e. phone calls, back into the Breakfast show and exploring. We walk around the beautiful streets in the daytime and go into the sex museum with Jane. We are greeted by a six-foot wooden penis. That info may have been discreetly dropped from our Breakfast content! We stay at The Hotel Splendid and they graciously give me a free towel! Recces are awesome as we get paid to do some work abroad and it feels like we are just hanging out in another city. Which we are, and getting paid.

Baz, Glen, Debbie and a few others have moved up from Essex Radio, our sister station. They launched Vibe FM with

Peter Andre across the East of England one year before I joined. Our listening figures roll in every three months. I don't know how long I'd been on Breakfast but one RAJAR set I can vividly remember. I push open the two seriously heavy wooden soundproof doors. Baz looks at me and says, 'Nix, the Breakfast figures are phenomenal.' He is truly ecstatic, if a little surprised himself.

Breakfast usually peaks somewhere around 8 a.m. to 8.30 a.m. with between 30,000 to 40,000 listeners. (I don't have all the old RAJAR figures, but it was an amazing jump up on that specific quarter. It was a dream come true.) We are delivering absurdly funny shows and now utterly staggering figures to confirm it. I like to think it's partly due to my love of crafting those little promos that go out all week. It keeps us fresh in people's minds, but I produce them with my humour and style. Make people laugh and they are more likely to tune in tomorrow.

I don't remember what we started on, but in the early days we used to say we had roughly a third of a million listeners per week. We grew up to well past 370,000. It continually grew with almost every single RAJAR.

## I WANT TO BE A DJ

Very early on, even when Bex was around, all the guys are DJing at the weekends and making a lot of money. Definitely Adi, Baz and Glen and maybe Debbie. It looks interesting. Bex and me think we'll have a crack at it. Glen shows me how to line up a track and grab the first beat on our old rack mounted studio Denon CD players. I mix… well, not just like that, but that's how quick I started. I grab a couple of CDs one day and get straight to it after my show. Bex does it for a bit as well, but I don't think she's sucked into it like I am. Beats and drums are my thing after all, and she has a face for TV. I have a head for headphones!

It seems like an easy extension to all the techniques I'm learning. Anyone working there has full and free access to all the music stored in the digital library. Thousands of tunes to scroll through all available to listen to or burn onto CDR. It's an extensive database of dance music paradise.

I decide to get into this DJ thing and throw any spare time I have at it starting in the Vibe spare studio. I practise and practise pitching up and down the beats, mostly on CD and some vinyl, and I jump on at any friends who have a full set-up at home. I bang tunes away for ages. I restart and rescue just two or three selected records over and over, then one night, pure magic happens. It goes from being a complete carnage of horrible chaotic messy beats crashing all over the place into total pure split hearing! One part of my head hears one track and the other can clearly and precisely hear the other. 'Holy crap, I can hear, I can hear!' I shout at the top of my voice, over the tunes.

I remember it like it was yesterday. With split hearing achieved in that moment, after that, it was just like any other profession. Practise, practise, practise and dedicating of all my spare time, whilst willingly sacrificing my social life, for the rest of… well, nearly all my twenties.

## MY OWN SHOW, OVERNIGHTS AND SWING JOCK

In April of 2000 I land my first solo show overnight. Appropriately it comes prenamed *Insomnia* which it also kindly gives me after about three months of living with the night shift. I resent radio's standard six shows a week, five days a week and one at the weekend.

Jane suggests it is a good idea to keep a folder of all my work and highlights. (This was well before the digital age.) It is helpful for interviews or to look back at what you were doing and when.

(Fortunately, I have this immaculate preserved photographic timeline of my working life. Which is bloody useful now, writing this, as my memory is shot to shit. Half of this section is from that little portfolio, as it's just so long ago and, with so many shift changes, how could anyone remember all that? Good job I'm writing my book now at forty-three and, as I have children, time has rolled into forty-four and now I'm trying to finish aged forty-five! Otherwise by the time I reach fifty it would have only been five pages long.)

## MY FIRST SOLO SHOW

Here's an extract from one of my first newspaper interviews for *The Girl Power Hour* with Gemma Cutting.

**How do you cope with the early mornings?** I sleep at any time of the day and if I'm on an awkward shift, I'll sleep up to three times in a day. I had friends once.

**What time do you have to get up?** I get up around 1.30 a.m., but I also cover everybody else's shift (swing jock). When necessary, I swap shifts and some weeks, I have done up to ten shows in a week. I sleep whenever I can and I'm always tired. Wow, don't I sound great company?

## OVERNIGHTS AND INSOMNIA

My friends will tell you I'm always in bed first. I'm a lightweight! I just can't stay awake till the graveyard shift show starts. Instead, I opt to go to bed around 9 or 10 p.m. for a couple of hours and then get up and go to work. After leaving work around 7 a.m. I drive home and go back to bed. After about three months I develop insomnia and I can only sleep for about three hours at a time, then my body wants to get up.

Of course, split sleeping like this is a stupid idea and I screw up. That's what I ask my body to do most nights and it begins to run automatically. It is an unfolding nightmare with terrible sleep and live shows to produce. I'm on coffee before the show! Also, as swing jock I can be on anytime, so I don't have just the night shift; I have other day shifts all over the place in the week too. I think that is where it's tough, but I take it. I'm never one to turn down the opportunity, no matter how hard it is. I'm young and I manage it somehow.

Once at least I do three shows in a day. There's roughly a total of six presenter-driven shows in twenty-four hours. That's fifty percent coverage from Nikki Elise. Lucky old listeners! My family always has Vibe on. My brother has jacked in farming and is working with Dad now, and they listen to the radio a lot. Monday to Friday 8 a.m. till 4.30 p.m. and they get to hear an awful lot of me, just like anyone else. On the crazy cover days, which is almost every week, you get six to seven hours (and once, nine or ten hours) of me in just one day! It's fair to say I'm working my ass off right around the clock.

I partially solve the sleep issue by meditating a visual walk down a green grassy, bird- and butterfly-filled pathway back to sleep. It's manageable. Nice but no, that doesn't work anymore. Nothing works for true insomniacs and most people can't fathom that at all. Even if you hit the gym factory for three hours, my dear old insomniac, there's no sleep for you. Nope! I just don't drop into the normal sleep zone or stay in it for that matter. It's annoying.

## DJ GEAR

I buy decks and I have, of course, been DJing too. Meet my babies: two gorgeous little silver Pioneer CDJ-100s. (If I still had them, they would be up on my wall like the artwork that they were. I do still have the same original Pioneer mixer, working perfectly after about fifteen years of solid beat graft, and it just sits in its well-earned retirement. I'm not a hoarder and would often sell my old gear to make way for new kit.)

At Mum's, half my bedroom has been turned into a working studio to practise the art of DJing. Mum is typically very laidback and supportive and doesn't mind me practising for hours on end with heavy beats pounding through the lounge celling. After all she likes the tunes and could tape *Eastenders* when desperate. It's not like she can hear anything else for two or three hours at a time in our little two-bed house. I practise with house and dance music several times a week for six months solid. I practise until I'm ready to go out, and I get my first gig supporting Adi, who is quite a renowned local DJ and Vibe presenter. Adi has an incredible deep smooth radio voice and is a lovely gentle guy. He takes me out on my first set in a village hall type place. It goes well and I have no mistakes, no clangers and no mic or crowd skills, but I give a solid start.

I think Adi was a DJ previously at Rollerbury (the skating place). This is one of our favourite hangouts as young kids and into our early teens. A big group of us go up there for the afternoon all weaving around the wooden floor at high speed. It's on another level as they have their own DJs high up in a booth playing out tunes and taking requests. I save up until I buy a pair of seriously cool black Roces skates and fitted big fat fluorescent laces. They are well used but in mint condition and would have lasted about 300 years if a mouse hadn't viciously chewed through all the inside padding when they were put in the loft.

Rollerbury is the coolest place in town. They have an entire themed end wall. The best one was city apartment blocks and skyscrapers. It's so inspiring that Dad's neat idea is to copy this, as he has all these big rolls of paper knocking about. It fully covers the probably seven-metre-long lounge wall. We paint and print black silhouettes for the city blocks with yellow sponge stamps for lights. He has quite a lot of house parties. Even one when he is stuck in bed vomiting from his migraine right before the party started and I host the whole thing without him.

My music collection starts in '99. The next few years are almost a total blur and total lack of sensible sleep! I do some gigs out with the guys as well as by myself. Very quickly Baz has put my name forward as a new talent. He has left his residency at Brown's in Stowmarket, moving on, and he says to the club's owner Dave Brown and Vibe FM's R&B and soul DJ, 'Nikki will be great for this.' I meet with Dave briefly and he hires me.

## MY FIRST DJ RESIDENCY

Around my twenty-second birthday I start my first DJ residency at Brown's. I always find Dave calm, fair and decent to work for. His son does the warm-up and when I go on, there's always something up with the mic. I sound like a chipmunk in my inexperience of club mixer desks and mics.

This is the first time I start to learn all the club's mixer functions, live. The ones at the club are way bigger than my basic two-channel at home. Each week I have to work out how to fix it, whilst mixing tunes, without dropping a beat. Almost all clubs and deck set-ups sound slightly different. Once I realise I'm inheriting this mic problem each time, I fiddle with the knobs until it works for my voice. I think he has a higher pitch voice than me and I confess in my early raw days I'm very shouty and just plain loud. So those two different voices don't come out well on one mixer setting. I sort that out quickly under pressure as it is do or die in front of a live crowd.

I bang it out in what I would become known for. I start to develop my own style. I play OT Quartet's 'Hold That Sucker Down', The Prodigy's 'Out of Space', and Baby D tracks. Then I slow it down a bit and play some garage and more chart stuff, maybe Daniel Beddingfield's 'Gotta Get Thru This', to fit in with the local expected club sound. My job is to build a crowd and a reputation, not alienate them. I play Stowmarket every Friday night for six months or more and plus other gigs on Saturday.

The crowd is exactly what you'd expect for a young group in a small town, but there is a girl who is dancing alone and always on the right side of the dancefloor. She is dressed differently to the rest, in her clubber's gear, hot pants, crop tops and big fluffy boots. Typical house gear. After a while she comes up and speaks to me about the tunes. She is complaining and saying, 'Why isn't it all banging tunes? You're playing some amazing tunes then you go and play R&B. What is this crap?'

It turns out (after she bugs me repeatedly for a few weeks) that she dances for Pam's House. She is a house head too.

I say, 'Come and talk to me after my set but quit bugging me now!'

We grab that drink and I explain that there are rules that you follow to please the crowd and owners in this type of smaller venue. The capacity is maybe 200 to 400, something like that.

She says she thinks I'm good but then I play some total shite. We laugh about how she told me so directly. 'Nikki, this is fucking shit. Sort it out. Where's Tag Team's "Whoomp! (There It Is)" remix?' Charlie tells me loud and clear what she wants every single week, funny complaints... the girl has character. I like her. Funny kid.

She wants to be a DJ and is stuck in a boring job that she hates as she has been made to drop out of school very young. At this time within her traveller family girls are not educated for long.

I say, 'I'll teach you how to mix.'

She is blown away by the offer and thinks I'm joking. I set some time aside into teaching her the basics on my decks. She comes round and I just leave her to play for hours. For me it's time well spent as I know she is serious, so I give her an opportunity. Dreams are meant for following.

She told me our first set together was in Fat Pauly's in Norwich where one deck was bust so they had to swap it over live whilst she carried on playing. She came to see me play at Debenham Dome. Even my mum came to that one! She got herself some decent gigs as Miss Charlie B (B is for Bird), the nickname I gave her, in the well-respected Club M in Newmarket. Disruption was a night she promoted and played Beats Are Banging in Jokers in Stowmarket. We might have both played it together one time. I have played there once or twice.

## I GET MY FIRST BIG DJ RESIDENCY!

Going back a year, there is a new player in Norwich. (Bars are going to almost take over from clubs in the decade to follow.) It is breathtakingly well designed with floor-to-ceiling glass walls on either end and the bar itself is one long flowing curve.

The size of this place is ridiculous with its vast wooden floors and two sets of mirrored sweeping staircases that roll around to reach upstairs.

Under a Vibe FM promotional night, I help launch Squares on Riverside. I tell the manager on that first night, 'What this place needs is a DJ.' It's begging for the final piece. I work a brief six months to a year at Brown's before the manager of Squares calls me and offers me Saturday nights. One year after I launched the venue, I go back.

We carve out fame and fortune for the super bar. I say farewell to Dave and his family-run club with his son and daughter in Brown's. (I went back for many guest sets over the years and Dave's birthday party with Baby D performing live. Given I'd played her iconic track possibly hundreds of times it was a pleasure to meet her in person, although she'd almost lost her voice at that appearance. Shows how hard performers try to stick to the schedule and not let people down.)

## RIVERSIDE

Riverside in Norwich is the new epicentre of nightlife along with Prince of Wales Road. We are tearing it up. I play at Time nightclub a fair bit and Norwich becomes my city; it is where I feel at home. I'm there all the time, and I know all the doormen along the strip at least by face and a couple by name. I know I'm becoming successful in my work when I say hello to all the bar staff and some of the enormous muscley guys on the door who can't look me in the eye. This is strange and new to me. I guess they are seeing the brand, the radio presenter, the DJ, not just me. I'm still just me at five-foot-four. Really, I'm not that scary. That's when you feel things are changing. When people can't look you in the eye. It's odd but you get used to it.

Squares is one of the first to have video walls. It's like four or six big screens together creating one big video wall with continually rotating pop videos playing silently alongside me DJing. With Christina Aguilera's 'Dirty' in her boxing ring and leather chaps playing over and over, no one complains about the view. We have our own team of beautiful dancers who are some of the best in the city. There are about six girls swapping on and off in their hot pants and boots. Lydia, Tanya and others dance high up on the middle part of the swirling wide staircases which double as club platforms. I don't remember all the girls' names. I name one Vicci 400 on account that she does 400 sit-ups to get the most incredible core! I said they were the best.

I build my own night from scratch but the whole place is a thrilling atmosphere. You can't beat it. Some of the best nights of my life are there with this crowd, right up close and personal. It's flamboyant and decadent. It's high-class music and social heaven.

I craft my nights as a cross between harder dance tracks and commercial dance music usually the twelve-inch versions and remixes. I play funky house, dance, trance, some hardcore and get into mixing a little bit of drum and bass. I like the diversity and change of energy and pace within my sets. It is like I throw away the rule book on one-speed house sets. Why one tempo, why? Who fucking says? I'm doing this my way. Nikki Elise style. All the dancers love Silicone Soul's 'Right On'. For me it's the signature track for that venue.

It isn't just my Saturday nights. We are also tying in live broadcasts on Vibe FM like the Boxing Day Special. (I still have that live set on CD amongst many I recorded, including New Year's Eve celebrations, and all of this unfolded over the next couple of years on my named Saturday night: Kinky with Nikki Elise, 2002 and 2003; I still have a few of those original flyers.) Glen has Fridays and we are fucking nailing it, for real. The numbers taken on the bar are insane. It's crazy spending.

Across the city and mainly Riverside my image is plastered everywhere on giant posters and flyers across Norwich. On a good night they take £20,000 on the bar. Capacity is either 500 or 1,000 but because it's a bar, people roll in and out all night long. We may get well over 5,000 people throughout an evening. I'm so utterly focused on tailoring my DJ sets for each venue that it is pretty much the place to hang out in Norwich. Much like the superclub, the super bar is born.

I know things are really taking off when people start chanting my name. At the end of your set, if you've done a sensational job, no one wants the night to end. I begin to create a following with regulars and new faces. Often times the crowd of girls and boys stand looking up chanting my name. 'Nikki, Nikki, Nikki. Just one more tune!'

In Squares I look across for the manager like, 'What is going on?' and sometimes he gives us time to play one more. It depends on what venue I'm in, the time restrictions and licences. It's quite a feeling and the noise… it's enough to give you goosebumps all over your arms. Your heart kind of melts humbly, knowing you did a great job. It is priceless.

In the early days I park my car on a strip of wasteland just up from the bar. I have, typically, a lot of company that night so we have two cars. This weekend a new barrier had gone in but it's up and there are no signs anywhere, so we just park and walk down Riverside as normal.

On leaving Norwich at around 1 a.m. the barrier is now down and locked. We are locked in, it was the middle of the night, I just finished work, and I'm really pissed off! If you had put a notice up explaining this, I would have gone to the multi-storey. I stand under the streetlights thinking about what I can do in the middle of the bloody night with my car stuck. How are we going to get rescued from this and if so, how long will that take? Ages?

Not one to be beaten I go to the boot and search for any stranded car tools that may be in there. I pull out the only one: the wheel wrench for flat tyres. I think it has to be worth a shot. I walk to the upright post and put it on. Amazingly it is the exact size I need and fits the four nuts perfectly. To my astonishment I just unscrew the post, take it off and move it out the way. We lift the barrier and some other people had arrived by now all watching and cheering. We jump into our cars and drive out in a convoy. It's such a massive relief and so easy!

We get about four cars out before neatly replacing the post and barrier back down. I put my tools away and wave at the security camera. I want to give them the biggest one finger salute ever but decide this blatant 'fuck you' sign may result in a parking ticket, so I simply smile and wave instead. We get home victorious and unbeaten!

## FAME AND FORTUNE

I stay around two years before there is so much demand that I can't stick to my regular Saturday nights. I ask Glen to cover quite a lot, maybe a bit too much, so I move on. I'm flexing my specialist DJ talent too and am playing as a guest DJ all over the East of England. From then on, I'm so busy I can only take monthly residencies. There is so much demand in both categories, either I'm playing commercial dance sets or giving them a good hard house spanking, *House of Elise* style.

It is the beginning of my face getting recognised a lot. Fortunately, mainly on nights out (Tesco's is still largely ok), so some normal still exists. I mainly get recognised walking out whilst wandering towards nightclubs. Sometimes by my voice ordering food or sometimes paying at the till. I'm quite a quiet person really. I'm not in it for the fame, just the job.

Photoshoots for the typical radio presenter cards and various promotions are frequent. Receiving clothing and merchandise has become the norm since my days on *The Girl Power Hour*. I receive a lot of artist merchandise and wear the coolest ones like, Mint Royale's Sexiest Girl in Jamaica, a black and gold vest top. I also wear the Thick D's Insatiable top which is a perfect description of the life I'm living. I challenge you right now… put any of those tracks on and try not to dance! Impossible! It's the groove. So good!

I did so much I can't recall everything. It's a bit of a blur with fragments of events that still pop up in my mind even today. If we were making a film, it would be easier to throw in a quick montage right here. Massive tunes, bars, nightclubs, outdoor events, racetracks, hot dancers, Vibe FM street team, non-stop Vibe radio shows, live broadcasts from foreign lands and superstar DJs.

And that's just the shows and DJing. Alongside that is all the promotional events for charity fundraising or station revenue. Under my friend Patsy as Vibe's charity coordinator, I go parachuting a couple of times and walk on fire with the Hot Coals Challenge. There are a lot of go-karting nights and racing track days at Lotus Cars. In the middle of it all I go to Cambridge for the week, and take my intensive full bike test at Cam Rider in Cambridge. I'm literally bricking it the first time I take a motorbike up the dual carriageway. I've always been more of an off-roader.

We have corporate functions from Stansted to Scotland, where I'd have been happy to wear my little black dress, if I had found one I like. I once bought a £200 dress literally wearing it once as I couldn't find a £50 one anywhere and I searched half of the city trying. It's about how it feels on me. That's my essential, it's me feeling comfortable in it. Otherwise, it feels like I'm wearing stress not a dress.

I go to a wedding in a £40 dress that is my new summer favourite, possibly as it's a Superdry. It's not about the price tag, it's about the feel. I pop down to the MOBO Awards in my 'standard DJ' clothes as I call them now: my regular biker chick or biker chic look. Huge chunky leather watches and silver chains sometimes swapped for more elegant jewellery depending on the event. (I lost quite a lot of it at festivals over the years.) Somewhere around this point in time the mighty Vibe FM Dance Party Weekenders are created, an island of weekend club life twice a year. Life is getting crazy busy.

In my early radio days with access to so much, we get the last train down and dance all night at the Ministry of Sound in London, my new favourite club, and once, we hit Camden Palace. In either 1999 or 2000 on New Year's Eve, I never remember which, we take a limo ride with Nick Bridges as he is playing a set at the Millenium Dome, and we watch Ferry Corsten be incredible in the main arena. I drive to Homelands on the south coast to see Faithless and with a handful of social trips to Norwich during my twenties. Around twenty-one I stop going out with my friends to my beloved Pam's House. Solely because there isn't enough time. I work with Vibe FM twenty-four-seven. I work so hard I don't go out again socially to any big music events until I'm roughly twenty-seven. Six years.

I go out hundreds and hundreds of times but only ever working, as my services are required on the decks constantly. Suz manages to continue a further eighteen years of clubbing. I will try to explain what the hell happens next as my life blows up from sleepy backstreet village into a hugely in-demand DJ.

The perfect song to summarise: The Chemical Brothers' 'Hey Boy Hey Girl'… 'Superstar DJs, here we go!'

It gives me goosebumps every time. It's one of the most perfect music tracks ever made!

# CHAPTER 4

# THE 00S: LEISURE AND TOURISM

## PRESENTER SCHEDULE

In the radio industry, the standard format for a mainline presenter is to produce six shows a week and we get four weeks of holiday or twenty-eight days if I remember rightly. We all work Christmas, Boxing Day and New Year's Day if it falls on a show. Plus all four or five bank holidays or state funeral days or whatever. If there is a gap for a week or more, I am away on holiday. There is almost never an empty weekend.

Not all gigs are written in my diary, as with a residency sometimes I didn't write it down. I stopped writing down my residencies at Brown's nightclub later in the year. A handful of Brown's DJ sets I took as a guest as I'm pretty sure I left there and went straight on to my new residency at Squares. I worked in Stowmarket for around a year before Squares recruited me. I started DJing in clubs during 1999.

## DJ DIARY 2000

January

Thurs 6 Jan: Barcelona

Fri 14 Jan: Brown's, Stowmarket. Joint with Debbie Mac

Sun 16 Jan: Austria for one week. Recce with Baz

Fri 28 Jan: I think a gig in Harleston… can't remember

February

Wed 2 Feb: Joined Baz in Peterborough, 12–1 a.m.

Fri 18 Feb: Brown's, Stowmarket, 11 p.m.

March

Sat 4 Mar: Kartouche, Ipswich

Sat 11 Mar: Somewhere in Norwich

Fri 17 Mar: Harlston I put as a possible! I can't remember (with Glen maybe)

Thurs 23 Mar: Go-karting

April

Sat 1 Apr and Mon 3–Fri 7 Apr: Cam Rider motorcycle training, Cambridge

Fri 14, 21 and 28 Apr: Brown's, Stowmarket

May

Fri 5, 12, 19 and 26 May: Brown's, Stowmarket

Sat 27 May: Liquid, Ipswich

June

Fri 2, 9 and 30 Jun: Brown's, Stowmarket

July

Thurs 6 Jul: Go-karting, Haverhill

Fri 7 Jul: Brown's, Stowmarket

Fri 14 Jul: Park Hotel, Diss

Fri 21 Jul: Brown's, Stowmarket

Sat 22 Jul: Kartouche, Ipswich, I think!

Sat 29 Jul: Parachute jump in Peterborough, then DJ at Lava Lounge, Ely

August

Fri 4 Aug: Probably at Brown's

Fri 11 Aug: De Niro's, Newmarket

Sat 12 Aug: By midday in Great Yarmouth. Sandstorm 4–7 p.m. stage work and DJ set in evening

Fri 18 Aug: Brown's, Stowmarket

Fri 25 Aug: 5th Avenue, Peterborough

September

Fri 1 Sept: Probably at Brown's

Sun 3 Sept: Ibiza for two weeks

Fri 22 Sept: Park Hotel, Diss

Sat 23 Sept: Ely (I think). Can't remember where

Mon 25 Sept: 5th Avenue, Peterborough

Fri 29 Sept: Lava Lounge, Ely

Sat 30 Sept: Easterns, Sudbury

October

Sun 1 Oct: Interview in Kent, Invicta FM with Penny at 11 a.m.

Fri 6 Oct: Adi and me at Debenham Leisure Centre

Fri 13 Oct: Probably at Brown's

Fri 20 Oct: Toxic 8, Cambridge, 11–1 a.m. I think it was a live link

Fri 27 Oct: Probably Brown's

November

Fri 3 Nov: Squares, Norwich (I think)

Fri 10 Nov: Brown's

Sat 18 Nov: Club Brazilia, Bury St Edmunds

Fri 24 Nov: Brown's (I think)

Sat 25 Nov: Corn Hall, Diss. Picking up women—that's a first! I left them there obviously!

December

Fri 1 Dec: Brown's (I think)

Fri 8, 15 and 29 Dec: Brown's

Thurs 14 Dec: Mildenhall Riverside, work's Christmas dinner. Drank boss' whisky (£8 a shot, apparently)

Thurs 21 Dec: Brown's

Fri 22 Dec: County Hotel, Ipswich

## ITINERARY. MY FIRST FULL WORKING TRIP IN 2000

Saturday 15 Jan: Stansted to Austria with Baz. Daytime work contains links back, usually into the Breakfast show, sometimes other shows.

Sunday 16: Snowboard lesson and blue runs. Dinner at 6 p.m. (Mum's birthday). Migraine? Stiff neck clicks.

Monday 17 Jan: Migraine. Ski and boarding (I hate skiing sticks). Pubs, Arena nightclub and Skidoo up a steep mountain to a log cabin for drinks. Get drunk. Two of the guys crash their Skidoo right down at the bottom through a fence leaving some nasty scratches and bruising. We look on as they don't stop, totally out of control, and career into it. Funny as hell… only on realising there are no catastrophic injuries!

Tuesday 18 Jan: Swim, sunbed, fondue dinner with the owner Eric.

Wednesday 19 Jan: Boarding, Ice Bar, dinner with head of tourist board. Recommended to eat dumplings (my most hated food). I manage two and politely decline the rest citing that I won't be able to eat my main meal. Yuck.

Thursday 20 Jan: Boarding and bobsleigh at Innsbruck.

Friday 21 Jan: Boarding and Arena nightclub.

Saturday 22 Jan: Leave at 17.00 and fly back to Stansted.

Sunday 23 Jan: Rest.

Monday 24 Jan: Shows all week and trip to doctor's regarding headaches. Feels like migraines but are not as severe.

Away from corporate dinners it's indulging in the ski culture in full spirit! Our company works with Kirk's company Radical Escapes multiple times over the years. He puts together tour packages that are custom built for clubbers, and Vibe joins forces for many enormously successful trips abroad including later on Ibiza. One evening walking through the minus-twenty-degree, deep snow-covered town, Kirk introduces me to Red Bull. This is the first time I've ever seen it and it's spectacular. It's like rocket fuel for party animals and we also drop tons of Jager Bombs. Both of these drinks are totally unheard of back home in the UK and it's all new territory.

I'm suffering on and off with migraine-like headaches. I've had about four this week. I suspect they're not true migraines as I can work on with Ibuprofen.

I see the doctor when I get back and find no answers. I also see a physiotherapist and chiropractors and they never manage to track any of it to the root cause. They are on and off for a nice round couple of decades!

I would learn in my forties that the left eye pain is caused by muscle cramps in my back left side. I wish I'd learnt that twenty years sooner. Eventually I figured out my back doesn't like sitting at a desk or my head looking down, plain and simple. Studio work was desk work, research was desk work. My whole life DJing was desk work! It's looking down at screens or to read or type. I need my neck upright or just level. Not rocket science, is it? Simply lift the screen. I can treat it with a heat pad and massage ball wedged in the pain point and count numbers whilst grimacing. Solution: keep my head and vison level! I learnt… eventually.

## BOBSLEIGHING AND PORN. YES, REALLY!

In Innsbruck one night at the former Olympic bobsleigh track, after an enormously long road trip, we get to have a go ourselves. It distinctly feels like sitting huddled together in a giant coke can. Flimsy as hell. It hurtles down the track's tight turns, rattling and squealing and it's exhilarating, quite a buzz. Bobsleighing, I'm all over it!

I meet someone on that trip who isn't with any of our companies. He's just tagging along. During one evening at the hotel bar this guy, who looks like a body builder, offers me an opening into the porn industry! He's quite serious and has connections of sorts or maybe a job himself—I don't ask! An irresistible work offer for me, surely? Thanks, I'm not expecting that! I explain that would be quite difficult given I have a fast-becoming recognisable face back home.

Doesn't he realise I'm here on serious radio presenting business, given we are working together all week, our two companies side by side, on this fucking massive radio *work* trip? Well, yes, he does know that, of course, but is quite keen to see me get… 'involved' perhaps we can say. Maybe he'll make some money… no shit! Such a gentleman and keen to please me, he persists a little further after my initial 'no, thanks' by explaining I can wear a mask. How very thoughtful of him, so sweet. I respectfully decline again citing myself as having a successful career and not needing another one right now. He looks disappointed but glad he's brought it up. Worth a crack, I guess. So, however big or small (the production) may have been, my big opening into porn has just been shelved, permanently!

## DJ DIARY 2001

January

Fri 12 Jan: Brown's

Sat 13 Jan: DJ set in Halesworth somewhere

Fri 19 Jan: De Niro's, Newmarket. Nikki and Ric Groves

Fri 26 Jan: Brown's (I think)

February

Fri 2, 9, 16 and 23 Feb: Brown's

Sat 10 Feb: Tiffany's, Great Yarmouth (take my CD decks). Classic house set, a nice a change for me

March

Fri 2 Mar: Brown's, Stowmarket

Fri 9 Mar: Easterns, Sudbury. Chart and commercial

Sat 10 Mar: Lava Lounge, Ely. Commercial dance and garage

Fri 16 Mar: Debenham, I can't remember!

Fri 23 Mar: De Niro's, Newmarket

Fri 30 Mar: Rendlesham Sports Centre plus Squares, Norwich

April
Fri 6 Apr: Easterns, Sudbury. One-hour set
Fri 13, 20 and 27 Apr: Brown's
Sat 14 Apr: O2 club, St Ives

May
Fri 4, 18 and 25 May: Brown's
Thurs 17, 24 and 31 May: Full-On Thursday at Pestello's,
Bury St Edmunds. Dance Anthems with Big Ben

June
Fri 1 Jun: Possibly Brown's
Sat 2 Jun: Well-earned holiday
Thurs 14 Jun: Full-On Thursday at Pestello's, Bury St
Edmunds. Dance Anthems with Big Ben
Fri 15 Jun: Liquid, Ipswich. Club mix live on Vibe FM
Fri 22 Jun: Club M, Newmarket, 10.30 p.m.–12.30 a.m.
Sat 23 Jun: Easterns, Sudbury, 12–3 p.m.
Thurs 28 Jun: Opium Lounge, Ipswich
Fri 29 Jun: Squares, Norwich, 9–11 p.m. Covering Glen (he's
on his honeymoon)

July
Sat 7 Jul: 5th Avenue Peterborough. I think live broadcast on
Vibe FM
Sat 14 Jul: Kartouche, Ipswich, 12–3 p.m.

Fri 20 Jul: Squares, Norwich. Covering branded 'Porn Stars' night

Fri 27 Jul: Club M, Newmarket. One hour live on Vibe FM

August

Fri 3 Aug: Liquid, Ipswich. Live Vibe FM

Sat 4 Aug: Snetterton racetrack. Party in the Pits. (Maybe Sacha and Ric Groves too)

Sat 11 Aug: Sandstorm, Great Yarmouth. DJ set

Sat 18 Aug: Sandstorm, Hunstanton. DJ set

Sun 26 Aug: Squares, Norwich, 9–11 p.m. Live link Vibe FM. Live broadcast East of England blah blah blah…

Thurs 30 Aug: Time, Norwich, 11.30 p.m.–1.30 a.m. Uplifting commercial dance and trance

Fri 31 Aug: Club M, Newmarket. Commercial dance

I don't know exactly when I left Brown's but I joined Squares for two years right about now.

September

Sat 1 Sept: Squares, Norwich (seven or eight shows and four nightclubs in last eight days!)

Sat 8 and 22 Sept: Squares, Norwich

Wed 12 Sept: Abroad. Happy hot days

Thurs 20 Sept: Ocean Room, Great Yarmouth

Sat 29 Sept: Corn Hall, Diss

October

Fri 5 Oct: De Niro's, Newmarket. Two people having sex on the couch… ew, get a room

Sun 7, 14, 20 and 27 Oct: Squares, Norwich

Fri 12 Oct: Hemsby. Probably a Vibe weekender. One or two were moved to Hemsby I think!

Fri 19 Oct: Debenham Dome (looks like it was live for one hour maybe)

Fri 26 Oct: Newmarket (probably Club M)

November

Fri 2 Nov: Liquid, Ipswich. Live on Vibe FM

Sat 3, 10, 17 and 24 Nov: Squares, Norwich

Fri 16 Nov: Zoots, King's Lynn. Live link/set on Vibe FM across the East of England

Fri 30 Nov: Club M, Newmarket

December

Sat 1, 8, 15 and 22 Dec: Squares, Norwich

Fri 7 Dec: Nottingham, somewhere in a club

Tues 11 Dec: Flying Dog TV presenter course, London

Fri 14 Dec: Hippodrome, Colchester. Was this the club that still had carpet on the floor, sticky? So odd!

Fri 21 Dec: Studio 2. Prerecord New Year's Eve mix ready for Vibe FM broadcast

Fri 28 Dec: Rendlesham gig (I think, absolutely no memory)

I took four days off work then flew out on Saturday 5 January. Gone snowboarding!

## GUEST SETS AND MONTHLY RESIDENCIES

Very quickly I'm averaging sixty to seventy DJ gigs a year. Six shows in forty-eight weeks (my maths is dodgy. I'm hopeful this is 288 radio shows). Plus what I do in my year as swing jock, so at least forty more shows doubling up covering others. So, approximately 328 shows or more during my swing jock time. My brother says to me as they are all listening whilst digging footings for an extension or something, 'Nick, you were on all day.' It's a pretty accurate description.

Some DJ stands are way up in the air, and I never like that separation. It's like there's something missing or a barrier in place as they can't just come up and say hi. I want to be with them on their dancefloor level. Obviously, the bigger the venue, the harder it is. In the biggest marquees, like the big circus double top tents, they have huge stages and sound and lighting rigs and you need to be up or the people at the back will never see you.

I get to know all the doormen by face, and they know me, as it's mostly all guys back then. At nearly each club I chat to people before, during and after especially where I have residencies. It's a sort of club life of night friends. It's good getting to know individual people to chat to before and after my set. It makes the place feel familiar and friendly. It's their club and tonight it's my home also.

The only exception to this is if I've driven long distances, or had multiple sets in a weekend. At a very few venues, I just turn up and play if I'm out of time. Often, I drive to and play two events over Friday and Saturday night and very occasionally three venues, usually over a bank holiday. Sometimes a Thursday, Friday and Saturday but I don't work many Thursdays in general.

In my time I've had monthly residencies all over Norfolk, Suffolk, Essex, Lincolnshire and additional venues in Cambridge, Peterborough and London. I allow an hour to pack up the correct style of music, put my makeup on and get ready, giving myself several hours to drive there to arrive between thirty minutes to one hour before my set, as late will never do. Don't think I've ever been late really. Late is not an option in my world. Usually, I'm booked for a two-hour DJ set then several hours to drive back home. On these longer routine drives I need to allow seven to eight hours per gig. I don't think anyone ever thinks about that. You just see the DJ turn up and entertain. On longer trips sometimes I have friends or work colleagues share the drive with me.

Mostly I'm hardened to it, but it can be lonely at times with all the night driving. Sometimes I take friends along to party but there aren't enough people to cover fifty gigs a year. You're centre stage of everything and then all alone driving cross country sometimes in sleet or freezing fog at 3 a.m., trying to come down from your performance. Freezing fog can lose me hours and my eyes and brain ache from the extra concentration. It's hellish driving in those extreme weather conditions on country lanes with ditches either side. Fog is not my friend! Once I even missed my turning and ended up backwards on the main road a mile from my house in deep snow. Ironically a minor spin on one of the last gigs I ever played. Fortunately, there's not a lot of traffic on Sunday at 6 a.m.

It's a weird existence from everything to nothing, every single weekend. Giving so much energy every time to deliver my always energetic performances to waving, screaming crowds. The job creates such enormous highs and then just silence as you lie there exhausted looking at the ceiling with three cans of energy drink filtering through your system. Sometimes the cats get up thinking it's breakfast time.

I have the two jobs, day and weekend nights, for all these years from 1999 to 2013.

## OVERNIGHTS: MY FIRST SOLO SHOW

For a year I work the graveyard shift. It's neatly prenamed *Insomnia* and I have my weekend show. Six shows a week is the standard for radio and on top I'm also the swing jock, which is a very old radio term for a cover presenter. If any other DJ, or disc jockey, is off sick, then I'm on instead. How old is the term disc jockey? It sounds hilarious to me.

*Insomnia* automates running by itself solely with music if I'm away covering any bigger shows. (Charlie reminds me that I would call her up and chat and say, 'Hi, hang on, Bird. I've just gotta get this tune on.' She's always awake.)

It's a real challenge to keep yourself awake at that time of night. I get pumped up on tea and coffee each night.

Conversation helps me in the lonely night hours whilst working at Vibe and although I guess we aren't supposed to, truthfully everyone is on the studio phone sometimes. Quite a lot of us practically live there, taking turns to sleep on the sofa in between show shifts, DJ sets and events. There are some listeners texting in but usually none between 1 and 3 to 4 a.m. and not many others in the studio at that time of night. Truck drivers can be chatty, but the rest are busy working or sensibly asleep. Some of the content in those texts can be a bit odd from time to time. Your average normal person is not very talkative at 2 a.m.

Glen, as presenter, DJ and head of music, has shared a lot of knowledge with me and explains the advantage of becoming indispensable, so they can't afford to let you go. I work hard at becoming exactly that by getting myself into all sorts of areas. I undertake travel bulletins, film reviews, audio production, Breakfast producer, pre-Breakfast, co-Breakfast, swing jock, DJing, plus I'm now assistant head of music. I train under and work alongside Glen using Selector to programme and schedule the station's music output for a twenty-four-hour period, excluding any specialist shows.

Production software feels like an extension of me. I love the skill, the detail, the craft of building sound. I spend hours and months and years of my life working with this kit and that's when I start thinking, one day I want to produce music. I love creating digital audio so much, except for the RSI in my mouse hand after about eight years. It aches a lot in my latter radio days.

## GLUTEN FREE

There is something up with my stomach. I regularly pull the car over driving home from work and spit out small amounts of white foam. Surely that isn't normal but it is for me. I just never bothered about it before. I have aches, cramps and problems digesting food in general. Sometimes it moves up higher causing pain around my ribs. I live with all this thinking it's normal. I don't know exactly when this happened, but I'd been playing for a few years.

I had no knowledge of food content whatsoever. I can cook spaghetti Bolognese and that's about it! But mostly I don't have time to cook. I eat half a can of soup for lunch or a salad and for dinner, often in the office kitchen, I throw in a microwave boxed meal.

Around here I hire a nutritional dietitian type person to hopefully prevent these pains and feeling sick. You cannot be on stage if your stomach is regularly not working. I'm a performer and being in front of thousands playing live every single weekend, there's a lot of pressure. You don't want any complications. I have no choice but to fix it. She sets me on a gluten free diet and almost all my problems disappear with this simple solution. I perform on stage with my shows for the rest of my career never worrying about this cause of sickness again.

I'd never heard of this intolerance thing so I have to start from scratch. In the supermarket, I read all the backs of packets I pick up, studying the nutritional labels on every item. It takes about a year, until I know what I'm doing. I do eventually take the coeliac test, which is negative. You're supposed to include wheat for around six weeks beforehand but there was no way I could do this or even get to the hospital like that. I can eat the odd sandwich, but I can't eat two or three.

Gluten sensitivity is far better understood now than it was back then. It was quite black and white at that time. It's a varying tolerance scale and if I cut it out, I'm well. It's simple when you understand it.

## THE HIGHS

On my shows I develop a good connection with people across the airwaves. Glen has always spoken about being yourself, being natural and sounding like you are only talking to one person at a time, not lots of people, even though tens of thousands are listening. The medium of radio is very personal; it's just you with your voice in between songs.

I become skilled at this important part of the job. My gift in the radio industry seems to be connecting with people and in a fun way. That's how you grow your listeners, sustain the best and hold mostly, if not all, the market leader listening figures. It's a very personal and fun type of work. Essentially, we're almost in sales. We want to get the biggest audience possible. I know I can confidently state I'm great at my job as I've definitely had a few jobs where I can confidently state I was crap!

One couple proposed on *The Girl Power Hour*, there was a baby named after me, and we gave away money, holidays and cars. The life-changing moments are just a joy to be a part of especially the really big competitions. It's one of the best bits of the job, delivering content and running big competitions. People, and often their whole family, would be helped in a now cliche phrase but genuinely 'life-changing' way from an enormous prize. On the smaller but more fun side, Baz and I on Breakfast had once been to a couple's house and cooked them bacon and eggs whilst presenting the show. It goes in the newspaper with Baz wearing an apron for the job. Fun times. The listeners love us and we love them.

Both parents and children listen happily on the way to school, at home, or work. My parents love it and so do my friends. It spans the two generations so perfectly. The music has soul, chart and dance, some from the seventies, eighties and mostly nineties. It is, as our jingle says, 'Feel good music.' There's a lot of pressure to get it right but as you grow with the job it all becomes normal. Running your entire life down to the half second, watching the studio clock tick-tock, tick-tock, fire sweeper, play song.

We are real, friendly, genuine, dynamic and fully in touch with our listeners, hence Vibe FM has such a massive, almost cult-like, following. They can see us at events and meet us in the clubs. It's a whole personal music and lifestyle culture. We are truly imbedded in the lives of people across East Anglia. Radio is such a personal medium and we are an awesome radio team and that's why I fall hook, line and sinker in love with radio.

## THE LOWS

The downside is it also captures a lot of unwanted and unsafe attention from all over the place, as we broadcast online, so we are accessible nationwide. There are a lot of strange things happening behind the scenes to some of us including me. It is immensely challenging to work through, and it continues throughout a large part of my early twenties.

It's so intense and at times overwhelmingly distressing and yet somehow, we all muddle through, and the shows continue to flow. Management from various places work hard together trying to figure out themselves what to do, and eventually with the police involved, it becomes clear I'm dealing with an unprecedented level of incidents.

To try to resolve any further potential problems the police advise me to call them if I need to. And when I do, they refuse to help. I feel so stunned, so fragile and alone. After all, the whole team around me has decided that it's time. I rarely take big decisions by myself. It's quite frankly devastating. The police offer help, then refuse. Great. I wonder what the point was. It's ruining my life. (I would like to add that their refusal was just that one time. Mostly they were helpful.)

At a school reunion a decade later one of my friends says I snubbed his email, and he's really annoyed with me. It turns out he didn't write his full name down so no one knew we went to school together. On writing a witty but slightly weird email it was put into the 'not safe' pile. Everything was taken seriously, and I was just trying to do my job the same as everyone else. Looking back now, I was just so young and struggling so much. Life changed dramatically.

## TAKEOVERS AND BUYOUTS

Brace yourself! Radio anoraks, get a pen and change whatever you like here! I'm doing my best to recall what the heck went on in my twelve years behind the studio desk. Typically, you get all these initials for company names when several radio stations or company owners merge together. Honestly, I don't even know what some stand for.

Originally, Vibe FM is part of Essex Radio Group, then Daily Mail (that we knew as DMG). When GWR get involved in a joint ownership with SRH, it's not for long. They are overruled as having a market monopoly with essentially too many stations or too high of a stake in the industry and that's just not acceptable. So, they are eventually forced to sell off some bits (us) and we are bought out by Scottish Radio Holdings (SRH). Some years after that, EMAP comes along and so on. Shortly after that, along comes Bauer who don't wait long and quickly rebrand us to KISS FM which we always thought was on the cards. Then we are called KISS 105-108 (East) and networked. I'm also on KISS 101 (West). The original station in London with independent programming is rebranded to KISS 100.

All of that plays out continually repeating like a loop, over and over, sale after sale. On a good sale no one notices much except maybe office software updates and equipment changes. On a difficult shake up, loads of people get sacked and new people arrive. So far and for my twelve years in radio presenting, I survive corporate reshuffles and buyouts, but you watch and learn. You know one day the axe will fall.

I adapt through all that right up until six months before KISS (in 2011) terminates both East and West regional broadcasting, by which time I'm definitely ready to bugger off anyway!

## ENORMOUS EVENTS

The most spectacular of our events is Saturday 12 August 2000: Sandstorm. We take up where Radio 1 left off. The first one we put on is in Great Yarmouth with sunshine on the beach. This is my first time on stage in front of a massive crowd (estimated at 20,000 plus people) waving and screaming. There's a nice pic of Gemma, Sweet Female Attitude and me.

I go on stage with Glen at one point as it is more presenter-based in that year of our first mega event. We do crowd games and stage entertainment mic work. It's nerve-wracking with that amount of people; I had real butterflies in my stomach beforehand for hours. (I don't feel them much these days but that day for sure! It was churning over.)

Sandstorm year two, even bigger, even better and we hit Great Yarmouth (with a 25,000 crowd) and Hunstanton Vibe style. Hunstanton is about 15,000 but I've no official numbers. Jane is auditioning for dancers looking to grow the show. Mainly it has just been the street team on stage before or whoever was around, and they want to put on a full show. Charlie Bird has her own team of dancers by now and is DJing and working some events. I say she ought to make contact. She gets an audition and brings her team of dancers including Suzie. They are mostly all Pam's House dancers by now. Her crew and the breakdancers impress and although they are quite a house looking crew (giant fluffy boots) and slightly less commercial, they join both beach parties. One time they are late, panicking due to being stuck in event traffic, but they do eventually arrive and perform alongside the DJs.

The second ones are bigger and better in every way as we've had practice now and the head coordinators have worked so hard (Jane and team) plus we have grown as DJs with stage work. I know I have. At the bigger one in Great Yarmouth, we have artists singing on stage throughout the day. Dane Bowers is headlining and performances from So Solid Crew and Cherise. Events have created a big backstage area, a bit like being in the pits at a racetrack. We have a Vibe FM branded motorbike backstage although I'm not riding it. I think that's Ric's job. The Lotus must have been around somewhere. I expect the boss had it that day. I see many friends there and some of my family too. If you love music, you are at this event. It is unmissable.

One of the days I'm DJing on Great Yarmouth seafront Sacha comes up and does some mic work for me. There are a couple of Vibe girls dancing either side of the stage. Sacha is so cool. She has the raw talent to be able to just walk up spontaneously and, almost like an MC, fit in seamlessly some mic work to my set. Bear in mind her genre is urban music, but she joins right in on my dance set for quite a while. (There's some early DJ set footage knocking around on YouTube under Sandstorm Parts 1, 2 and 3.) I'm on after Ric Groves and I start with Ian Van Dahl's 'Castles in the Sky', a dirty ass remix of 'Bass for Your Face London', some old skool vibes, and of course Darude's 'Sandstorm', the signature track.

I'm looking out into the night sky with a smaller crowd than earlier in the daytime but still probably 5,000, maybe more, people in euphoria on the warm sandy beach. The backdrop is the black night sky and then, I don't know it's coming, but a ton of fireworks explode just to one side. That bit is electric! On the beach and in the air! It's such a moment to be alive. I'd been DJing a year or two by now and you get the pressure off once your first couple of tunes are in. It's so surreal. I'm standing up there entertaining this screaming crowd in the vast open-air night. A bit later, Just Glyn, Sam and the others come on stage. You can hear the raw emotion in their voices at what we have all achieved. It's mind-blowing looking out over Central Beach.

A few things disappear from the edges of the stage and off the rig. Some people are after anything branded they can get their hands on, and a few of the giant flags walk. The brand is very cool and everyone wants a piece of the event.

If I ever try to explain it now, looking back to that time, I say to people we were living a rock star lifestyle. It was beyond a job and we were travelling to so many new events and places. We were always on the go and half the time I never knew where we were going to be in a few months.

But we were not rock stars… we were DJs.

## I BECOME PART SPECIALIST. *VIBE NATION*

Following that, late into 2021, aged twenty-three, I land a big new show: *Vibe Nation*. I now present a mixture of specialist tracks chosen by me along with Vibe chart music on weekday evenings 7–10 p.m. with five local guys in the mix. The new boss is confident about his big brand idea and that I should take that job.

*Vibe Nation* has five different DJs in to mix live each night: Fluff, Krazy Kev, Chappers, Dan Stone and Neilos. Each evening a different guy pops into the studio to mix live and have a chat. We are tearing it up live, Monday to Friday. It is so much fun, and it's an evening shift plus I end my swing jock role. My working life is more balanced for the first time, without any insane extra shows.

I work for Vibe FM from 1998 to 2006. I research, write, produce and present my own shows. Finally, I'm getting some decent sleep again… well, in between nightclubs.

## VIBE BRANDING

The new boss hires Sacha Brooks who is a woman with smouldering appeal on and off air. She is the person I looked up to. Sacha has come from one of the Galaxy FMs and brings with her charm, cheekiness and plenty of urban flavour. The boss knows she is the perfect woman to expand our music and brand.

Seriously, she is a good presenter, a little bit naughty, and we get on like a house on fire. I call her Brooks and she calls me Knickers and that's how it is. Very grown up! Sacha creates the urban show.

When I first saw her DJ we were working Liquid in Ipswich. The way she talked to the crowd, played with them, interacted and teased them… Her mic work was like liquid gold, so strong and confident I'd never heard anything like her before. It was mostly all blokes this way in the clubs. I have so much to learn as I'm still a bit 'yank the music down, put your mic up and shout loud' and 'let me hear you make some noise' which is ok for the first few times! But Brooks is in another league. I'm in awe of her mic work. From our DJ booth she shone with confidence and capability right across a packed dancefloor. She is a breath of fresh air, so clever and skilled. What a performer, what a woman! She is my industry icon. She knows this business inside and out.

## MODELLING

The new boss invests heavily and sets about rebranding us. The standard in any station I've ever worked with (and I do mean *all* stations) is to have the quintessential logo branded radio mug! It's part of the heritage and the very fabric of broadcasting! But this guy thinks out of the box and way beyond. We go through several new logos, boxes full of baseball caps, whole wardrobes of clothing, stickers and keyrings and loads of other cool stuff arrives. He has a clear vision of how we should be seen, and he bases this new look on a race car team.

I'm modelling with the other DJs and this is just another normal day's work for us at the station. Whatever is going on, we are involved.

I can assure you this is as far as any modelling career will ever go! 'Just do that while you're there please, Nikki' while wearing clothes for the camera is not my bag and never will be. Or not wearing clothes as it turns out.

We are modelling the merchandise for sale: T-shirts, hats and puffer jackets. All black with orange details. It starts off well! Nice black fleece with my hand up on my head... a pretty decent nice relaxed shot. With Sam from Breakfast in a matching black vest top. It is all going fine.

Sam has either gone or it is the next day, but I'm wearing the gilet or sleeveless black puffer jacket with orange collar and zip tags. Ok, so now I'm in my bra. Fortunately, it's plain black so the shot looks good. A sort of matching accident. Let's bear in mind this is taking place during office hours and the other twenty plus staff are on the other side of the closed window blinds.

During this photoshoot my good friend Jane is looking after us with the photographer, a fairly non-descript bloke. This is just a normal working day for us with another shoot, or so I think. Black zip-up jacket, where the feck has my bra gone? Somehow, I'm now modelling braless with the jacket. I do recall Jane politely holding my assets up for a while trying to fit tit tape (standard office Sellotape). I'm a bit uneasy, but oddly not too bothered all at the same time. It's just work. Jane is sure they need a lift for the 'perfect' shot! Really? No one ever mentioned that to me before. So, there's Jane carefully hoisting them up a fraction higher, sticking bits and replacing the black jacket neatly over the top. And me, working the shot somehow the best way I can with no prior modelling knowledge. She is very professional about it and so are my 'norks'. Jane's excellent word instead of boobs and it needs repeating, so go on say it loud. Norks! Ha-ha!

And this shot… WHY DOES IT HAPPEN? Next up, wear a black Vibe bag. NOW I'M *TOTALLY* NAKED FROM THE WAIST UP. I probably have something covering my front aspect before we capture my all-skin back view shot wearing a bag. A bag! What is going on? All this for a £10 drawstring bag? And yet, worse, is the last one. A clear plastic see-through poncho. I shit you not! (The world's uncoolest item.) Yet again we go for the back shot fortunately. I'm basically naked now, at work in a small central side room. Well, all except for my trousers. I'm half-dressed and it's only 11 a.m.

We all know a poncho will be fucking hard to sell, so sell it naked *naturally*! (Someone told me years later that they'd peeked through the gaps in the blinds and got an eyeful. Great—not!) They are funny photos.

I agree to it all and I'm a hundred percent ok with that. It just surprises me how quickly I'm able to get my kit off for the brand, with no clue or experience in this department. Had it been laid out in a dossier of today's to do list: write, present and produce show, followed by model clear poncho (a plastic bag) and a rucksack half-naked in the office with your colleagues outside on the phone, I may have said, 'No, thank you.' Hindsight! I really don't care though; it's quite a laugh.

The result is good work actually! And I'll be honest, maybe she knows a thing or two about photoshoots, bare skin and cleavage in the centre of an unzipped jacket. The fact is that shot gets used a whole lot on club flyers, posters and selling the merch online. We use it across all four counties in our patch. In the evening, I'd be walking down Riverside or just out in the city at night and I'd walk past myself on a four-foot window poster thinking, *I actually look quite hot, but thank God for the tit tape!*

(I'm hopeful the rest were lost through time, except for my original prints in the old portfolio. This was before computer storage or decent 'back-up' was really a thing. Lucky!)

**SNOWBOARDING**

The year 2002 starts well as I'm in Austria on a recce with Trailer Boy who works on the Breakfast show. We are staying in Mayrhofen at Hotel Strass and our job is to provide links on Breakfast and other shows when we are available.

When we arrive, there is some confusion over the room as previously only one room was required for two radio staff and we are like, 'Oh, well, we definitely need two rooms please.' With that little potential bed sharing worry resolved after a very long trip, we hit the sack, separately! We'll carry on with our radio business tomorrow. Our business is to get involved in all the cool stuff, record it and talk it up with live links back to the UK studio and audience. Promotion is such great fun!

High up in the crystal-clear Austrian Alps we are snowboarding on my second work trip. We spend time working, which is exploring and playing in the snow. We pop up to look over the glacier and one day we go up the Ahorn to record sound bites. Usually most of the morning and lunchtime are spent working up on the Penken each day. This is my dream job: sports *and* broadcasting! At times I wonder how I got here, standing on top of the world breathing the crisp mountain air, then I get the audio recording gear out and do some actual work. Really, come on, as if it feels like work at all. We do work hard though. We are a dedicated little team.

I'm meticulous with detail on all my audio work. One job is to capture and record sound bites for when I get back home to complete the production. It is on-air promotional material to aid the sales team to drive up bookings. I am quite obsessed with aspects of individual sounds; audio is a passion for me.

I set up my gear and record myself snowboarding, whilst explaining the details, riding steadily down a blue run. Your job on radio is to paint a picture. I drop my mic right down low to the ground to get the exact distant crunch of boots and boards across fresh powder snow. Sound production is an art form and I love it. I can still recall how well that came out when I put it together in the production studio some weeks later. Bliss in my cans (headphones) like being there all over again. It is audio heaven.

We wrap up and walk around. It is continually well below zero at night. Once, it reached minus ten, but we still stomped from bar to bar in the crisp freezing air. One morning after a very hard night out in town where the social rules were drink till you drop, we meet up in the hotel room for the joint phone live link to the Breakfast show. Somehow I do a silent but enormous burp. Trailer Boy is young and picks up on it immediately laughing, 'Oh my God, that stinks of alcohol.' It is basically pure alcohol and if anyone had lit a cigarette, we would both have gone up in flames.

We'd knocked back some serious drinks, shot after shot as that was the spirit of young skiers and boarders: party hard, on and off the slopes! Anyway, no alcohol reference should have been made on air, accidentally or not. Especially *not* on the Breakfast show with kids listening. I professionally gloss over it by moving on the best I can. Later off air, I apologise profusely to the rest of the studio team back home.

On another normal day's work (snowboarding at the top of a mountain), we all add a cheeky lunchtime shot to our hot chocolate. I try to board back down ever so slightly pissed. The straights are fine but on every single turn I slump over a fraction too far and just sit down. It is totally idiotic, boarding a fraction pissed. I may well have been able to drink for England back then but not at 1 p.m. I decide not to do that again as it is a complete waste of an hour's decent upright boarding.

Later on, I do a spot of paragliding with Stocky. (I think he competed at a high level, maybe even been a champion. I don't remember now as it's a long time ago and he now works with tourists' flights.) He is a real cool guy and also DJs in the hotel's Ice Bar and Arena.

Stocky sets up his kit all neatly laid out on the ground up the mountain then I'm harnessed in just in front of him. The wing and cables are all behind us as we walk forwards, then run a bit until we generate some lift and start flying off down the mountain. Remind myself after lift-off that this is my actual job. I have the world's best job! Morning radio links back home, lunchtime hot choc, mildly drunk snowboarding followed by afternoon paragliding! Come on!

The view and the sheer silence are breathtaking. It is an utterly wonderful ride with long periods just drifting about slowly in the sky. The coolest way to get yourself down the mountain. Until we reach much lower down then he says, 'Ok, here come a few turns.'

He only demonstrates about three very gentle spin ones, but, with turning tight circles, comes the G-force on the ground followed by the continual sick feeling. I feel sick as a dog for the next couple of hours as I'm hopeless with motion sickness and that was too much for me.

BBC news presenter Jane Hill is on Austrian TV as basically the only English-speaking thing on, so seeing her is always comforting. Whenever I see her in the next decade she reminds me of Austria. I love the place. All good things must come to an end and at some point, we have to fly back home. Make a few more shows, turn up at a ton of nightclubs and fly straight back out to Austria again, yeah?

## LEISURE AND TOURISM

On Saturday 30 March we get back on a plane for the Vibe FM In the Snow listener trip. Unbeknown to me this will be the most gruelling week I ever live. I pretty much think my body will give up on me at one point. In beautiful Mayrhofen they have since hosted Snowbombing, but at the time it is the Brit Games 2002. There are a load of DJs there, with some playing up the mountain or in the clubs. Ric Groves and I are playing in the arena under the Strass (I think it was).

It is a clubbers' winter sports paradise. I guess when I tried unsuccessfully to study leisure and tourism, this would have been the ideal job. I'd struck gold! It is hard though and so draining. There are times when we break down in tears due to sheer tiredness. This is new to me; my body is not coping at this level. My friend Ziggy works on the hotel desk, having become friendly, as I'm there so many times over a few years. She is always kind and helpful even in those tense times. It's like a second home for a while.

It is a combined workload. There is behind the scenes pressure and then front of house. It is hard work interacting with the listeners day and night. The bus full of listeners on holiday with us are all amazing and never any hassle. I suddenly realise how hard being a travel rep is. It is intense with long hours and snowboarding, plus playing DJ sets. It is clear to me after day two I can't cope anymore physically with the fourteen-hour and sometimes up to seventeen-hour days. I can't do it all, so that has to stop. I have a lie-in after a late DJ set. We aren't worked to death. I'm just saying it is very full-on.

We go out to the bars at night and Ric and I both entertain our listeners with DJ sets in the Arena nightclub around midnight hence the very long days we all work. I stop boarding around day three and after that decision I pick up again carrying on with the rest of the itinerary better. Cutting the boarding out really saves me; it is disappointing but it has to be done. Focus is the key. I'm there to work.

Jane and I are sharing a room this time. I do sleep then but it is a bit sketchy to be honest. I move about a fair bit, turning, trying to get to sleep and she is so funny, the exact opposite. She lies down on the bed flat on her back just motionless. I think this amusing as she looks like a corpse and all I do is scuffle about. This gives us the genius names of Stiff and Rustler. It cracks us both up all week. Be quiet, Rustler... Are you still breathing, Stiff? Silly humour.

One night, the coldest I've ever been, ever, in my entire life, we spend the night up the very top of Penken mountain. There's a ski resort up there with a bundle of buildings together: bars, restaurants and sleeping rooms like a big dormitory, but Jane and I are feeling the burn of work. We are given the choice and so opt to sleep in a separate small church-like wooden spire to grab an hour or so of downtime. An available room looks nice and peaceful, just what we need. Jesus, it's a serious mistake! Up the mountain it drops to what, like minus twenty or something? It is deathly cold in the little wooden pointy roofed hut.

After hours and hours, I say, 'Are you awake?'

'Yes,' she says.

I say, 'I'm not being funny but I'm so cold. Do you want to sleep on one bed to share body heat? I am that cold.'

'Yes, I'm freezing too,' she says.

By far the coldest I've ever been indoors in my life. I get a few hours of sketchy sleep but not much as it is just so bitterly cold.

I get down from the top bunk to try to survive the night better together. We sleep in all our clothes, coats, hats and socks back to back.

'Have you got any food?' I feel I'm starving. Another problem.

She may have had a snack bar of some sort or eaten it earlier. I'm so incredibly hungry and so cold.

With bugger all sleep we get up around 5 a.m. naturally and get dressed… Oh no, wait, we are fully dressed.

After a truly horrendous night we struggle up and pull our boots on and go outside to meet the others. The hardcore group have got up to see the sunrise so we have to be there too. It is almost worth the pain to see such a majestical sight. We wait for twenty minutes for the sun to peek over the crystal-clear mountains. Then quickly back inside to warm up and find some bloody food with the others who have obviously had a much more normal night and all look great.

## DOWNTIME

In October of 2002 we are in Cancun, Mexico. I start taking frequent big holidays very far away to escape the pressure and strains of my career. I spend a lot of holiday time in the Caribbean too. I usually crack a bit just before my holiday; once, I literally cried at work, then I disappeared for two weeks. Downtime is my essential way of coping and I fill it with pure delights! Quad biking, swimming, running, tennis, dinner out and hotel clubs or any nightclubs and in this case the smoking hot Coco Bongo.

We meet an awesome group out there and the eight of us visit Coco Bongo, one the hottest clubs ever. It has almost a theatre-like feeling to it with high sides and rows of people dancing, a stage with acrobats and the central bar. We get up and dance on the main central bar naturally as this is the best spot. We become good friends and stay in touch. We join Terri and her girls much later on regularly out in Ibiza. I also meet up with Annabell who comes to see me play with The Prodigy in Essex.

That's one of my favourite club memories along with some scuba diving out at sea. Just beautiful. Except for a bikini wardrobe malfunction on the boat ride back. I shit you not. I was so busy I didn't have time to buy any new clothes. Any that actually fitted! A VERY *BIG* MISTAKE! I genuinely had no time to shop or do anything at all other than work, hence the bottoms did not fit. Hardly anything fitted. That's as much as I want to recall for you following scuba diving and sitting exhausted on a boat in an ill-fitting bikini.

It was bad! Serious note to self, wear swimsuits that fit! Harshest of lessons learnt that day. I wondered why the woman opposite me on the boat was staring at me so oddly. She didn't say anything. Why on earth not? If I'd seen she was in a spot of bother with her clothes I reckon I'd have helped out my fellow woman there! If someone had pointed that out to me, I'd have had a chance to rectify my worst ever wardrobe malfunction! At least it wasn't anyone I'd ever see again. I suppose I must always be grateful for that, if nothing else!

In future, *must* make time to buy beach clothes… Embarrassing on another level.

# CHAPTER 5

# INTERVIEWS, IBIZA LIVE AND *HOUSE OF ELISE* IS BORN

## PROPERTY

At work there are lots of nice rides in the car park and I do like a nice car but I never spend a crazy amount on wheels. Instead, I invest in bricks. I buy my first property, a buy to let, age twenty-four and run it as a rental, a business, giving my accountant another job. It comes complete with a tenant in it who covers the mortgage and I continue living at home. It ticks over in the background of my working life unless it is renovation time or I need to fix the odd thing.

## INTERVIEWS

During my first few years I amass a lot of various types of interviews. Our patch TSA (Total Survey Area) or the transmission area is Norfolk, Suffolk, Cambridgeshire and

North Essex on FM and DAB online anywhere. We're based in Bury St Edmunds, Suffolk because it's central to our region. This location is efficient for work and travelling throughout East Anglia, but it does mean we don't always get all the celebrities and artists who constantly pass through London and other big cities. We fight hard for our share.

One of my first interviews is 'Kernkraft 400' for Zombie Nation, arguably one of the most defining dance tracks of that era. Being new to interviewing I have to learn from a producer how to technically hook up our spare studio to Germany. I'd written down questions following my research on the artist. After setting up the recording software I'm ready to go. Sometime before, one of the other DJs had said to me, 'Ask him this question.' I'd written it down and worked it into my interview. I don't really follow the question or answer well as it references something before my time. During the interview I'm thinking I need to get out of this and on to the next question to get back to common ground. Right after that interview I decide not use anyone else's suggestions again. I trust my instincts and carefully develop my own style. Later on, I factor in listeners' questions if we're live, but I need to be in charge of my own style.

## 2001–2002 ARTIST INTERVIEWS

So Solid Crew, Groove Armada, Dannii Minogue, Liberty X, Matt Darey, Smoke 2 Seven, Ladies First, Nigel & Marvin,

Tilman Uhrmacher, DJ Pied Piper, Oxide & Neutrino, Static Revenger, Ian Van Dahl, Paffendorf, Public Domain, Agnelli & Nelson, Scooter, DJ Sammy.

Andy and Tom, AKA Groove Armada, are playing at the Junction in Cambridge, so I go over to meet them. The guys are nice and totally normal even when I mildly fluff a question. Andy just chuckles a little bit and continues smiling and talking. It's about my third ever interview so I'm young and chatting with the *iconic* Groove Armada, already legends of music. So, no pressure at all!

I'm trying to say, when he'd done a couple of things successfully, that it's 'like another string to your bow' but somehow, I muddle it up with notch on your bed post (which is obviously a vastly different thing all together). Aww crap! I get out, 'Another notch on your belt.' Oh no. I try hard to keep my composure and he can see how young I am and it's no big deal. I'm carrying my little recording unit so I can edit that out later. God, I love a pre-record!

Interviews are a complex beast especially if they are live. For one, you're producing your live show whilst driving the desk, presenting, back timing songs and so on. Then either hooking up your studios to another in the country or greeting guests in through the door stimulatingly whilst the music plays. Then you continue to produce your show flawlessly, remember all your questions in your head or on a bit of paper, then keep up the flow and answer naturally. Sounds easy, right?

When conducting interviews, your head is focused on the next question, as they answer the current one. You must listen well, respond correctly to that and then get onto the next, or take some live listener questions off the screen. Essentially one half of you is on working the desk producing, the other half presenting a list of hopefully memorised and/or live questions, the other half is processing their answers and responding and adapting what you're saying next. The last half is watching the studio clock and delivering it all seamlessly and back to the music and remembering to switch all the mics off! As you can see there's an awful lot of halves with my brain splitting directions. After years of practice, it all becomes second nature like any other job.

## MISTAKES

Depending on what show you're on, there are maybe 10,000 or 35,000 (or networked maybe 70,000ish) people listening live and there's that crushing feeling if you make one tiny mistake. There is nowhere to hide. You can only drill yourself to get better and not make any mistakes, *ever*.

For some time to come, maybe around a year, I work with my mistakes list. A so simple and yet so effective paper sheet. I draw up a cause and effect and potential resolutions chart. Most errors come down to poor sleep or too much coffee. It is so obvious looking at it this way. With this self-reflection I can reduce my mistakes to zero or as near to perfect as anyone can get, year after year. Except for this one time when I step back too far and kick the amp switch off with my foot, taking the hole station off air immediately. I frantically look around the studio trying to figure out what the hell I had done. I'd never even noticed that particular black switch before, located way down at ankle level.

In the early days (shhhh, don't tell anyone) I'd taken the station off air accidently dozens of times, literally loads, but usually late at night! I can confidently state a hundred percent that I've made every single mistake in the book. I doubt anyone has made more mistakes than me but that is how I learn, by trial and error, devising a plan or pattern to stop repeating it. My brain doesn't remember information well, so I learn the pattern instead and that takes a bit more time.

If I want to leave the studio, I have a double check list that I follow every single time, so I can't screw it up standing in the kitchen making my essential cup of tea. I also limit myself to one coffee a day or my mouth will run away with me. I try to get optimum sleep (which is quite hard with the *Insomnia* show) and eradicate the rest until I hardly ever mess up anymore. Eventually I turn pro!

The DJ bathroom break! That double check is essential as there is no way of monitoring the station output whilst washing your hands. I can confidently say almost every single presenter has popped to the loo at least once and the song has run out! It's so common, it's barely even worth mentioning it. It's a junior, early days mistake, a schoolboy error! So, if you ever wonder what the gaps are at the end of a song, that's us screwing it up! You learn to get to the bathroom and pee very fast, usually in well under the three minutes and thirty seconds of the average song length. I pop out to the restroom quite a lot. Say, every single hour! Only because I enjoy walking about. I feel it keeps me more active. Literally it keeps me on my toes. Whether it's correct or not, I don't really care. The sales staff often look at me oddly going in and out the building. It is like a little routine I build myself. After double checking everything, fling open the heavy doors and take a three-minute break! Also, it means you are never caught short with the feeling of wanting the loo but have too many junctions and songs to play. A step towards perfection if you like.

Interesting how I never swear on air, isn't it? Given I do swear rather a lot and have since I was a kid. I do once by accident say 'fuck' at about 9 p.m. on *Vibe Nation*. I professionally gloss over it and carry on. Hopefully no one will notice! Ok... you want to know how I screwed up? During a studio chat I accidently spit a tiny bit of saliva across the desk onto Dan Stone and he says, 'Ah, you just spat on me!'

I feel emotionally disheartened and spontaneously say, 'Oh fuck.'

Two texts come in. Yeah, they heard! 'Nikki, did you just say that?' Like my mates asking me a question but fortunately there is no drama. That means no complaints to the station or Ofcom. I apologise to the boss the next working day as there is nowhere to hide on air. I try to put right my wrong.

He says, 'We'll wait and see what happens.'

Nothing happens. Luckily.

I write it on my mistake list. Don't spit on people. It creates the wrong emotionally charged response!

## BITS FROM DJ DIARY 2002

May

4, 11, 17, 24 and 25 May: Squares, Norwich. Friday 17, cover Glen. Friday 24, live on Vibe FM

June

1, 8, 13 and 15 Jun: Squares, Norwich

3 Jun: Summit, Wisbech. Live on Vibe FM. It's an unusual bank holiday Monday night gig

22 Jun: Phat Feet, Peterborough. Vibe FM DJs Dance event, 6,000 people

23 Jun: 6 a.m. Stanstead to Ibiza

24–28 Jun: *Vibe Nation* Café Mambo studios

July

5 Jul: Thetford Sports Club

6 Jul: Squares, Norwich

11 Jul: Edwards, Peterborough

19 Jul: Club Brazilia, Bury St Edmunds

20 Jul: Marina Centre, Great Yarmouth

And so on…

## VOMITING IS GAME OVER

On Monday 8 July I take five days off radio sick. It is so rare for me and it is the first time it has ever been written in my diary. Definitely there is something extremely wrong with my stomach here. It is hard to manage as I've never felt so ill. It feels like there is something alive in my stomach, like little aliens moving around in there. Weeks later I test positive for salmonella. It is vicious!

Anyway, with severe stomach cramps, pain, diarrhoea and vomiting, *ideally* the show has to go on if I can leave the bathroom and stand up! Nope! My radio show is off for the whole week. A big new Vibe promotion has been booked for a venue in Peterborough on that Thursday night. With the paid advertising, station activity, street team, my DJ set and whatever else, revenue is probably somewhere around £3,000. The adverts are playing for weeks on air with my name on them.

I dig deep to keep it on track and deliver. I physically cannot eat for the pain, not to mention the rather dodgy consequences immediately after eating! So, I don't eat anything at all that whole day to make it to that gig. It is an important one and I deliver as usual. Had it been two days earlier, I would not have been able to stand up. That was the fourth night I had my unwanted guest.

My Friday show is covered so I can rest in bed from working the night before. Normally I never do that. We get in at 3 a.m. all the time, sleep a few hours (often on the work's sofa at the weekend) and then get up and do the show. It takes a lot of energy to get to Peterborough and stand up on that night. For a smaller more typical event I would have got the guys to stand in. Glen covers me at Squares that Saturday, and as we cover each other's night so often it is no big deal. That Squares night is the only paid DJ set I've ever missed.

## PHAT FEET

It's worth a mention not just because it has a daft name but Vibe is so bold in constructing the gigantic events. We have new bosses again, following the mid-year sale of the station. There is a problem with the original name Phat Beat, so it has to be changed. The entire team, events managers, street teams and DJs all perform from an enormous stage in Peterborough and we thoroughly entertain all afternoon to a 6,000 strong crowd. All the Vibe DJs play unless anyone is away on holiday. The next day, with the rest of our events, production and DJ team, I fly out to my favourite destination, the White Isle.

## BROADCASTING FROM CAFÉ MAMBO, IBIZA

For me the most insatiable working project is coming. The rest of the team spend six months to a year planning this type of station revenue and branding. Vibe Live in Ibiza is heaven on earth! It is the dream destination as by now I'd been several times; I'm a seasoned partygoer and I know the place well. A truly magnificent week of live broadcasting lies ahead coming direct from the world's most famous and iconic global brands of Café Mambo and Bar M.

There is just something magical about the place and, when I was younger, it was the ultimate clubbers' paradise. I've been seven or eight times to the point where I've lost count. We stay in a not very glamorous hotel somewhere deep in San An. It is noisy at night with large groups of drunk people walking past cheering and shouting. The team notices that they don't change the bed sheets all week and are not very impressed. Anyway, bed sheets are not that important right now.

It is such a privilege to be involved with this ambitious week of live shows and DJ sets and, for the listeners, an epic holiday they'll never forget. A big team of us fly out and everyone works their arses off. Although when you have to work on a beachfront studio and walk out onto the balcony looking at my new neighbours, Café del Mar, it doesn't feel much like ordinary work! Except for all the usual industry tech, time pressures and drama, whereby all the all-new studios are so new they haven't actually been built yet! Anyone spot any issue with that? Me, I do!

My main job is to broadcast my show *Vibe Nation* from the Café Mambo studios and so we do… eventually. We arrive at the beach after the short walk down from our hotel. The air is very warm on early Monday evening. By now it is about 5 p.m. so there are a couple of hours before my show is live at 7 p.m. We walk into the studio (a small empty room) and there is nothing there. I mean nothing at all! It is full of cardboard boxes. I shit you not, boxes! No studio anywhere!

Apparently, they ripped it all out during a big refit and no one had yet refitted a single piece of the equipment. What the hell… What are we going to do?

In true radio fashion we start opening everything at the speed of light and my producer Momo has to assemble the entire thing before I can start my live broadcast back to our expectant audience in the East of England. On-air promotions have been running for the trip for months by now. The hype is huge.

He works his nuts off and you gotta hand it to him, we get on air live only twenty minutes or so late, somewhere around 7.20 p.m. Very impressive work and thank you so much, Momo, you're a legend. It was said that these were to be the new Mambo radio studios and we were the very first broadcast. *So* first at the time, they were not even built yet.

As a presenter we run and produce our own shows. Normally I can test out, or at least look at, a studio desk to try to familiarise myself with all the knobs, faders and settings before I sit down to present my show. This time I figure it out in the moments before I go on air. Basically as Momo is building it, I'm trying to learn as fast as I can, so I don't fuck it up!

I'm presenting *Vibe Nation* all week live from Ibiza. Ric Groves pops in one night and Chappers another, so we have a chat on air about the day's antics, the food, the sunshine, the beaches and promote all our itinerary for the week. There is a little window that looks out to the side, and I stand there thinking, *Is this really happening?* I'm just twenty-four and now paid to work here at Mambo. Ric is a well-established funky house DJ of many years and plays a set in a room over at Manumission, although I have to work and can't attend his night.

Gemma's job is to present from the rooftop above the famous beach club Bar M. I often walk down to drop in for a chat on her lunchtime show, and we both sit in our shorts and sunglasses gathering a tan, beaming with job satisfaction. The job is setting the scene and detailing the sights, while overlooking the water lapping the sandy shore on the bay below. We casually discuss all the funny moments and our upcoming events. It is pure working heaven, I ain't gonna lie!

Dinner at Savannah is one of my favourite hangouts in the warm breeze. If you have been you know it looks out over the sea with all the little white parasols stretched out overhead and this time, I get to DJ there instead. There's a little room just a bit inside and I play there. This kind of chilled out, warm-up music is totally new to me. I searched it out high and low planning well in advance. It is a really careful selection to complement the Savannah evening mood, so that it will go down as seamlessly as the views. Balearic beats and blissed out funky sun-kissed grooves, anything that fits neatly. The style and the atmosphere here are crucial. I have to match the brand.

My other venue is a set at Kanya just along the beach. This one is during the day in the afternoon where we throw down a little house party. It has a great relaxed warmth to it with a small swimming pool at the front. Most of the team come and, of course, the listeners. I get everything down to 128 beats per minute for this Ibiza beach party. This set is also custom planned to have the Ibiza essential chilled tones but more upbeat for dancing. It is party time!

Back home in flat East Anglia I take on some new clubs, such as Summit in Wisbech which feels a bit like an industrial factory. It is an enormous building with a vast rectangular main room. It has that warehouse feel to it and is more the size of a superclub. Even room two is large. I play both for several years.

From this venue I deliver huge dance nights and it feels epic because of its sheer size. The stage is high like in a lot of superclubs and after climbing the steps to get into the DJ booth, I feel I'm a bit disconnected from the crowd. I prefer to be down with them, face to face, up close and personal or ideally just a fraction higher so I can see everyone right to the back of the room. The view is great though and you can see all the way to the bar sometimes through the smoke and lights. I'm there for several years with a monthly residency playing in the main room where I first play alongside icons like Lisa Lashes then Judge Jules and Tim Westwood, although Tim (who's very tall) is in the main room that night. I'm in the second room.

## PHOTOSHOOTS

As my work expands and my shows grow, I need more and more photoshoots for PR. I started in college and got passport style ones but with a smile, head and shoulders typical studio shot with big curly hair. Hair straighteners were not invented yet. With a work colleague back at her place, she has a camera and a wardrobe to try out. We muck about with different clothes, indoor and outdoor locations, and a plastic gun. The best one is tight black trousers, pin striped shirt and a plastic pistol and absolutely no use whatsoever, but I'm learning.

One time back at my house she gets a cracking couple of natural shots on my black sofa. More media presenter type shots and some of these I send out. I have to learn about lighting, angles, clothing, colours, makeup, good colours, good backdrops and be natural. You have to grow into this role taking time working out what it is you are trying to capture about yourself. You can see this in some early shoots with Angelina Jolie and I look at them and think she probably went through this trial phase. How to get comfortable with yourself and the camera, lean that way, go for cheeky, fun or smouldering. I am not a natural, so it takes some work.

I don't think this kind of stuff is said to the guys at the time, but it is clear there is more pressure on women in the industry. I was also somehow talked into half my clothes off as I said previously. Again, not something the guys did, did they? And I have been told that one freckle on my face is a bit big (what about the other fifty?) and I've been told my face is a bit wonky. Looks good on camera this way but not so much in profile! And this is constructive feedback, not vicious in any way. I'm also told that I have a good figure but my tummy sticks out. It does. That's my food intolerance damage over many years of not knowing.

Maybe I don't go hard enough on the makeup. I'm referring to the freckles. I've never been a massive fan of tons of makeup. Why? Why cover up your face? It's my face! It has a right to be as it is! Why apologise and shovel on fuck loads of gloopy spot generating crap up on it? I will wear it when it's needed and that's about it.

That was every day when I worked in an office and a hundred percent on stage but not now, nope. Honestly, I can't be arsed! It may be the only thing Gwyneth Paltrow and me may have in common! I just don't see why I should. I don't want to apologise for my skin. It's being skin! I used to wear makeup all the time for twenty years. That's long enough. I will if I've a photoshoot, perhaps a dinner or a wedding, but that's about it now. I'm very different to my younger self in every way.

Anyway, modelling is not my job and I don't have to take constant criticism like they do. I'm told once to 'get a look' by a big agent in London and I was already wearing a £200 leather jacket and thought I looked all right, but obviously it just isn't enough, and I did bother to dress that day. They are probably right but I'm never that great with new fashion trends. Now I think they only wanted Holly Willoughby looks and she is lovely and all, but that just isn't me. I assume I'm not dressing feminine enough, not enough like a lady. Please do fuck off! (Although I really don't recognise this at the time.) I would eventually evolve style-wise just enough to do the job or for a photoshoot and stage performances. I'm a DJ; I'm not into TV anymore. Essentially when the internet came along and rescued me from clothes shops, it was magnificent. I'm sure it was purposely designed just for me!

That agent also says Davina Macall is about as blokey, matey or masculine as the TV industry will tolerate. I can't remember the exact word. Davina? Are you kidding me? She's all woman. WTF? Davina is a fucking amazing presenter. The ideal person you want to chat to if you ever had the chance. I never thought of Davina as being any different to any of the other female presenters and even after I processed that, I was being told by a big agent that she was on the edge of acceptable. WTF? Just because she's not Barbie? That is confusing, but I know what they are saying. I don't fit the mould they're looking for. (I thought later on… Fuck off then!) I think I said, 'Yeah, ok, sure.'

Two decades later fortunately life on TV, radio and media and life in general has changed quite a lot, hasn't it? I see people all the time and I've no idea if they're a man, a woman or a gender fluid individual. Only Graham Norton was allowed on TV back then! Fortunately, anyway I was a DJ and in house music you can be whoever you want to be. It tolerates everyone. There's room for all.

I have another shoot in Ipswich with a photographer friend in my mid-twenties when I'm still trying to figure it all out. I'm pretty dull with makeup here but I do get better at it over time. We try a range of clothes and different poses and a couple are good enough for flyers. This time we end up with a variety of shots including my only little black dress. No use whatsoever. (Although my nan still has this photo on her sideboard.) The one shot uses a white racing biker top, a blue denim skirt and the old faithful leather jacket. Finally, I'm starting to get the hang of photoshoots. This is the first time I get something useful for print. It is used for a lot of stuff including flyers for me and Lisa Pin-Up at Funky Bunny's birthday bash, another residency of mine.

A few years later I only work with one professional photographer. It's worth investing in a good photographer who really can get the best from you. She is so easy to work with, highly skilled and creative with her style. Working with her I achieve colours, backdrops, angles and what is going to work for my look. I also learn I only have one or slightly two good angles as not surprisingly I'm not a model. So, I learn to work with what I have. Work with only those angles and clothes that spell out you. She can make me look excellent in a fake fur hooded coat and an eroded brick wall. Hired.

## MY BRANDING

The first thing is what name to use on air and how to spell it. It's common in radio to drop, change or shorten your surname depending entirely on whether it sounds cool enough! I try some adaptations in my head but I quickly settle on Nikki as the more female sounding version of Nick. I spell Nikki that way as it looks better with my signature next to Elise. Essentials: sounds good, looks good and easy to sign quickly. Job done. So now I'm Nikki and at home still Nick.

I'm in the media for fifteen years and during that decade and a half my brand style is evolving to meet the ever-changing market. I start with a guy for a few years who then disappears and therefore I lose my initial website, the .com and all associated branding. Having invested around a grand from websites to stationery, CDs, letterheads and so forth, I never hear from him again. Although after my initial frustration and cost losses wear off, it is a good thing as the design does not represent anything I do. Many lessons are learnt, even from the bad moments.

After this, my next batch of gear is more identifiable and much more in tune. Glossy design-based artwork, CD covers and business cards featuring a close-up shot of the vinyl grooves in pinkish purple on a black background. It is elegant and serves me well for a few years although I don't remember how or who produces it.

After that I turn to my cousin with her own business. She creates an elegant website with a gallery and sub-areas of information with neat little rectangle white photo boxes. It looks awesome. Later on, another cousin shoots and produces one of my promotional videos filmed at Big Ben's Dance Island in Cambridge. It is a huge festival spread across five or so arenas with around sixty DJs. At the 2008 festival I'm with Ric Groves and Steve Smart but I don't stay as my schedule is manic. Due on after us are the Audio Bullys, Freemasons and Stanton Warriors. In 2009 me, Chappers and Steve are also scheduled, then later I see some of Chicane, but leave before The Shapeshifters and Pendulum.

Next, I hire head of production Momo to design my new logo, a tribal dragon sun logo. So perfect for that era. We spend time choosing the perfect design that best represents the hedonistic house music era and endless sunshine party days and tribal tattoos are everywhere, including me and Suzie. We have a matching pair but laid out differently, although hers is upside down! (She says mine is… it's an ongoing joke.) We get these together when I return from snowboarding.

By now I'm on my third website design and I hire Lotty, the station's tech girl who can build and design websites. Plus, she is always around in the office which makes things so much easier. This is around the time Facebook is beginning to take hold but I have no time to get involved as I'm maxed out already, so I learn to delegate! Lotty also becomes my online content manager running everything: my website, Myspace, YouTube, Facebook, uploading and editing content… I pay her to look after all that, as I have no time to do anything else myself. Hiring and delegating is the only way forwards as your business grows. After all is done way in advance, we leave work on Friday at 3 p.m. and go get mashed up in the hot tub or swim in the pool or whatever is occurring in my house. I know because it regularly says in my diary: Lotty 3 p.m. Must have been on the rare occasion I'm not working a club to depressurise every few months.

Lotty plays bass in a band, loves music, sometimes brings her guitar round, has a beer and is full of energy and fun. Next friend in, we spend a lot of time driving, cruising about in my car and listening to the latest music tracks, free. We also take our mountain bikes out and then pour Bacardi, cider, wine or whatever is on the menu that weekend. All of my friends are party people; it is the way of life to me. I may have dunked her in a bit at the deep end really, as she joins Vibe halfway through college around seventeen.

We are in the epicentre of the dance generation: work, rest and play. My house is a crazy fun place to be, and we are never short of company. One time we put a bottle of bubble bath in the hot tub! That's just too much! I'm twenty-six or twenty-seven by this time. It must have seemed a bit surreal to Lotty and Shaun being college age. Shaun works at the station too and starts to hang out more and more; I don't really notice him in the early days as he is just so quiet. He is also hired much later on to build and manage websites for me and eventually blends into my family life.

## THE ART OF VINYL

I'm working a lot at Club M in Newmarket and they have a lot of promoters' nights putting on specialist hard house events with guest superstar DJs. Then there's Dave's Night Dilemma and various other venues. In the nightclubs I need to up my game to deliver on twelve-inch. I learnt my trade initially on CD, having hardly ever even seen a piece of vinyl. Mum has a record player but it is never used. The more time I spend in clubs, the more it becomes apparent that if I want to succeed in the big game, I have to learn vinyl.

Once I set my mind on vinyl and after my research is completed, I have to go shopping. The best kind of shopping *ever:* record deck shopping! I buy Technics 1210s Mark 2. I learn vinyl and it is hard for me. I think it's harder in general, but totally achievable. It is just practise, practise, practise.

I can openly admit I'm never quite as good on vinyl as I am on CD. It may be the other way round for others. House with its big beats is more chunky and raw, more banging, and that's the point of it. Not being as good with records is not about mismatching or dropping beats, that doesn't happen. For me it is about starting and exiting at the exact point in the music track where I want to and sometimes I miss those.

So, you move on to the next point, no problem. The crowd don't really notice imperfections like that, not in house. Just personally I would like to be better, more often. Like I say, I am better with CD, my first love. Trance cuts you less slack.

It would be a couple of years before I realise the vinyl decks move at continually changing speeds. No one ever says that to me and finally I realise after much confusion. As the needle moves across from the start, it's a big distance at the outside edge to a much smaller distance at the end of a track near the centre so the music speed changes, every time. So as a DJ your beat matches (your next incoming track) all nice at one point, ready in time, and boom, it drops down and very swiftly it is already running a fraction out. This confuses the heck out of me for a long time and live. I have to work very hard to fix it! Lessons learnt… it seems so obvious now! That is why vinyl is harder in my opinion. Allowing for that change can be learnt. It would have been helpful to have learnt it sooner but I'm self-taught all the way. CD, vinyl and later digital Serato (although I prefer the look of Traktor) and VirtualDJ. Once I'm asked to cover a new room at the last minute with R&B and play a set on software I've never even seen before, and I somehow manage that with no mistakes.

**DAYTIME RADIO**

At the station, heads have rolled, again, with more shakeups. The Vibe Tribe changes so often it is hard to keep up but they all work hard and are nice kids. Some stay on and move into the office roles. When Patsy and Jane move on to new ventures, new people join, Kelly becomes head of sales and Mike is our new events manager. Sally, who is station coordinator, much later on becomes my part-time PA.

Sally spends a lot of her time fixing my mistakes. To manage me better she kindly sets up an automated spreadsheet so I can add up my monthly show invoices properly. I can't do this one simple maths thing right! She proudly says, 'There you go, Nikki. Even you can't cock this up.'

We laugh. Well, yes, after the first month of smooth-running invoices, I can cock it up. Sally rolls her eyes in disbelief. We laugh some more and then she patiently fixes it with me again.

In July of 2002 I get the daytime shift 10–1 p.m. Daytime shifts are so normal. Oh God, what a relief. Finally, some normality in my insane schedule! On my weekend show I have Deano, one of the tech ops (TOs), co-presenting with me. He is a calm and gentle chap and we are quite funny together. We laugh a lot, have good on-air chat together, and it flows well. He buys me some cool black boxing gloves, probably as a birthday gift, or maybe just as a gift to go with my punch bag. (I still have them!) When we are at Vibe, we are so free with content and we can try features or people on air and see how they work out.

## CONTENT OUTLINE FROM MY EARLY DAYTIME SHOWS

Unique perspective, it's personal. The thing with Nikki is she does things 'differently'; it's a topical format in an amusing way. The other day she was doing yoga on the floor with the strain on her ham strings and rush of blood to her head. 'If Meg Ryan's doing it in the street, I'll do it now.' Noises from the back of the studio… 'Oww, ahhh, it's a bit difficult but not bad.' Nikki combines questions that invoke and really pull in the audience, along with entertainment news, chat lifestyle and fresh ideas.

She creates a demand judging by hundreds of emails asking for the website address, building a cult following. When Atomic Badger Racing was the latest craze, all the listeners who worked in offices were playing. The Vibe FM reception phone was jammed with people needing the address for a fix. People across the East of England were drawing up score boards to stop outbreaks of cheating in the game. That's demand by creating a real need for people to do and to be involved.

People are copying the show's catchphrases with the current text line and emails are full of 'Thank you, do you want a fish?' and 'Dinosaurs with moving eyes', phrases from the ad played on the station. People are saying them out on the street and making toy dinosaurs for the show. You can't take the adverts out of a radio station so why not incorporate the best bits into the show. Subconsciously even the ads make people smile.

Nikki's passionate about the whole feel of the show writing and producing her own dry liners and sweepers, the show's sound FX. With self-aimed silly liners, the jokes are on her. Music beds (the background music to the show) are carefully selected to add cool beats, attitude with fun and recognisable rhythm. A lot of time goes into these productions. She produces all her own interviews which brings it all together with the Miss Elise touch.

She combines her knowledge and love of music on the show. The 'Sound Test' is a chance to play new music tracks where we are really open and encourage people to say exactly what they feel. She'll also drop 'Old Skool Dinners' over lunchtime, with the very best from the nineties, a trip down memory lane. Maybe some SL2, KLF, Baby D, En Vogue, Faithless, TLC or 2Pac.

Drop some interviews with actors, TV presenters and book writers, including Paul McKenna, Wade Williams and Shaggy. Who can forget Shaggy's personal ident, 'Nikki Elise… moist'. Naughty humour. And with Dannii Minogue's track, she asks Dannii, 'You sang "Put the Needle on It"… where do you want the needle to go?' 'Oh, doll, you know exactly where.' Both ladies lost it in hysterical laughter.

Thrown seamlessly together with humour, music quizzes, sketches and games, it gives you all-inclusive memorable radio.

## ME NOW!

I *CRINGE* at that Shaggy ident now! 'Nikki Elise... moisssttt...' Gross! Back in the day it was all *Loaded* and *FHM*. Everyone in programming lived and breathed lad culture. Honestly, at the time we all thought it was cool as he was a big star and it was funny! Even me. I played that ident constantly.

It shows you how much culture, mainstream media and acceptable language has changed in a few decades. Shaggy and I recorded off air three or four various types of name tag idents. As it was not live, we always messed around, just having fun. Everyone did. He maybe thought it was a joke and it wouldn't get used, so he had no idea whether we'd use it or not. That was up to us.

I was responsible for the station's brand (target content) within my show and ultimately all content on all shows was cleared by the boss. We liked it as it was edgy, which had to be cool! Now it seems shocking and it would never be allowed on air.

Michael Lewis on *Drive Time* used to play an ident whenever I walked in his studio. I never knew the name but it came up on YouTube last week and reminded me. It's by KRS-One's 'Sound of the Police'. He'd sing along with it... 'Woop, woop, that's the sound of the Elise' and repeat twice. Ha-ha. It was so cool I wanted to use it on my show, but I wasn't one for using someone else's creativity, so I never asked. It was hilarious though. Nice one! Idents and creativity were essential, and I was meticulous with my show's branding.

## MOTORBIKE COLLECTION

On Christmas Day over at my brother's, I squeeze in a spot of bike riding, getting splattered in mud racing round the motorcross track. I buy my rugged quad bike, a big red Honda 300cc, and it lives there waiting for me. I pretty much have all a woman desires now (well, depending on your desires). I have my dream job (well, actually two dream jobs), two cats, tropical holidays, a lovely group of expanding friends and my motorbike!

The missing £99 Argos kids' bike has accidently led to a small collection. Following that, I buy a petrol engine midi moto bike replica Yamaha R1 blue and white for about £400. It is a working piece of art and lives briefly in the kitchen until it gets thrown out into the garage. How rude. A little later I pick up a blue PW 80cc mini dirt bike until I have three motorbikes in my garage. This is what happens when you delay your childhood dreams. Wait for the drum kit!

On 31 December I'm in the Caribbean for two weeks. When I first see the Caribbean Sea and stand on the immaculate white sandy beach looking into the crystal-clear turquoise water, I cry. Which surprises me. I thought I was better at holding it together than that! Woman up, woman!

Honestly it's just so beautiful and I don't come from the package holiday generation. I was sixteen when Mum took me on my first ever package holiday to the Canary Islands. I'm overcome at how I came to be looking at this incredible tropical landscape, purely from my commitment to following my dream.

In 2003 I change shows again. Now I have 9–12 Vibe weekday mornings and the late 10–12 shift on Saturday, *House of Elise*. We've been bought out by SRH. For some years I've been contemplating a new project. I draft out, perfect and pitch my new concept. It is my dream show. I take a meeting with our new Scottish head of programmes as half of the new team has arrived from Scotland. I am very passionate about this idea and confident and I put in a lot of time designing my new show. I must have delivered well because he loves it and he commissions my new show. What a day!

## *HOUSE OF ELISE* IS BORN!

Keeping weekday daytime, I turn specialist at the weekend. It is produced as live in the week and plays out by a TO initially on Saturday nights because I'm mostly out working clubs. I'm told I can't be a specialist DJ and also a daytime presenter. Why ever not? I never understood this way of thinking… I ignore it! Anyway, here we are again and 'yes, I can'. This boss believes in my vision of a hard dance show and I take Boy George's space. He only arrives weekly on a mini disc anyway.

I'm much more real and embedded, in your kitchen, lounge, workplace, gym, car and across the entire East of England. We rock every single weekend. I never miss a *H of E* show in seven years (to the best of my knowledge).

*House of Elise* is a big production. I have new TOs for driving the show, usually Lotty and sometimes Paul or Shaun. It plays out 10 p.m. to midnight every Saturday and I and Ray Keith are often fighting for mid-week studio space if he turns up on the wrong day to record his *Breakage* show. Usually, I accommodate him by moving my schedule on the grounds that he's driven further than me! He's a really lovely guy. We have a laugh and he gets me a nice white Von Dutch cap, an essential at the time. Paul also helps me with interviews and event coverage. Paul is street team but, when I can't fit in any more hours, he picks up things like interviewing BK playing at the club. In *Fusion* I organise our weekly guest DJ sets from the best globally and some of our homegrown regional talent.

This is where I now find myself listening sometimes on a Friday night (if I'm not DJing) with some Bacardi and the stereo. I find myself pulling up the occasional mistake on air and then talking to the team next week about how to perfect it. Just like when I was a tech op for the other guy's show. Why do people listen to their own show live? Weirdos! To see how it sits, to see how it feels, to hear it in real time. To assess it and fully submerge into it after dark… and get smashed with some cracking tunes!

Dave Austin promotor and DJ joins the team from his Roobarb nights. He researches and writes all the house music news for me. Absolutely everybody in the UK in the hard dance and house scene is on my show after a while. I use my record shopping trips to acquire the best new material. Bird and I go record shopping at Rapture Records on St John Street in Colchester when John is running it. It is bliss quietly sniffing around all the record boxes and pilfering banging new tunes. You eagerly and carefully place it on the deck and put the needle down. What will my ears be graced with today? I go to a couple of other record shops but that is our favourite.

Once only, on my way home from a Norfolk record shop, I briefly fall asleep at the wheel of my car. The only time it ever happens. I hit the rumble strip in a few seconds with the noise opening my eyes wide. It startles me enough to know that I'd shut my eyes. Jesus, I'm lucky there are rumble strips. Driving in the warm sun around 4 p.m. is dangerous. Noted. It is a warning sign flagging up daytime driving. I never suspect daytime driving would be a threat to me given that I'm continually driving at night. I am hyper aware driving at night. I have once pulled a trapped mother and son from an upside-down car in a ditch and I noted it was 5 p.m. The dangerous time when you're not expecting it. No one else was injured. He just drove off the road with no recollection of what happened. They both blacked out on impact as it was a while before anyone spoke from the wreckage.

## CONTACTS AND NETWORKING

Once I've bought all the records and driven them back home, I place them on my Vibe office desk. I set about contacting each one, until everyone is on board with my show. I may have spent about a year sorting it all out. They add me to their mailing list and send me brand-new material continually. That is all the major players in the UK and some from abroad. I have hundreds of contacts nationwide.

After a while there is no need to buy new material as it all arrives on my desk. Research is always valuable though. I still look for new stuff and once pull out a lovely little mix of Tim Deluxe's 'It Just Won't Do' (the Secret Squirrel remix) from a store in Trafalgar Square. I have contacts everywhere. Here are just a few: Ministry of Sound, Global Gathering, Cream, Ibiza clubs and all the big labels like Tidy Trax. Just everywhere.

We have plenty of ticket, festival and event giveaways and all the latest albums such as Gatecrasher's Club Anthems, Euphoria CDs and of course all the artist albums like Sander van Doorn, Tiesto and K90. Often, I receive packs or duplicates for prizes. I give most gear away via listener competitions and I wear the black bomber jacket with a white Cream logo on the back for several years.

*House of Elise* is my dream. From all the networking, content, programming and carefully constructing it every single week, we grow to be a key industry player. Everybody is on *House of Elise* in some form or other. Tiesto is on so often that later I ask him to be on the lunchtime show too if he has a track in the charts. It is an enormously successful show and brand. I'm confident I beat Radio 1 in almost or quite likely all our RAJAR figures (but I don't keep the figures now). Those little numbers were the benchmark of work success.

I produce my own radio demos every three to six months and having two show styles, daytime and specialist, it is twice the work. I'd been for (job) interviews from the south coast Power FM to Galaxy in Newcastle but London is my goal. I am offered a couple of roles and but they don't fit me or my more south-based lifestyle so I decline. I spend a lot of time in London dropping these off and having meetings with a few big stations including KISS FM and Capital FM.

I go to Radio 1 three times, lastly meeting a specialist producer. Initially I meet the boss of everything, Andy Parfitt. On my next train trip (12 May 2003) I meet the head of mainstream, Ben Cooper, for a coffee. He likes my work and we keep in touch. I DJ at a big venue in Great Yarmouth with Annie Mac and the Stanton Warriors. As she is up on stage gearing up to hop on the decks right after me, I say to her, amongst the regular 'hey, how are you?', 'I've sent demos to Ben.'

She kindly says, 'Just keep trying.'

The thing is there is very little room at the top and as Annie is mainly doing the sound and style that I play, they don't need both of us. In the last letter, Radio 1 suggests I may benefit from an agent. Once I joined KISS FM I was so busy I didn't search for an agent and stopped looking towards other radio companies. I always keep my demos up to date but seriously it has to do for now.

I am increasingly interested in music production. I work with Ray Keith as he is our drum and bass show man and I meet him at his Dread Records studios. I spend the day with Divine Inspiration at their studios. A few others, including Dan Stone and Louis Napoletani, show me around their home set-up and I decide that's where I am heading now. Music producer is a career I want and crave.

**POST**

I enjoy nothing more than putting a heavy tune on loud and sitting in the car or standing in the middle of the speakers to feel it. To feel the rhythm and beats pulsate, physically pushing against my body, travelling through my skin and connecting to my mind. It is just bliss. A downside to spending all my time editing production for the shows is how bad my right hand has become from repetitive strain injury using the keyboard but mostly the mouse. All my waking hours are spent producing audio, mixes, sound bites and bits for the show. The aches and cramping-like sensations are growing and constant.

I have almost unlimited access to glorious new sounds and fresh beats and opening the post is unpacking exciting new discoveries all the time. Music is on a parallel with my existence. It is kind of like a legal substance where I get a fix. It is my addiction, my passion, my working career, my salary and my social life, and it is my up or down time. Music is in every taxi or bus, restaurant or shop. It is in the studio before and after and during my show. In my office, my car, on at my parents' house or my friends' and on holiday in the clubs. Music is my all, music is my everything. My whole life revolves around music.

In daytime radio I get sent so much from all over the place. Stuff from listeners like cards, music and mixes, and anything they think is interesting. Then contacts, PR events, merchandise. I have piles of T-shirts and clothing, such as movie merchandise. I have glossy *Terminator* photo books, an *X-Men 2* watch, a *Walk the Line* guitar plectrum No 35. (I've kept my *Mr. & Mrs. Smith* black bath towel; it lives in my swim bag even today.) A collector from Essex has sent me a replica *Blade* hieroglyph and bank notes used in *Total Recall*. I never have the time to look at everything as there is just so much coming in. I do my best with prioritising.

I had literally no idea I'd been sent porn until I put the VHS tape on in front of *my mum* in her lounge! I thought she could use a spare video for her regular taping of *Eastenders*. I say I'll just play it to see what's on there first. FUCKING HELL, WE BOTH GOT A SHOCK! You try standing there, trying your best to explain that shit to your mum!

Although she does believe me that I had no prior knowledge as to what was on that tape. That video had been in my radio station office drawer for God knows how many years. A whole drawer full of stuff gets launched in the bin following that day. Take no chances on anything anymore! What the hell?

It seems unbelievable but yes, that's a fact and that did happen, right in front of my mum!

# CHAPTER 6

# JOINING KISS FM EAST AND WEST NETWORK AND RENOVATING A HOUSE

In the middle of all this, it feels like a good time to spend twelve months renovating a house. Eventually, my partner and I buy a house together. I tell my friends we are moving in for financial reasons! Which is partly true, as I have no desire to live with someone. That seems like a very big commitment that I just don't need. However, I do perhaps need my own home at twenty-six! The house comes complete with 1980s pink walls and green carpets and, as I embark on our first working project together, everything is fully renovated. Everything, except for plastering the ceilings which comes the next time around.

The work starts by taking down an internal bathroom wall, moving it over and building a stud wall to create a bigger space. The sledgehammer swings back and smashes the front of the toilet off but still working. That's how it stays for eleven months. It must have been summer as there is a photo of me in action wielding the sledgehammer in my safety bikini top! After carrying out a wall of rubble into a skip, I help build a new one: plasterboard, plaster, paint, and eventually after nearly a year, there is a working toilet in the all-new bathroom.

Just to explain how the loo works for the remaining eleven months, I have to keep a bucket there for the duration. Our friends come round and ask to use the toilet and I explain there is a bucket in there. My other friend Charly (there are two now) looks a little shocked, thinks for a moment and politely asks, 'What's the bucket for exactly?'

'To fill with water to flush the toilet.' All totally normal to me.

'Of course,' she says. 'I actually thought you wanted me to piss in the bucket for a second.' She'd taken the 'use the bucket' instructions at face value and was trying not to be rude thinking, *Well, this is a weird freaking house.*

Glen jokes with me that I only come into work to get a rest from my life and he is so right. It is physically hard but I'm young and fit, so can take on anything.

After a year of solid graft, I can enjoy the freshly renovated house and entire landscaped garden. It is so extensive that our neighbours think I'm a property developer for that first year.

If ever I'm free on a weekend, which is rare as I'm temporarily juggling three jobs at once, I usually get drunk and go completely off grid losing all contact with the outside world. A sort of mini hibernation accrues. It is my escapism for the relentless pressure of on-air and live performance perfection.

In my younger days, having a drink and being on holiday relaxing were the only ways I knew. I didn't know anything else to destress me. I've been there, done that, got the vest top, grown up and quit it.

There is a little book that someone at work mentions and I buy a copy. It is called *Who Moved My Cheese*. It has a very simple message about staying stuck or embracing change. I also learn there are really only two choices in life: change it or accept it. If you can't change it, you must accept it (even if it's temporary). If you can't accept it, you must change it.

## BEING A DJ, BOTH ON AND OFF AIR

I've always been told overall in radio presenters have to choose either daytime or specialist. You cannot be both and shouldn't attempt it (although my regional bosses are very supportive of me). Well, quite frankly, bollocks to those rules. Who were they created for? Not me, so naturally I don't listen. If they mean due to time allocation, then they are perhaps right. There's not nearly enough time to breathe, produce all your shows and collect music, plus travel to all the different places. Perhaps they are right, partly. It's not that I can't do it, as I bloody well do!

Many of the decisions I make feel like a good idea at the time, and then somehow they swallow up every single aspect of my life, until I become saturated! If you are going to present, then that's a great choice but adding in DJing on top can become hectic. A lot of radio presenters choose DJing as a natural extension of work. It's a logical progression, good business sense and bloody good fun.

Things become more intense when I work up to a specialist DJ, but I just keep going. I say 'up to' only because I start out with commercial mixing on CD; neither is up or down. They are just different. I just find vinyl harder, so I have to work harder until I play both. Not many people choose such a range of music, as it's so demanding with the collection time and continually stocking your weekly library. Most people choose either commercial or specialist or maybe commercial and then just funky house. Funky fits in most clubs or events and you can just collect the twelve-inch version of the track or more unique tracks and it'll all fit together. It just feels natural to me, as it is something I can do, so I end up doing it all.

Eventually I'm collecting to play around eight different genres of music, and a huge amount of time is spent on my record collection. I have chart and dance, including garage, a small amount of R&B, a fraction of hip hop, drum and bass and some commercial hardcore. All this music is at different speeds and beat layouts.

Then on the specialist side I'm collecting tech house, hard trance and hard house and hard dance (which are similar really). Then later, playing a vinyl breakbeat set in Essex, plus a tech trance in London. Oh, and dubstep is just in at the end of my time, so some of that too. I kind of like rising to the mutual genres' challenges within my live sets. Keeps me on my toes! If I want to play a certain club, I find the music, practise, then go and play it. I also end my DJ career with all my trademark Nikki house and dance but also, chart and pop, having never *ever* touched pop before. That's gay bars for you! Or at least this one. They're not all the same. I've played many types of clubs.

## COLOUR CODING AND COPING!

I have so much music that when I go to play a set it is hard to look at a CD wallet with maybe eight CDs on a page each with ten to twenty tracks so my eyes are scanning over more than a hundred tracks just on one double page. Thousands in a whole large CD case. And I always have a minimum of two full cases and up to four, or sometimes five, depending on the club.

I try to separate them into commercial and special folders and that makes it a bit easier. *Always* remember to take the correct folders out with you on the right night. And *always* remember to take them home. I've only ever left one folder behind at Club M and had to go back in the week for it.

I lend Goldie my headphone jack adapter over in Peterborough. He is on after me and somehow doesn't have one to fit the mixer. It could have been an on-stage drama! I need to leave so leave it with him. I let Goldie keep it. He needs it more than me.

The best thing I find is colour coding everything, so if I've broken into a bit of hardcore or hard dance, I can locate it much faster. Over time you also build up a memory of the pages and where everything is stored. I have red R&B, light blue is house and dark blue hard house and so on. Yellow is crap as you can't see it in the dark of your DJ booth. Reprinting everything in colour labels from then on drastically increases my speed to find the exact track I want to drop at that perfect moment. It's your knowledge of the music and what the crowd needs from you that helps you create the most electric performance, and I have a huge range. (Digital kind of removes all this effort now.)

## WHAT DOES IT TAKE TO BE A GOOD DJ?

Every club is unique. It may have a different sound, monitor (or no monitor sometimes... nightmare), desk area and spec set-up. Most of the bigger clubs have the industry standard Pioneer and Technics but by no means did *all* of them! This is the tricky part: using crap kit! There's always room for error and you throw yourself wide open to a new live audience every single time. You learn to deal with it all at that moment, live! Lots of pressure!

When you're on stage, you are the epicentre of everything. You play with the crowd and they play with you. They look to you to deliver the best moment of their world, their weekend, month or clubbing history!

I have another big turning point mid-set at Funky Bunny one night. (I wondered what to call it for many years, then I saw it on the film *Black Swan*, referring to a ballet performance. It's called transcending.) I transcend the technical ability to play, to be able to deliver magic, with the crowd on a whole new level. I feel the shift and it is electric in my mind and body. A goosebumps moment mid-set.

On that night I lift away from the confines of the technicalities of the job, and become greater at my performance. I've watched loads of other superstar DJs and played with Lisa Pin-Up many times. I notice she has the ability to make the crowd go crazy. She achieves this by holding just one index finger in the air to wind them all along with the peak of the song. She knows how to work the crowd, the little minx. She's a lovely legend. All of us women are working friends and I'm friendly with a lot of the promoters who are mostly, but not all, guys. There's a lotta love and support as we're all in the same business together promoting and working venues all over the country. It's like meeting up with your family out on tour, in different venues and countries.

I build myself, through passion, practice and dedication, a pretty decent reputation as a DJ. Some of my listeners call me the Lisa Lashes of the East which is obviously a massive compliment! She is widely thought of as the number one female DJ at the time. I master how to plan and adapt my set perfectly over time across a wide variety of genres to audiences everywhere. I'm probably best known for hard house though, my signature *House of Elise* style. And second, funky house.

I learn to look at the crowd and see how they feel many times throughout my live set. I read their faces individually and as a group whilst they dance in front of me. I assess their immediate response. Do they feel happy, bored, excited, tired? In need of a stomp or a huge emotional trance lift? They look to me for that, for their fun and excitement, their moment. Their weekend is in my hands.

That is my role as a DJ: give them what they want. When I read to that degree you need to know your music and be able to drop exactly the right tune, at exactly the right moment. That's what we do, we create moments, some of the best times in our lives. Friends stand shoulder to shoulder covered in sweat in front of the DJ. I've stood there hundreds of times myself. I know what I want, what they want: to be lost in bliss or willing the DJ to deliver their high! I've danced in venues where the combined sweat of hundreds drips from the ceiling onto your face and it is all ok because you built that together. There is a oneness, a harmony and it usually comes from complete satisfaction, a very tribal moment of euphoria.

I'm always really particular about what will make me dance. A lot of places I just stand there stiff! I can't just dance to anything; it has to be perfect to make me move. Maybe that is why I'm extra choosey with music, and it helps me put together the best sets for dancing. I have been to plenty of nights where I haven't danced because the tunes are quite frankly shit. It's a massive let down. You're looking for that hit, the musical reward for the energy, and to let yourself go.

A shit DJ takes your night away from you. Must be a bit like going to a race and being told you can't run; you just stand there wondering what happened. All your pent-up energy, expectations and hopes are ruined for the whole night. That's your life, your weekend, all crushed. And all because the person playing doesn't understand the crowd or possibly care about the crowd. Being shit or having crap tunes or no interest in the crowd's needs, only their own, is where it can go wrong. Even when I have club rules to follow, especially in the early days or with certain nights or brands, I still try to tailor it for that crowd, every time, and do my thing for them. It is a two-way experience.

## I BEGIN PUTTING ON WEIGHT

This is something that affects my life dramatically. It affects my career, my confidence and my whole wardrobe for the next nearly two decades. It is just something I have to deal with, somehow. It's pretty devastating at times. It wrecks my body. Radio is not such a problem although women are still expected to be thin in media. I want to look a certain way and wear the clothes I want on stage but for some reason I can no longer achieve this. What happened?

I'm aware that I'm putting on weight which is basically not tolerated in media. It is particularly frustrating as I'm fit, running four and a half miles, twice a week. I also have the treadmill and am biking but I have many food intolerances, which does not help. I've been wheat and gluten free since I was twenty which has made a big difference but still there are a lot of foods I can't eat.

I try hypnosis for losing weight, but it doesn't make any difference to me as I have plenty of willpower. Willpower does not look like an issue for me does it, really, honestly? Anything normal doesn't work for me including exercise, diet and thinking myself thin. I can't do that. It just doesn't work and I don't know why. It is massively disappointing for a person who is really physically fit. I usually work out five times a week so why is this happening to me?

I steadily and continually (and disappointingly) put on weight, all the time. It is noticeable around twenty-nine onwards.

## BITS FROM DJ DIARY 2005. TWENTY-SEVEN THIS YEAR

January

11 Jan: 11.45 a.m. Interview with Paul McKenna. He's got a book coming out. I like him as he's empowering, warm and easy to interview. We've spoken twice for his different books. I'm into this mind training stuff… I like it.

February

11 Feb: Daytime show interview with Anna Ryder Richardson. Then Time, Norwich. Live on Vibe FM, 12–2 a.m. Hard dance set

26 Feb: Corn Exchange, Ipswich. Big and Slinky Easter Ball. Ben's gig and this is staggeringly good. We have to stay and dance after my set which is unusual for me.

27 Feb: Funky Bunny at Zoots, King's Lynn with BK, 12.15 a.m. Run by Marty. Great guy

July

16 Jul: Tickets for Creamfields (one year we sent Dave to enjoy/review)

22 Jul: Roobarb at The Waterfront, Norwich. Nick Sentience and Nicki S are both playing

20 Jul: Lisa Lashes, fusion guest mix H of E

28 Jul: Live broadcast from our hired mobile unit, like an Airstream retro silver caravan

29 Jul: Live broadcast day two from Lowestoft Air Show. Biggest event in the East

30 Jul: East Coast Extreme Cruiser event. Old Bentwaters air base. DJed off the back of a lorry. Awesome event! Where they film car stuff like *Fifth Gear* or *Top Gear* occasionally

August

6 Aug: Big Live at The Junction, Cambridge. Either with Lisa Lashes or she was on *H of E*. I can't be a hundred percent sure in which capacity I was working with her!

Hold up! I have the flyer. I can confirm it was Big Live on Vibe FM Big & NC Arena Nikki Elise and Lisa Lashes with Big Ben, Paul Wilkerson and Mark Hughes. Also The BeatThiefs, Tee Vegas and Henry Hacking plus guests.

When I first stepped foot behind on stage that night in The Junction it was so loud my eyeballs were vibrating, for real. What the actual fuck? My eyeballs were shaking! Never felt that before. Welcome to The Junction. It was insane! With the hard stage floor and the noise so loud, wearing heels, as I always did when I worked, made the vibrations literally shake right up through my bones and into my eye sockets. Never happened before or after anywhere! A lot of these gigs were pre noise limits being put in place. I don't remember when the noise limiting rules came in that affected some venues like city buildings with neighbours complaining more than isolated places.

December

2 Dec: Liquid, Peterborough, 12–2 a.m. Dance and house music. A huge buzz in a massive venue

3 Dec: Oliver's, Huntingdon. Commercial

26 Dec: Funky Bunny at Zoots, King's Lynn. Hard house. Harder, faster… love it

31 Dec: Ely/Cambridge. My brother is in Australia and I call him after my set en route home (which was legal then before hands-free). Happy New Year! It's lonely always being on the road at night. He had visited or was about to go to the Great Barrier Reef. I was about to finally visit home and bed.

## 2006: THE YEAR WE BECOME KISS

I take a big relaxing hot holiday at the beginning of January, two weeks in the Caribbean, as I've pre-recorded up to three weeks of Saturday shows. *House of Elise* has no cover as we never need any, such is my dedication to it. I just cover myself pre-producing way in advance if going away. Very little illness occurs and if it does, I often lie on the floor between links trying to catch my breath with the sales staff looking at me strangely as they walk past the windows. This is severe viral-related asthma as yet undiagnosed. I have no idea. My asthma had gone after school… or so I thought.

## WHO IS ON *HOUSE OF ELISE*?

Interviews, mixes, albums, tickets, merchandise giveaways, etc.

Dave Austin, Marco V, K90, possibly BK again, Nicki S, Nick Rafferty, Big Ben, Edison Factor, Sander Van Doorn (nearly melted when I interviewed him!), Jan Loper, Anne Savage, The Tidy Boys, Tiesto (deffo interviewed him, but not sure for which show), Dave Clarke, Lee Haslam, Nick Sentience, Carl Cox (interview and mix).

## DJ DIARY 2006

Oliver's, Huntingdon. (29: Covered Gary's show 4–7 p.m.)

Liquid, Peterborough. Taken Suz

Gone with friends to see Robbie Williams at The National Bowl, Milton Keynes. Basement Jaxx were incredible. I mean, Robbie can sing (I had an album or two) but to see the Jaxx absolutely smashed it! Danced my ass off!

Oliver's, Huntingdon

Liquid, Peterborough. Separately, quad bike riding!

Big Live on Vibe at The Junction, Cambridge

Oliver's, Huntingdon

Park Hotel, Diss (where I used to waitress, serving up of a different kind…) Big ass tunes!

Lester's, Bourne

Oliver's, Huntingdon

DPW (Dance Party Weekender). Shipwrecked theme

Oliver's, Huntingdon. Ibiza dance party

Funky Bunny at Zoots, King's Lynn. Tidy Extreme tour

Oliver's, Huntingdon

3D Events Company, Essex College. Classic old skool. That was a cool gig!

Lava Ignite. Funky house and club classics

Liquid, Peterborough

Funky Bunny at Zoots, King's Lynn. Hard house

Cambridge event (don't know what it is)

Mercy Nightclub, Norwich. I have played there but I don't know if it was this year or if I was just drunk dancing on a podium when Glen was playing there... that happened too!

Ignite (can't remember where)

Pink Festival, Cambridge

Liquid & Envy opening (I think I was there... my life is soooo blurry)

Oliver's, Peterborough. First birthday

Funky Bunny at Zoots, King's Lynn. Anne Savage

## I JOIN KISS FM (CURRENTLY NOT CALLED KISS FM)

On 29 August at 11 a.m. we have a conference call with big boss Andy, head of programmes for KISS or KISS FM or whatever they are called that year! Marketing meeting is coming up next week. Rebranding to KISS. We have approximately four days of Dalet training (new radio software), then it is on air for us at KISS 105-108: Nikki Elise weekdays *KISS Lunch* 12–3 p.m. (East and West stations networked), Friday night's *House of Elise* 10 p.m.–12 a.m. (East of England) and Sunday 12–4 p.m. (East of England).

After Stu, Glen is now our new programmes controller and swing jock. Stu is on Breakfast with Kaz and producer Thomsta, and Sam moves on before KISS (I think). Yet more people get chopped for the new line-up and new office staff all round. Kelly makes a committed speech about who's left (survived the mass sackings). It goes something like this: 'We are all still here for good reason and we have much to do and much to deliver.'

I nod in agreement. It is exciting to join this big heritage brand.

With takeovers this time, we have all-new studio software and all presenters prepare with Dalet training. It feels so intensive. Just a few hours for four days straight after my show. Then there you go, get on air with all the new equipment and be perfect! Oh crap… no pressure then! That is the last time my head physically hurts every single day after work. (It hurts for many reasons in your forties!) My brain is overloaded but copes somehow with such fast-track training and joining the new brand overnight.

We launch the rebranded KISS 105-108 with mine as the only networked show broadcast from Bury St Edmunds in the East and reaching the West station KISS 101, automatically doubling my lunchtime audience. London KISS 100 sends some new, mainly specialist, shows over the weekend evenings and nighttime to all three KISS stations. I am now responsible for a massive *seven* shows a week on KISS. More than anyone else… probably. I've not researched it.

## CONTINUED DJ DIARY 2006… AFTER I JOIN KISS

Oliver's, Huntingdon

Roobarb at The Waterfront, Norwich, 11.15 p.m.–12.45 a.m. With Dave Austin and guests

Casino's March KISSTORY set, 11 p.m.–1.30 a.m. Then I still gotta get up and be bloody amazing on air Sunday 12–4 p.m. Seven shows and two nightclubs. I'm starting to feel it's too much!

Oliver's, Huntingdon 12–2 a.m. Halloween. Sunday 12–4 p.m. show

DPW (In the future, rebrands to KISS Weekender). Both Saturday and Sunday DJ sets and on-air Sunday 12–4 p.m.

Funky Bunny is three years old! Zoots, King's Lynn, 11 p.m.– 12 a.m. Nikki Elise and Lisa Pin-Up. She freaking rocks! Set recorded onto double CD by Marty (promoter)

Central's Stamford KISSTORY. Old skool set

Mercy Nightclub, Norwich, 12–2 a.m.

Route, Colchester, 11.30 p.m.–1.30 a.m. Dying in my own body. Have to get up for work for the Sunday show 12–4 p.m. A realisation that this warp speed of shows production and events *CAN'T* CONTINUE LIKE THIS

We were in PRS for a couple of days again. Do not screw anything up on air or in the music logs. An accurate broadcasting record was essential here. We were in PRS a lot, several times a year. It's just really boring so I didn't mention it till now! Ha-ha!

Produced a special mix for New Year's Eve, *House of Elise Christmas Eve: Ignite*, 11 p.m.–1 a.m.

Last gig of the year was New Year's Eve at Jack's, Wisbech, 11 p.m. –1 a.m. Floorfillers and commercial dance

## SEVEN SHOWS A WEEK HURTS A BIT... WELL, THE GIGS REALLY, NOT THE SHOWS... SOMETHING HURTS!

My schedule is now insane, but I have everything I ever wanted and work for KISS FM! I don't know if anyone else ever makes seven shows a week but I do, for four years solid. I never miss one *House of Elise* show as it is my dream project, but something has to give for me to keep up the new level of perfection and presenting on air for a national iconic brand. I decide I have to cut some of the nightclubs to focus on my KISS shows. I drop to about one club or event per month and that feels more manageable. Bits of me are falling apart!

I work for Vibe FM for eight years and continually live in that building. I sleep on the sofa dozens and dozens of times. I'm there twenty-four-seven and now with seven shows a week. Lunchtimes are networked out to South Wales and the West on the old Vibe 101, making me the only network presenter on the East, and Neve has London's Lunchtime show.

It is a very big day for me getting the green light to work for KISS. Finally, after all my demos and efforts, Andy has given me the job with the biggest audience. He says he wants the two women working as one across Lunchtimes. Lunchtime is the perfect shift for me. I love it and there is no rush hour driving!

Women don't really get the lead Breakfast shows at this time in radio. However, I'm not really suited to Breakfast as you have to be more character based. I've trained to be a solo presenter on daytime. Honestly, getting up for the Breakfast show at 5 a.m. is not very nice. I've done it and I'm grateful I don't have to do it again. Especially as I'm a club DJ and constantly working late shifts, partying the night away all over the country. Breakfast hurts!

## THE BRAND: BIG AND DIFFERENT

With Vibe there is a great deal of creative freedom to try out sketches, humour, games, competitions, etc. When I write and plan a feature called 'Sixty-Second Babble On', my boss just says, 'I don't like it.'

I'm really disappointed as I believe in this one. I talk with one of our producers about it and he advises me to produce it, make it and then demo it to him in full.

I take that on board and with his help set about voicing and producing beds and tails (intros, talkover music and exit point). Then try again! This is my new feature, the Sixty-Second Babble On. We get listeners on air and give them a topic with no notice and no prior warning, then hit start on the one-minute clock, the production sounds package.

Their job is to talk and entertain us on whatever is thrown at them, i.e. transport, pens, dogs or shopping. Finally, I get the green light from my boss to air it. I wonder if anyone will call as there are no prizes attached, no money, no incentive but they do call, every day, and play. It is probably one of my best features. (The only one that I remember to this day. It sounded cool and it was fun.)

*None* of that freestyle creativity is required anymore with KISS, not on my show anyway, so I erase it. It is a different beast of a brand and the presenting is different. It is more music based, some or a lot of the songs are cut and shuts, KISS short edits, so they can get more music tracks into an hour.

There are a lot of scripts and new promotions to read live from your show's paper music log copy (the playlist). It mirrors the on-air music playlist. I work with two logs: the show's music log and I have my own content log where I plan my links, features, competitions and chat pieces. Most people write their show notes on the music log but I can't read it. The space is too crowded and I struggle to follow it. It looks so hectic in my mind. I can't focus on it and it is like black-and-white ink overload. So, long ago I developed my own strategy with my content paper log.

## WHAT DO WE DO IN THAT STUDIO?

One time, Nic P from school drops in on my weekend show, previously saying over the phone that I didn't really have that much to do, except sit around and play records! So, I vividly encourage her: 'You'd better bloody come in then and visit me with my *easy* job: the live broadcast!'

I direct her. 'You sit down silently in the chair behind me and don't move anything. Don't make a sound. Not a chair squeak, not a whisper, not a cough and do not breathe loudly. You catch my drift? Studio mics pick up everything!'

She is impressed at just how much stuff we have to work with simultaneously linking it all together.

In my studios there are like three computer screens or maybe four with playlist music and adverts, sweepers and jingles, texts, emails, internet, on-air output, etc. Although I have no picture to back me up I know where everything is: the entire mixing desk, with the rack of amplifiers and other on-air kit, mics and standing idle during the day over in the far corner, all the DJ mixing gear, the decks and mixers.

My job is to keep us on air then open the mic and seamlessly link all the changing music tracks together entertaining with target content and factually correct info in an amusing and friendly way. How I love my job so, sooooo much. Weaving it all together down to the split second to fire your adverts, news and jingles. Plus running competitions with listeners on air and timed perfectly every second of the day. Flawless live production... it is a joy to have been part of the product.

## LIVE READS AND SCRIPTS

The station scripts are getting longer and more complex under KISS. I notice they are well spaced out and laid out on paper for the presenters. Most times you can read them before the show. Very occasionally one is dropped on your desk during the show. Usually with directions like, 'Just fit that in before the news break.' But it is impossible for me to rip and read. It always has been. In the early days we print out info, rip it off the printer and run into the studio at top speed (if nearly late) then read, hence it is called 'rip n read'. Essentially, you're taking something at the last minute live. A lot of people can do that just fine, newsreaders for example. Nina, Dawn and Neil are all wonderful at reading. Not me... I've never been able to do that.

All my scripts, every one, have to be read fully, many times, in advance of the show. I struggle a bit with the scripts and I have to practise and practise. The others can just do it with minimal prep, one pre-read. This is why I have my own show plan sheet as I can't add to the music log like most. I struggle to see the complexity of it. (It makes perfect sense now that I struggled to read. It was the dyslexia. It's like chaos in my brain and my mind wants to run away from it.) I have previously run into real problems on air, pronouncing things wrong and have to pre-work at my scripts so hard.

One day, in Vibe times, I run a listener competition and take the caller's number down. Now competitions in particular carry a huge weight behind them as they have to be carried out professionally, according to the rules. The rules are serious business.

It's do it right or risk the wrath of Ofcom, get fired or possibly chuck away your radio station's licence should you fuck it up spectacularly! Anyway, so I run to my boss frantically saying, 'I can't call the listener back. I got the number written here and I've tried six times. The line's dead. I don't know what to do.' I need the winner back on air or to notify him of his win as it is our legal responsibility. There are huge laws and massive fines around conducting competitions to the correct standard.

After a while he says, 'How can that be happening? What's the number?'

I tell him what is written down in front of me on my paper sheet. The area code '73301' for example. Panic is setting in as I have the wrong number.

He says, 'What?'

So, I repeat it again.

He says, 'That's impossible as no phone number starts with those digits...'

I look at my sheet wondering how it is possible when I've written it down. As I stand in his office doorway staring down at the numbers, the digits move about on the paper. It is so weird. I see them move and line up in a different order. Then I read it back to him again, for example '01733...' It is a real realisation. The moment I find out I cannot read numbers correctly.

It is a sort of disbelief. How could I have read it exactly wrong about ten times, typed it in wrong, then the numbers just switched into a different order in front of my eyes. I see them move across each other. Finally, I call the winner back. Following that near radio fatal crash, I decide to get some help. I search and find a diagnostic company assessing and working with people with dyslexia.

I'm twenty-seven and it is a wonder how I got this far without knowing. Really, how? I knew I found some things hard but learnt to adapt to make it work. I know I'll never be able to read live news, even with our brief one-minute bulletins. I have zero chance of reading that. Even with my travel bulletins I use only a few words and draw symbols for roundabouts or traffic lights to cut down on the amount of written text. It is easier for me to see and read live without making mistakes. Less text is best.

I get an assessment booked for something I didn't know I had. It is clearly affecting my work though. Hopefully I'll find some answers.

# CHAPTER 7

# I'M A DYSLEXIC, AN INSOMNIAC AND HOUSE OF ELISE BECOMES A MAJOR PLAYER

At twenty-eight, following a private assessment, it concludes that I have some difficulty with letters and numbers. I'm dyslexic and also with numbers, which is a total surprise to me. I didn't know anything about it. I didn't even know you could be. Is that dyscalculia? I'm honestly not totally sure. (It's hard for me to read the spelling then type it. The letters are so confusing to look at. It took me three attempts using spell check to get 'dyscalculia' typed in the right order.) I find it hard to see the letters in the right order, and if they're in the wrong place, I can't see it. From my test score, I'm mild to mid-range but not severe. It just explains so much for me. I still recall the record company plugger emailing me and saying, 'The artist is Prok & Fitch, not Pork & Fitch.' Just so embarrassing!!!

I had a lot of trouble copying at school particularly from books or worse the enormous text spread all over the huge blackboard. Every single time I looked up or down I lost my place all over again. I didn't have much luck with spelling and some trouble reading, especially aloud, if rarely I was asked in class. I only started reading books by choice around sixteen apart from the Snoopy comic strip books I did particularly well with as a child. And when you had read the book, you were expected to write about it. Nope, no real memory, even though I'd just read the whole thing. Sometimes I used a ruler to keep my place on the page. And I sucked at maths. Even when I thought I truly understood what was required, I couldn't get the answer right and that was deeply disappointing. I learnt to accept that I couldn't do it, particularly maths where I gave up altogether.

There must be a void in my head between seeing the numbers and then physically typing out numbers. Today numbers are worse for me as spell check can get about ninety percent of words right except for when I'm so far off it can't even take a bloody guess! I have on/off trouble with debit cards; the long numbers on the front are usually the hardest bit. I literally can't type the numbers in the correct order no matter how many times I try. I have to phone the help line eventually after six increasingly frustrating failed attempts to spend a £20 gift voucher online. Next, I read the numbers to a nice lady in customer services then she types them in. Oh yeah, then it works! What the hell is my brain doing? And what has it been doing in an oddball random sequence (sometimes working fine and sometimes just not) my *whole entire* life without me noticing?

After three attempts to transfer Suzie back her £8 on my mobile phone banking app, I give up and thrust her my phone, stating, 'Just do it please. I can't bloody do it.' She can do it on attempt number one, of course. Transfer £8…? On a good day I can!

I have trouble with phone numbers. I tend to write down sequences wrong so I often start with the second number or letter, then try to write the first! What I've written makes no sense. I can barely even read my own handwriting. I'll be walking round the supermarket looking at my phone's photograph of my shopping list wasting time standing there trying to work out what the hell I've written down as it's illegible an hour later.

The whole thing still causes problems and every single time I am required to write the word annual, I try to write 'year' instead. It's just safer that way. I must google to make sure I don't accidently put anal… every single time! That's a horrifying typo disaster, right? An annual event is quite different to an anal event, isn't it? I still to this day mix up 'now and know' and 'how and who'. I have to say and spell out who or how every single time. Utterly ridiculous. I've been writing for nearly forty years!

To be honest I'm really glad I didn't know I was wired this way for all the little imperfections it has caused. I think I may have been scared off my dream of presenting. The number of scripts and reading and in general being on air may have been terrifying. Had I known that I would have to read complex competition scripts live I think I may well have gone, 'Nope, I can't do it. I never even learnt my times tables. I don't think I can live read on air about the competition rules to win a £4k luxury holiday.' I've got to five, ten and bits of the six times tables. Go me!

There's probably a lot of awareness around it now but back in the dark ages with blackboards and chalk, no one had ever really heard of dyslexia. And let's face it, mine is mild. Confusing at times but we learn to adapt, don't we? Like my travel news with pictures of traffic lights and spreading out all my scripts onto a separate line with space between each so I could read it confidently. Reading the eulogy at my grandma's funeral with my fingers tracing the end and start lines down the page otherwise I lost my place on every line. I wanted to get that right.

I feel I adapted and developed a good overview and I could see things far down the line in multiple directions. I can't give you exact maths to anything except maybe ten plus twenty but I can get to an average within a percentage or two quicker than anyone who's good at maths. As long as my job is not maths based or on a till, I get by. Even my till work was usually only out by a few pence, nothing major. It was likely I was just handing back an average amount of change for your cigarettes and packet of crisps.

This week I have *just* realised that with rebranding for the delivery people Hermes to ERVI, it is in fact EVRI! I literally had no idea! I've been saying it wrong… the whole time. That's about a year now. That's a hundred percent the truth! Ha-ha! I can't even see the difference when I've written it down here. They look the same!

Why bother to get tested on anything? I didn't go through with taking any extra help or courses as I figured I got this far in life ok. Because I know now and literally had no idea before, I can always double check everything I do. I have the awareness that my brain will see and write it backwards. I still can't get to a hundred percent but at least it gives me a better chance. Especially with numbers I can try to catch out my own mistakes. I have to add things up at least three to four times to get the correct answer. Previously I'd have done it once and not known I had it wrong. It helps massively just to know.

## SPIRITUAL COURSE

On the opposite end of the glamorous, rocking stages, full-on DJ lifestyle, I join a church! Not just any old regular church though. I join a spiritualist group based in the function room at the back of the church. Over in Ipswich every Monday night I sit in a circle (for over four years) on my spiritual journey. If you want another name, how about we call it a universe aware personal development group. Our group of around ten learn with my teacher Carol guiding us through our first meditations. I find it very grounding and detracted from my manic, busy autograph-signing twenty-four-seven schedule. I know I will struggle to put even one new thing into my diary. I force myself to find the time for this unknown adventure. It is a big deal for me to commit to one extra thing in my life and I want answers to life's odd questions that most people ignore.

On the journey we are active in personal growth and openness, meditations, energy healing, channelling, readings and inner mind adventures. Gaining trust and knowledge is hugely enlightening and it is what I need to discover for myself during my late twenties. If you have a spiritual side then best to tap into it and train yourself and get it under control as opposed to thinking you're just fucking nuts! Well, that is the best route for me anyway. I know others who prefer to shut it down and if that works for them, that's good. Everyone's different.

The best thing for me personally is learning to meditate. It becomes (and still is) the bedrock of my life. I have given up all forms of me trying to escape myself by smoking and drinking and for long periods give up serious vices like coffee.

Or cheese, the toughest of all! Why? Because I don't need any of it anymore. I replace it with something better. The cheese thing is a real challenge for the first month and I don't think I can make it! I give it up for Lent. Which is an odd teaching as I'm not religious, but I just think, *Well, I've never tried this experiment, never, so try now.* I accidently consume it twice which thrusts me into the position of choices: go forwards or fail. It is change it or accept it. As I accidently consumed it, I decide to accept this screw up and continue on my test rather than give up. Allowing for my mistakes I may learn more. I clear a month and realise dairy makes me sweat badly (and basically smell terrible) so I pretty much give it up after that. I wish I'd known that in school when Mum had to boil wash all my light blue shirts. (I eat it very rarely now. I prefer to smell better. A valuable lesson I may not have discovered any other way.)

An equally important change accrues in my thought process. It teaches me to view life differently, and gradually I start looking at a much bigger picture. I realise if I am constantly being challenged or in plain English, things keep going wrong, what can I learn from this? If the test is being repeated many times over in the same or different scenarios, then I haven't mastered it yet. What is life trying to teach me from this experience and more importantly what can I learn? Even disasters I begin to view as the hardest teachings, so ultimately through all the pain, it is very enlightening.

There is another opposite shift in me that happens over a much longer timeframe. When I start on this path, I am drawn to the mystical and unexplained and over time I come out very keen on healing. What person doesn't want to make things better? And that can be as simple as giving a hug, sending a text or therapy, healing and general wellbeing. There are so many remarkable areas to explore here and I continue to read about healing (and still do). Time though is always present, and I know this is not for me now. I also know I will be back to it one day. After three years I get all the answers I want although I continue until I'm twenty-nine. I learn all the time just in different settings.

Lately I've learnt to balance my chakras. Such a powerful tool in body and mind wellbeing. I channel colour vibrations too; it's awesome when you know how. It can alleviate some blood pressure issues and body shock system settings, like chronic stress or fight or flight. I like to chill and listen to easy peaceful visualisations on YouTube almost daily. Jason Stevenson is my main stopping point. He's great. He's known in my house as 'my other boyfriend' as he's on so often! Check him out sometime. I'm better at relaxing down layers with him (his audio) than by myself and there's not many people I can say that about.

## INSOMNIA, FOR REAL

My insomnia gets worse as time goes along and is made worse by all the shifts, nightclubs and energy drinks. I can say honestly I never sleep properly after a gig. Not once, not ever, not in *a decade and a half*! I wake up all the time. Some people take shift work in their stride and just say, 'Oh, I'll sleep some now and a bit later,' or go to bed for twelve hours and don't wake up. Wow, what the heck? It's such an impressive life skill. Credit to you. I wish I had that talent. That kind of oblivious and can sleep anywhere for any amount of time skill is badass combined with the fact you may live longer. Handy.

Around 100,000 DJ miles later on the clock of my sleek black Honda Civic VTEC (after I crash it a little bit at twenty miles per hour. Insomnia, thanks), I go to speak with the doctor. I buy a convertible with a much bigger engine. It is a beast and the bonnet length is half of the car. A red three-litre BMW Z3.

The other toy, my big red quad bike, has been replaced by a sportier very clean ex-demonstration Honda EX 250cc. I buy it personally from the Honda dealership who contacts me thinking they have a bike I'd like to see. I decide to pay for a road legal conversion so I can ride anywhere anytime when it moves parking locations and back into my garage.

Meanwhile, back in the studios, in a very exciting twist, we now get Christmas off work and KISS just networks all the show output from London! Great! Except you can see the obvious here, right? *Blindingly* obvious… You see it? I see it a mile off knowing the industry well. If they network all the shows directly out of London, currently called KISS 100, what exactly do they need us for? The answer is crystal clear.

They don't! So, beware, the axe is about to fall again sooner or later but I know it will be a while as radio transitions need time or they lose all their listeners overnight, which means losing money from advertising revenue from listener figures etc. I know it is coming so I enjoy the last leg of my radio ride.

It is cool though as in the meantime I get a Christmas Day and Boxing Day off work for the first time in most of my eight years on Vibe. Obviously, there are still a few clubs. I spend Christmas Eve at Ignite (although I don't recall it at all). And floorfillers/commercial over at Jack's in Wisbech for New Year's Eve. That is a Sunday, so my show is 12–4 p.m. and then later I go to the club.

## SOCIALISING AT LAST!

I begin to scale down the sheer volume of gigs to focus on my radio work. Well, a bit. It's no surprise that a few gigs and interviews aren't in my diary, even I don't know why. There's probably some I've forgotten. I know I play a gig or two for work events somewhere in London and interview Slipmatt and Alexandra Burke just after she wins *The X Factor*. I watch whilst putting my makeup on for the clubs, keeping up on topical shows to use as content on *KISS Lunch*. Fortunately, I pick up the phone to vote for her and she is the only time I ever call. A helpful coincidence.

Eventually, when I have a few less DJ sets, I get a social life back. It has been mostly absent for six years or so and I start going out again for the first time properly since I was twenty-one. It gives me some great memories and more stories to tell on air. Going out gives me more travel, good times and target content as it is a lifestyle. I'm always kind of working even when I'm not!

## INTO 2007

I am very focused on working hard to deliver great content for the KISS brand where every second of on-air material has to be a perfect match. Andy the big boss of programming is always listening. I don't look for an agent as I have reached national brand level working with my two regional lunchtime audiences. On average 350,000 people tune in each week on the East side and a very similar number also on the West station. It is probably around 400,000 plus by the time I leave.

My head is always mulling over new ideas. I want to produce records but have zero time to do this. How can I achieve this? I don't have the answer yet.

In the meantime, I begin combining work with Ibiza trips and I usually fly out twice a year. The strength of the KISS brand reaches far and wide and abroad which brings exciting new opportunities and many that I create. From all my contacts and networking, I've been working with artists internationally on *House of Elise* for years and now I can review anywhere, practically anywhere, I choose. It is like being part of the PR list from heaven. I have guest list places and tickets, clothing, records, albums, guest lists, superstar DJ interviews… it is going from strength to strength. It also shows up clear as day where we wipe the floor competition-wise. That's the RAJAR figures where we beat Radio 1 all the time. We reign supreme on our time slot. In essence, *House of Elise* rocks!

With the full team, myself, Dave, Lotty, Shaun and Paul, we are firmly established as one of the big players in the radio industry. This is reflected in the calibre of guests and mixes. Here are just a few: Mauro Picotto, Guyver, Jan Loper, Ed Real, The Tidy Boys, DJ Choose, K90, Dave Austin, Johan Gielen, Pierre Pienaar, Michael Splint, Phil York, Chris Lawrence, Dan Stone, Scot Project, Yoji Biomehanika and Amber D.

Amber invites me to join her on holiday in Ibiza but I'm too busy to go. This happens a lot due to my schedule and so I miss out on the party. Paul joins her instead of me and says it was a lot of fun. I wish I could have been there.

## BITS OF DJ DIARY 2007

February

24 Feb: Dave, Mike and I drive to the Brixton Academy in London. We're on the press guest list and working at this year's Hard Dance Awards. We spend some time in the crowd of thousands of clubbers watching the winners collect their awards up on stage and then we head upstairs to the interview room.

We meet and interview a lot of DJs; everyone from the industry is there. I record and chat with Ed Real, Lisa Lashes… I also think I interviewed Anne Savage and Amber D. There were so many but I forget now. Probably The Edison Factor too.

March

2 Mar: Cassanos. Funky house

April

6 Apr: Lester's, Bourne, 11.30 p.m.–1.30 a.m.

8 Apr: Funky Bunny with Lisa Pin-Up. I'm 11.30 p.m.–12.30 a.m.

30 Apr: The Loft, Norwich, 12–2 a.m. (I don't remember but looks like I played there)

May

6 May: Funky Bunny's fourth birthday. I can't recall if I DJed this one… I think so as I'm at most

25 May: Modified Nationals, 10 p.m.–12 a.m. Funky tech trance.

God, this gig was insane. There were thousands of people in a massive tent or marquee and I was high up on stage. One of the best DJ buzzes I've ever had. I completely went over the edge on this one. I gave so much energy to rocking the crowd that the next day I could barely stand up. It was a real revelation to me how much we were feeding a circle of energy. I gave so much I had nothing left after that performance. I physically couldn't get up the next day and I lay knackered on the couch; I had nothing left in my body.

I decided that I had to hold some of myself back for self-preservation to function the next day and week. I had seen a DJ lying on the floor behind the decks before in between his stage performance which was so crazy. He was jumping up and down non-stop hyping the crowd. There was footage of this night on YouTube but someone uploaded it with the wrong tag but it was deffo Mod Nats

27 May: Funky Bunny and The Tidy Boys. It says me for a one-hour set, much later after my Sunday show 12–4 p.m. I have played with The Tidy Boys but I'm not sure on this exact night to be honest. It's in my diary anyway. Occasionally the promoter Marty would move me to the next one depending on how full the line-up was.

I was trying to scale it back, wasn't I? Ah man, it was so hard when the gigs were so epic! There was a constant stream of clubs, promoters and events trying to book me so I tried to select the most suitable ones as much as possible depending on brands, events, other bookings, travel times, locations, etc. Three still felt like quite a lot but I managed it for a bit.

## WALES

In June, Saturday 16, I play the first of three years consecutively for Escape into the Park. After I present my Friday lunchtime show I go home, pack and drive down to Wales. I called Dave a day or two before and asked if he was free for the road trip. Dave was on board immediately!

The headliners for 2007 are Calvin Harris, Erick Morillo, Armin van Buuren, David Guetta, Above & Beyond and The Shapeshifters. The main stage is an enormous outdoor rig dotted around the trees and open grassland. There are four or five big marquees hidden between the trees. It is a beautiful site across the sloping grass dotted with big tops. This year I'm playing the Polysexual Arena with Lisa Lashes, The Tidy Boys, Rob Tissera, Amber D, Hixxy & MC Storm, Alex Kidd, Andy Whitby, Cally & Juice. I've worked with almost all of them before and nearly all have been on my show.

The noise from my first Escape is insane, especially trying to work at that volume with the sheer size of the venue. Playing flawlessly all the time leaves my ears ringing for a couple of hours and me shouting afterwards as I can't hear properly. That happens every year I play there! The buzz of playing probably to 5,000 or 6,000 screaming partygoers in the daytime is heaven. You're all in this same moment together where life feels insane on adrenaline highs and you give the best performance. Perhaps one of the best in my life. I don't know… there are many. The highs, the pressure, the relief of getting the performance perfect… The life we lead as superstar DJs up on that giant stage is out of this world. Nothing much can top that feeling.

Spanning all three events I interview Kenny Ken, Sander van Doorn, Amber D, Lisa Lashes, Nick Sentience, Matt Hardwick, Hazard, Adam Sheridan, Ferry Corsten, Fedde Le Grand, Scratch Perverts, High Contrast, Norman Jay MBE and some others too. Some are audio and some are video on YouTube.

In 2008 Mike and I stay late into the evening to watch Underworld dazzle on the main stage. As dusk falls, it feels almost hypnotic. It is an amazing night but the long day of work and the drive home hurt both of us. Mike's eyes nearly give up at one point so I take over so he can rest around midnight. It is worth it though.

## IBIZA REVIEWS

I work weeks in advance pre-recording the *House of Elise* show to cover me while I'm abroad. I use the chance to air some special shows featuring various guest DJs as my office drawer is crammed full of DJ mixes all very keen to be on the show. It is mid-June and after Escape we fly out to Ibiza on Monday 18 for the first week of two trips this year. I can dance, review and meet people. It is the best job ever! Having been performing behind the decks for so long, it is a welcome return to the carefree nature of being in the crowd on the dancefloor. I always like to pick a good spot to lodge myself into the night's groove. Both are amazing (DJing and dancing) but I have almost given up dancing for fun. Being there deep in the crowd is very liberating and free. Being on stage brings travel, pressure and the ultimate high of landing your gig flawlessly. DJing is a very solo event; there's no backing singers or band. It's just me and you, the crowd. Being in the crowd is exactly the reverse!

## HEAVEN, LONDON

On my return, and trying to recover from the indulgent twenty-four-hour clubbers' paradise, I have to prepare for Heaven in Charring Cross. I deliver my first ever tech trance set on Friday 29 June. I play many different genres but this one is totally new and it is a very prestigious club. It has to be right. I have to get my beat down from usually 145 beats per minute into funky territory, 130 beats per minute, or so I think. I search, collect and put together a set well in advance with practice to make sure it sounds right. I have this big remix of Robyn's 'With Every Heartbeat'. It is a risk as it has such a big break in the middle with almost emptiness, just strings and her vocals, but it is so impressive and I like to stand out. I may have interviewed her but I can't remember for sure!

I go with Paul and the street team as Mike has taken himself to hospital with tonsillitis and glandular fever instead. The KISS street team comes to give us a dancefloor presence. When I start my set, a guy from the club comes up and tells me to slow it down further so there is room to go up tempo later. I have to drop to maybe 127 beats per minute and it is the first time I've ever played that calm! The set is amazing; I can feel they are a different crowd with more chilled out feelings than my usual sets. The crowd is calmer and more laidback. We record this mix and it transmits on all three stations across the KISS FM network.

## IBIZA. I'M A PROFESSIONAL PARTY HUNTER!

On Tuesday 26 September we fly back to Ibiza for the closing parties. We meet Terri and her group of girls out there again. There is often a huge group of us as we half live there in summertime!

I pull a really fit Italian girl dancing on the beach at Bora Bora! She asks me back to hers and her friend's eyes slowly move away, somewhat uncomfortable, like, 'Oh no, not again.' I decline, sparing her friend's awkwardness.

My friend is very jealous. He says, 'How did you do that?'

I say, 'It's the skirt and bikini top. You should try that sometime!

## IBIZA REVIEW

This is part of my official press release (the playlist came afterwards).

Listeners: 20,000 listeners per show, 10,000 monthly online via KISS Kube.

KISS 105-108 Fridays 10 p.m. or anytime online

Show: *House of Elise* 'The Ibiza Special'. Transmission Date: Friday 8 September 2007

## THE IBIZA SPECIAL: EVENT COVERAGE DETAILS

The Review:

It is full lifestyle coverage from the clubbers' point of view. We are going through each event in detail the following Friday night on *House of Elise* with an 'Ibiza Special' here on KISS 105-108. Our aim is to cover as many venues as possible in a week.

| **Club Review Schedule:** | | **Guest List** |
|---|---|---|
| Tues 28 | Tidy Ibiza at Es Paradis<br>Interview: Amber D, 3.15 a.m.<br>San Antonio | Tidy |
| Wed 29 | S.A. Tranzaction at Club Basement<br>Interview: Michael Splint<br>Bar M, Café del Mar | Michael Splint |
| Thu 30 | Xtravaganza at Space<br>Interview: Alex Gold, 2.15 a.m.<br>Cream at Amnesia | Sliding Doors<br><br>Cream |
| Fri 31 | Manumission at Amnesia | Manumission |
| Sat 29 | (Unknown) at Heaven | Most Wanted PR |
| Sun 30 | Café Mambo and Savannah | |

After a few days in I realise I've booked too much. Aww crap! With bookings and promotions, I've taken on a list that not even I can defeat but I give it my best shot. The party schedule is incredible but also draining and we don't manage to arrive at every single venue but I make most. I see Amber D's set and I meet up with Alex Gold in Space after his set where he gives me his mix for the show.

One day we somehow manage eighteen hours solid of partying, moving through three different venues in spread out locations and quickly catching the Ibiza cold. It is such a waste of time and it costs me my attendance to one of the events. Just two of us get hit hard by the Ibiza flu. It is a TKO. The whole next day we are coughing and spluttering in bed. The other two are not so ill with it. We attempted just too much in one day; it was way too much for any physical body to handle. It's like throwing big kids into an infinite theme park, a giant ball pit of Haribo's... someone's gonna be sick! Ibiza is the ultimate clubbers' paradise twenty-four-seven. If you peak too early, you're gonna die fast. Fact.

We start around midday and just kept moving on, loving hours of Ibiza beach bars and clubs right up until eventually we collapse into bed! I never attempt such a long day again. I learn the hard way to pace myself. Personally speaking, eighteen hours of clubbing is insane and it's the most I've ever done! I've done many all-nighters out there with Cream and various promoters at Amnesia, for example. Usually, I go out around 8 or 9 p.m. and arrive at the club somewhere around midnight. I usually go through till 6 a.m. My feet hurt so much walking to the hotel often I walk barefoot for miles and maybe get in about 8 or 9 a.m. It is hardcore out there night after night if you can handle it.

OMG, let me tell you about the Amnesia ice cannon. That is an incredible piece of club kit. I never knew exactly what it was. No one knew where it was in the club and I never saw one anywhere else. Freezing cold steam like a thick fog descends everywhere within seconds and you completely lose sight of the people in front of you. It can be disorientating for some but I love it. It feels so intense! I think it's like a thirty-second blast or something. The noise of the crowd screaming is insane. I can still hear it now.

There are times when I go back into work and Glen greets me saying, 'Hey, Nikki, how was it?'

I'm like, 'Dying a little. Hey, please ask me in the week as I'm too tired to talk. I'm not being rude but I need the energy for the show.'

He understands. 'Yes, of course. It was good then?'

I nod and he lets me get my head down and start my prep work for the show.

And so, I trot back and forth everywhere spending my next few years like this.

## MARRIAGE? NOPE!

Lou is getting married in September and I have to wear a dress as the matron of honour (I have no clue what that is)! I do wear dresses sometimes, usually if work requires it. I have some confusion over her wedding dress and what to do. Who has to hold the trail? The what? The train? What? What the hell is it, the big bit on the end of the dress? I genuinely don't know. Fortunately, Lou does! Dresses are not ideal but I commit for big occasions and it is Lou. She gets what she wants on her big day because that's what best mates do.

So, Lou gets married. How very grown up and I'm totally avoiding that. I'm not big on marriage. I never feel I need a church and a bit of paper to confirm I'm in love (ok, you don't even need a church now). But also, I don't like all the princess dresses, all the people, the planning, the time and the money. It all just looks like a *major* stress to me and I try to avoid that entirely! I mean, great if you do like all that, that's cool, but it's just not for me. So many confines, you have to do this and that, wear this, sit there, dance here! At least I'm told I look like Amy Winehouse with my black hair, purple bridesmaid dress and tattoos. Cool.

## DJ DIARY CONTINUED

September

14 Sept: Roobarb at The Waterfront, Norwich, 12.30 a.m.–2 a.m. Dave's event, hard dance and hard house. It's storming and so much fun.

29 Sept: Dilemma. Tech trance to hard trance. Vinyl set as lots of my specialist sets are now on vinyl. Trance is harder and it's far less forgiving than dirty big ass house beats where you can cut, drop, fader fuck, mix and shake it up however you like. You have to be more structured with a smoother transition into your next record. Trance is really the pretty side of house and you need to play it with the respect that it demands.

This was another of Dave's gigs in some kind of underground bunker or some really obscure place buried deep in the Norfolk countryside. It was cool as hell! I got lost at 3 a.m. trying to drive my way out of windy tall hedged dark country lanes. I had no satnav at the time but it wouldn't be long before I realised it's bloody hard to find obscure venues by yourself in the dark with a torch, a paper map and a steering wheel! I hated the time wasted getting lost as I could never be late for a set (ideally). I don't think I ever have been.

On the way back, come the end of a very long week covering hundreds of miles, I didn't want to piss about trying to work out which way was north or south. There were often road closures late at night and I could spend hours on diversions just trying to get home, sometimes bolting on extra hours to my week. It was frustrating and tiring. I bought a satnav years later at the first opportunity. It was much better at night.

October

2 Oct: KISSTORY night at Essex University. Classic old skool. I think I played a broad selection of dance, anthems and anything in that genre.

Somehow around this I fitted in family coming to stay, plus photoshoots and more singing lessons to keep my working voice at the top of my game.

November

2 and 3 Nov: I have two sets at the KISS East Coast Weekender: Friday and Saturday 12.30–2 a.m. and the Sunday show 12–4 p.m. It actually says 'rest' after that for what was left of Sunday evening! You do whatever it takes to make your dream a reality. No matter how gruelling it was.

9 Nov: The Loft, Bourne. Probably floorfillers. It was such a long drive. It was one hour forty-five minutes on a good run.

13 Nov: Salt House, Ipswich. There was a big staff do on the waterfront. I did a bit of quad bike riding at the weekend and got the physio on my angry back.

16 Nov: Liquid, Peterborough, 12–2 a.m. They liked it hard there, so I played some quality hard dance, trance and anthems. It's a great venue.

Mum had had her knee replaced and following the surgery recovery period she couldn't walk much at all. The MS means her legs don't work properly to carry the weight and so she couldn't walk with two non-functioning legs. We put a little bed in the lounge to avoid the stairs and I moved in with her for a month to fetch and carry her dinners and cups of tea. Just to be useful for a bit, until she was back on her feet again. It went well.

December
23 Dec: Sonic Nightclub, 12–2 a.m. I can't remember where now

## MUSIC PRODUCTION

Finally, my dream of producing music is getting closer. Louis has a show on Vibe FM and amongst other work he is producing music at a studio in Essex. I catch up with him there and meet Jamie Ritmen with his hardcore music background and he is a producer for Anne Savage amongst others.

Through November and December, we create our first dance track together. Jamie is going by the name Gridbreaker here to help separate his music genres. I spend the next month or two running back and forth to his studios in Essex twice a week. He is working on Cubase and very musically minded and together we make a storming track. It has a phat beat naturally and some big synth cords for a trance breakdown in the middle. It really is a great example of my DJ style of music. We just click with production and together we make a track I'm really proud of.

If I try to summarise that year it's far easier to point you to the final music log from the *House of Elise* show.

**HOUSE OF ELISE TOTAL RECALL.**
**FRIDAY 28 DECEMBER 2007**

**Parts:**
1. Hard Dance Awards, London
2. Gatecrasher's Summer Sound System, Leeds
3. Escape into the Park, Wales
4. Peach at Heaven, London
5. Global Gathering, Stratford-upon-Avon
6. Ibiza

**Playlist:**
**Tracks and Exclusives that Represent the Events. Mix: Dave Austin**

Hard Dance Awards: BK's 'Systematic' and The Edison Factor's 'Love Parade'

Gatecrasher's Summer Sound System: Mauro Picotto's 'Maybe, Maybe Not' and K90's 'Ghosts in the Machine'

Escape into the Park: Nick Sentience's 'Carte Blanche'

Global Gathering: Technikal's 'Overdrive'

**Escape into the Park. Live Mix: Nikki Elise**

Booteck's 'Block Rockin' Beats'

Public Domain's 'Acidanimal'

Vinylgroover & The Red Head's 'Filthy Rock Chick'

Randy Katana's 'Play It Louder'

**Peach at Heaven, London. Live Mix: Nikki Elise**

Robyn's 'With Every Heartbeat'

Artist Unknown's 'Soul Heaven'

Richard Grey's 'Warped Bass'

Josh Wink's 'Higher State of Consciousness'

**Four Big Tracks of the Year. Mix: Nikki Elise**

Captain Tinrib's 'What You Waiting For', Tidy

Big Ben vs Xlab4's 'Megatron', Big

Greg Brookman and Section 2's 'Texas Saw Bass Massacre', Traffic

Johan Gielen's 'Magnitude', Black Hole

**Ibiza Mix and Guest DJ: Alex Gold. Set Taken From Space**

With thanks to all the guests, the *House of Elise* team (Dave, Lotty and Paul)

DJs Alex Gold, Alex Kidd, Cally Gage, Amber D, Fila, Jamie Ritmen, Lee Haslam, Lisa Pin-Up, K90, Mark Sherry, Vinylgroover and everyone else.

On seeing the show list above, I'd totally forgot that we also went on a social review of Gatecrasher's Summer Sound System in Leeds. Not surprising, is it?

# CHAPTER 8

# QUITTING RADIO AND BREAKING MY ASS

just want to drop this in here... Until I was thirty, I bounced! Then I started to break.

I've fallen off skateboards, roller skates and snowboards and I've fallen off horses twice until I sensibly quit because there are too many legs and not enough wheels. The last horse ground impact caused some limping and wet eyes where I landed sideways with all my weight on my right knee! My leg hurt every Friday night in the club for six months following that horse crash. It signalled the end of riding!

I've come close to falling off motorcross bikes and hung on for dear life preventing myself from going over the handlebars. I stop tackling big jumps following that near miss where I was trying to land it on the tabletop. I now prefer riding and trekking, not so much jumping! I even narrowly escaped by leapfrogging on my hands and knees in a woodland pit. That was a mild crash with my quad bike rolling backwards down a woodland slope very close to being on top of me. Man, I even set myself on fire once, just a tiny bit, and I've even drunk petrol. That was accidental! It was horrible. It repeats, scorching your throat with burps for hours to come. Don't syphon your motorbike fuel out of your dad's generator. A painful lesson.

So just hold that in mind for the next few chapters... I bounced! Until I reached thirty.

## GIGS... I HAVE TOO MANY

You may have spotted my less gigs theory is just a theory and not really manifesting itself. I try again! And finally, I set myself new rules. To be at the top of my game I have to spend less time DJing at events.

Look at my progress here below... Less gigs... more or less... It is pretty hard when you're in demand.

## 2008 DJ SETS

Roobarb in Norwich, The Loft in Borne, Spectrum Warehouse, Royal Norfolk Showground, KISSTORY Innocence in Newmarket, KISS Weekender East Coast, Modified National in Peterborough, Essex University, Escape into the Park in Swansea, Dance Party Weekender East Coast, Puzzle Project in Club 414 in Brixton, Dance Island in Cambridge, Heights in King's Lynn, and Big Old Skool, Club M and Innocence in Newmarket.

Thank goodness for that as I was struggling to write all the events with the correct dates. You know me and numbers… it isn't easy. Lots of these were residencies so they were multiple appearances. Trying to connect all the events in a timeline has taken a vast amount of time in this book. There's a good chance I'll have buggered some of it up as I can't see everything I write. So, I've given it my best shot and that's all anyone can do. If I worried about that I wouldn't be able to write the book. I strive for my best effort if not perfection. Perfectionist thinking is a mild form of self-sabotage. It's not me.

I'm sure if I have made any mistakes a few people will make a massive deal out of them online or the delightful platform of social media. Good for them. If they have the time to type out and post up such cataclysmic life concerns then congratulations! The rest of us do not, do we? I'm not a fan of social media. Ironic given I spent fifteen plus years in media. Media and social are two different things. I prefer a quiet life. I never sought fame; it was just a small dose that came with the role and it wasn't all good. Small parts were horrific and that is a fair statement.

I spent about fourteen years trying to work out if we'd ever seen Fatboy Slim play! Had we, or hadn't we? I asked everyone that went and none of us could ever remember what happened! Genuinely my mates would be going to see him play in the UK and I'd always be like, 'Oh, Fatboy. He's amazing. The one that got away.' After a few years (ten) I started to suspect that I had seen him live at Space, Ibiza. It turned out I was right. About fourteen years later I found the original flyer! He was playing under his other name: Norman Cook. Tuesday 25 August: Norman Cook AKA Fatboy Sim. It was so buried in my mind it took years and years to surface. Each year I was working with or seeing hundreds of DJs play. Sometimes it's just a blur. Eat, sleep, rave, repeat!

## MY LAST IBIZA TALE

I'll just add this last one. At home in the UK, I organise all the clubs well in advance so I'm pre-aligned with all the guest lists. It is July and as we fly in again, we touch down and the plane is rolling down the runway where we pull up next to Tiesto's private jet. His name is about twelve feet long down the side, so you know when he is in town. It's then I begin to feel the excitement rising. (My diary says we were going to visit Space, Pacha, Privilege and catch up with some of the DJs.)

**Club Review Schedule:**
KISS 105-8, *House of Elise* 'Ibiza Summer' show
Transmission Date: Friday 18 July 2008

Azuli, Ibiza Beach Party
Space, Carl Cox
Privilege, Tiesto

I attend and dance my socks off at all of the above on three separate nights. Tiesto is such a legend in one of the world's finest clubs. As seasoned partygoers we always stay in Playa d'en Bossa. The rest of our time in daylight hours is spent down the road in Bora Bora and sometimes dancing on the tables. It has such a sexy chilled little vibe about it. It is our home; it is where we belong. It is my favourite beach bar and I've certainly spent the most time there. They get the party started right after lunch which is perfect as we are on it! Shades on and a Cuba libre *por favor*.

The Azuli beach party review requires us taking a cab into the middle of nowhere not knowing how to find our way home. It is the most exquisite event I've ever attended. A personal favourite because it feels so secluded driving down a long dark lane and most people don't know it is there. There is a bar to one end with a DJ and a chilled-out party stretching along a narrow sandy footpath carved into the side of the cliff edge. In this most discrete party location, everyone is just so chilled out dancing under the stars. The hunting of parties is like a game; with this one, we have struck gold. It is big game hunting. I don't dance a great deal as the tunes are very laidback but the views are breathtaking and I'm just happy to be alive and a part of that very special moonlit night.

## GLOBAL GATHERING, JULY 2008 AND 2009

I'm speaking of both events here together. We go armed with our VIP press tickets to review, having worked the deal in with the show's competition ticket giveaway. I use the VIP only to catch up with Tiesto on stage mid-performance. I pop up briefly to check in and say hi. He is good and so I leave him to get on with being Tiesto!

The Saturday night everyone goes to see Armin Van Buuren but I don't feel well. I become incredibly unwell and am eventually shipped off to a medical tent unable to walk. This is the worst low blood sugar I ever experience (although I didn't know it at the time), and my body shuts down. I mostly ignored it as it had never been this bad until now. The blood sugars are a real worry though; I'm so ill I can't speak properly. I'm slurring so badly they don't bother much with me when I arrive as they think I'm drunk. I keep saying I've drunk nothing since about 4 p.m. and it is around 11 p.m. now. Eventually another guy takes my blood sugars and it is clear they have bottomed out badly. I lost three pounds in forty-eight hours and that physically hurts your body so much. It is a dreadful feeling.

I'd packed all my specific travel foods I need when I go away anywhere but the bag got left in the car and that was three miles away outside the main entrance. It is impossible for me to raise my blood sugars and that's what half kills me. No access to food at night to raise my dangerously low level. Slowly we sort it out with five sugars in tea. Not a good solution but all we have till I can speak again after an hour on the recovery bed. Then searching out chips. I desperately need protein and fats but there is nothing available after midnight so chips it is. It keeps me alive.

After this disaster (I miss Armin's set) where I'm very close to passing out, I book in with my GP and he books me a hospital appointment. Eventually I go and have the glucose tests where I'm told I'm borderline hypoglycaemic. The doctor at the hospital mumbles, with no further explanation, 'It's above the cut-off point so no, you're not. Go home.'

I feel very confused after I face such a severe reaction. What the hell is going on? At home in my GP surgery he says, 'Hmm, well, your test shows that you are 0.1 away from reactive hypoglycaemia, so basically you are.'

To get to the hospital I have to eat after my dinner again with supper at 8 p.m. or I would have woken from hunger and not gone back to sleep, making driving to the hospital trickier. I don't know how long I've had this or where it comes from. One thing is apparent. I have to eat regularly or my body will go berserk and it is not fun as I feel so ill, so quickly. Now I have to follow the hypo diet as well to stay level at all times. Always eating healthily and regularly and every three to four hours something has to be consumed. It is annoying but necessary, there is no choice. Hence, I'm putting on weight steadily but it will take me many years to realise that is the link.

## RAF

In November my week's itinerary is promotional videos for RAF Wittering in Peterborough. My producer and I are shooting promotional videos for the RAF suppliers. My role involves listening carefully and learning job skills which feel quite daunting, standing and presenting my piece to camera whilst working alongside the real team of RAF professionals. I just learnt it an hour ago! I'm trying to finish pitching the supply tent, refuelling trucks and loading kit. It is an interesting fun week.

## THE DJ MAG TOP 100 AT MINISTRY OF SOUND, LONDON, 2008

It's late October and my flight gets in at 10.45 p.m. on Tuesday 28. Our big boss requests me to work the next night's event as KISS press at Ministry of Sound. In my diary I'm granted the Thursday off work due to working so late. I rock up in a short skirt, black leather biker jacket and an excellent tan.

All the world's greatest DJs have flown in for this. It is the Oscars of the DJ world. Many are playing sets in the main room and you can hear the bassline though the walls. It is a very lavish star-studded event. We are mainly in the press room preparing for all the interviews. (I don't remember exactly where it was in the club.) My job is to interview the winners and as many as possible for the KISS network and to create bits for my upcoming Friday night show. DJ Mag's

Top 100 *House of Elise* special. I run many specials; they are just so much fun to make.

I run many interviews over several hours including all of these (some are missing due to their DJ sets): KISS' very own Armin Van Buuren is always pretty laidback even being crowned number one again. Number two: Tiesto, number three: Paul van Dyke, number four: Above & Beyond, and number five: David Guetta. I also record with Andy C, Fedde Le Grand, Mark Knight, Markus Schultz and deadmau5. (I think that was all of them on that night.)

Deadmau5 does not appear comfortable at all in front of a person holding a microphone. He is possibly the trickiest subject I ever have to generate a flowing conversation with. I think maybe he is really shy or the quiet type, hence his big mouse head for on stage. David is the exact opposite, a naturally confident chatty guy. I ask him how he is and he says, 'I'm very happy, of course.' (I may have interviewed Tiesto there or he could have been next door in the main room playing his set. I've interviewed him several times on both of my shows.)

## FIRST RECORD RELEASE

From 2008 into 2009 eventually our track is mastered and signed, and it soon brings my first release: Nikki Elise & Gridbreaker's 'Forgiven' on Presence Summit records. Playing my first track on my show, *House of Elise* on KISS, is a special night for me because my production dream has materialised. We send it out nationally and it gets good response from all my fellow DJs and some say they've dropped it in their sets and it goes down well with the crowd. That is what it is all about.

I begin to grow a little bit bored! Really, I do… Not the obvious day to day bored as I'm constantly required to do new things but I can now run the shows with my eyes shut (so to speak… I've not tried it). After a couple of years with KISS I stop looking for work and agents. I'm working hard on delivering all seven shows a week and DJing along with interviewing at more festivals and uploading on YouTube. Work life is good. I've mastered my craft. Well, as much as I'm ever going to. The concrete does not call me anymore like it did for a decade. I love being there but that is enough for now.

## 2009

There are various nights in Newmarket with my monthly residency at Innocence. One of Big Ben's nights is with the Rat Pack and Slipmatt in town. Some are for Big Ben's big promotions and some are for KISS. Deja Vu in Bury St Edmunds, Dance Island in Cambridge, Xcel in Stowmarket. Modified Nationals at the East of England Showground in Peterborough, Escape into the Park's Polysexual Arena in Swansea, and two sets for both spring and autumn East Coast DPW (renamed as KISS Weekenders) and the West Coast

KISS Weekender in Bristol (it says Bristol in my diary but Mike thinks it was in North Wales. I don't remember).

I'm out in Ibiza twice starting in late May for the opening of Space, my favourite club on planet Earth. I just catch the end of Carl Cox's set and many others with their all-star line-up. On 23 August 23 we go for the end of season. I'm there so much I pick up some very basic Spanish phrases. I really struggle with foreign languages, so this is a new thing for me.

At home, I have a bad tequila hangover from swimming in our pool with friends! It is so bad it's noted down in my diary. It is a monster hangover. It is the only time that, on waking, I realise I must have had an out of body experience. In my dream I can see myself sleeping, lying in the bed a few feet below. The room is dark with a faint night light. My head is on the pillow and I'm facing the ensuite door. So, I must have been above, around ceiling height, to have seen this full view of my own body. It's no joke… go steady with a tequila bottle! I can honestly say that's never happened before or since.

## MARCH 2009, SNOWBOARDING IN FRANCE

I meet with Anna and she is going snowboarding so naturally I'm going snowboarding. We hook up for some practice at Milton Keynes' Snozone. I'm aware in the few months before I go that I think I'm going to break a bone, but I'm going anyway. I've never broken any bone so far. I think it happens on day two of snowboarding in Chamrousse. I slip from just standing on my board mid-way down a blue run. I fall. I basically sit down on my bum hard and fast on the ice but feel a click. I sit there for a while and I can see Channelle looking up the slope to see if I'm getting up. I had a pretty bad night's sleep, which is rather typical, waking several times.

It takes me ages to get slowly down the mountainside to the cafe at the bottom. Boy, does it hurt. I order a rum and coke for the pain and am advised by Chanelle, a former army paramedic turned police officer, that drinking is not the best solution after an accident. I say it most certainly is given the pain I'm in. I back this up with, 'This is how we deal with pain on my home building site,' a house in various renovations. Then we go off to the doctors on a bus.

She says I'm talking half pissed junk… something about self-harming followed by marmots! On my arrival it is immense pain getting my trousers off. They do nothing as they can't see anything anyway, so it is just Nurofen day and night. The team feels maybe I have just bruised it as bad bruising there can be bad. We walk a half mile out for dinner and when I return, I lie on the bed and tears silently roll down my cheeks. Silent pain tears… that is new.

Back in England with my ongoing bum agony, A&E states, following the X-ray, that I have a suspected fracture of the coccyx. They also say to check my hips are ok as they can't see from the X-ray, but the long recovery time, intense pain and lack of movement were an obvious explanation. They say 'suspected'. They don't say 'fractured coccyx' as they can't quite see it. Odd, isn't it? I know it's broken because it is fucked. I can see the X-ray on the screen and I can see the tip of my spine bent to the left side. But on my own I'm in no state to mention it. It takes quite a lot to walk in the hospital from the car park opposite. I take codeine and sit on a rubber ring to eat dinner and drive my car for a full six weeks. I can also feel it is out of line in certain sitting positions.

I told friends at work, probably Sally and Lotty and whoever else I could bore with it, prior to the trip that I thought I'd break something. Just an insight I felt and not of any use really, was it? Might have been a pure guess. It doesn't matter either way. Being right is not always helpful!

Dawn from news laughs and says, 'Oh, look. Here comes Nikki, walking like John Wayne again.' Dawn is very funny, and it is very amusing, so we all crack up. Laughing is part of our office policy; it is a great place to work. I have to move everywhere with my legs slower and slightly apart to ease the pressure on my lower busted back bits. I walk exactly like John Wayne for quite a while.

**PREMONITIONS**

Breaking something was just a feeling I had. It was the first dream sometime after that I realised it appeared to have actually happened. I would have been around eight to ten years old. I dream a car went through a brick wall. Lou says a few days later or that week that a car crashed through their brick wall. There is a massive hole in the wall where all the flint stones fell out. I just think it is such an odd dream to have. I walk past and see it a lot. Maybe coincidence you think until you have dozens and dozens and as you get older you can give more and more detail.

I don't think it's the right time to get fully into it, but I've had many premonitions in the dream state. The overlapping of time when I'm fully asleep. I see a lot of them on the news usually a few months later.

In some dreams I can actively take control, know I'm dreaming, then go where I want to go and call people to me to talk to. But that is rare even for me. It maybe happens just a couple of times a year. I have by no means mastered this level! These are not standard dreams as there's no background features, just darkness. Typical dreams are usually very colourful and full of detail in a short timeline. If there's no background, it's a different state. Perhaps everyone does this, I don't know. If you were running a brain scan, is it possible you'd see a different level of activity? The different levels of sleep?

I like to sleep travel but not intentionally as it just happens sometimes, visiting other places and countries. I mostly see things with land and water or people. I'm strongly connected to water from sitting quietly by rivers as a child, to keeping tropical fish and bodyboarding as a teenager, and swimming as an adult. It's my main element and it crops up a lot in my sleep. Sometimes I hang out with famous people or check in on my friends. I can call them later in the week and tell them their current emotional state from a detailed dream and it'll always be right. They confirm it themselves. I like to call it 'sleep working'. I become really interested in dream states from a teenager onwards.

Other times I can draw you the face of my mate's next partner. This can be a fun game. Sometimes it really annoys them too! I can effectively swipe left or right on their dating app with my own built-in pre-knowing facial recognition software. Nope, nope, nope. I watch them date. Here comes another with no point. I think, *No chance* (and don't say). Then hold up… wait, that's the exact face shape, hair and features I have seen in my mind. Time saving effectively for me, isn't it? I don't need to waste time. I've always been funny about wasting time. Again, ironic given I've 'eternity' tattooed on my arm.

I dreamt something just last week actually. 'Has he got dark hair?' I say. 'Yes' is the answer. I've got to be pretty close to someone to see this detail. It's not a built-in universal software. It's more about special connections with friends. Last year I saw a break-up, so I just keep quiet unless I'm specifically asked about what I've seen. You don't always see good things.

One last story? Go on then. A clear scene occurs one night at one of my New Year's Eve house parties where I've drunk my way through half a bottle of rum or so like a pirate in training. My friend and I are the last two up as everyone else has gone to bed. I tell him around midnight I can see him with a backpack, possibly at an airport, and that he is going travelling. He says that is impossible as he is scared so doesn't fly. Never has and never will. A few years later there is a wedding (which at a separate time I said would happen) and with practice, he now flies all over the world on holiday.

## DIZZEE VERTIGO

On Friday 17 August, we take a few cars down to Wembley Arena. Charly 2 has sorted tickets and we all tag along to see The Prodigy with Dizzee Rascal supporting and the noise is insane. I can feel my left ear moving inside my head. That's not normal, is it? I put it down to the astronomical bass from Dizzee's set. It is pushing about something inside my head only on my left side. I notice this only happens with Dizzee not even when Keith from The Prodigy is singing up on the stage. It's not like they are a quiet group, is it?

This is the first time I realise loud noise exposure has directly affected me and severely. Two weeks after this concert I develop vertigo and am off work for several days. I drive in just fine and roll up to work on a very typical morning. When

I walk into the studio, I look at the desk and the whole room begins flipping over and over. The dizziness is accompanied by a travel-sick feeling and I can't focus on anything. It is like being on a fairground ride that is flipping me over and over in circles. I keep my head very still, but I can't work as I can't see straight. Glen is the boss and swing jock so he covers my show sending me home immediately. He is worried about me driving. I sit in the car park for quite some time before managing to slowly get home trying to not move my head. That is the worse I've ever had it.

I've had three or four bouts of vertigo throughout my twenties. It is quite incapacitating at its worse. I'll be stuck in bed and other times it can be milder. I have to brace myself, pushing my hands against the walls to walk down the short corridor to the bathroom. I keep getting pushed off balance falling repeatedly into the wall on the left side. It is like I am ludicrously drunk at 9 a.m. but it is a horrible feeling that doesn't wear off. If you've ever woken up drunk and the room is flipping over and over, it's like that for three or four days and nights.

You learn quickly that movement makes it worse especially head movement. If I lie in bed with my head and eyes dead still, I can nearly get my vision still or the stillest it can be for that day. The slightest movement of my head will set it off again like a fairground ride. I can only lie on one side as lying on the other side means the flipping won't stop. It is horrendous and perpetual on the other side. I do manage to sleep the night, remaining still in the one position. I recover and go back to work. I'm ok so I crack on.

## MY LAST TROPICAL HOLIDAY

In 2010 we take our usual big two-week holiday abroad. This time in the Cape Verdi islands. I take my new MacBook as I'm teaching myself to be a producer. After I check out Dan Stone's studio in Norwich, I fall in love with Logic. I sit up on the balcony with my bikini on and my head in the Logic manual. Finally, I'm learning music production. Along with hired quad bikes, I swim and play tennis every day. There is a sports coach on holiday and he pops down to the courts by himself like me. I book myself a court every day at 5 p.m. thinking I can play against the wall and he turns up every day and coaches me for free. My backhand has always been crap and with him I learn a decent shot. It is the most, and best, tennis coaching I've ever had and for free on a beautiful tropical island.

In the clubs I'm playing East and West Coast KISS Weekenders even after I leave KISS later this year. Plus, I'm playing all my various gigs and residencies, like Electric Boutique in Essex, and including clubs in Stowmarket, Stamford and Bourne. I play my last of three Modified Nationals car shows in Peterborough, Pink in Cambridge, and Santa Pod in Bedfordshire.

## SANTA POD RACEWAY

I manage somehow with extreme determination to make time to attend my cousin's wedding after-party in Poole on the south coast. All in one day I drive down to the south coast then back up to Bedfordshire in time for my first Santa Pod DJ set, then east to go back home. It is a very, very long day. I play off the back of a truck or similar stage rig. I've done a few of these and it always feels very rock star playing at racetracks. I take it from zero people on the ground in front of me, as they are all in their tents, to around 500 screaming totally bonkers up-for-it people and so I cane them as that is what they are begging for: banging house. All that weekend excitement has to go somewhere and so I take care of that. I do all that with my poor dad trying to nap in my BMW dozing to Radio 4 in the car park. He looks very tired when I finally make it back to the car! I'm absolutely shattered the next day.

At home on Fridays after work I hang out a lot with Lotty. (It is marked in the diary often.) Play some tennis with Lou, and once Mike, and ride my bikes. I sold the smaller ones but my Honda quad bike has moved back home into my garage. Trekking is my favourite past time, just me and my bike. I feel so free on a motorbike. Not much else comes close for me, except snowboarding. I love the thrill of riding my quad bike on the open road. On my mountain bike I build up to two lots of twenty miles a week, a half decent ride.

Indoors, we are chilling with Wii Sports, including Shaun White Snowboarding.

## CHANGE

I start to think more about being with our family at Easter and odd grown-up things like that, which I've never thought about before. But it is a solid party at home and the two thoughts are not compatible with this lifestyle. It seems like a religion that we have to party every single holiday. It isn't really what I want anymore. It isn't fitting well and it doesn't feel quite right anymore. These thoughts are unusual territory for me. What is happening to me? Am I finally growing up? KISS has been cutting shows on the West station and Ric's *Vinyl Decadence* funky house show goes first. I know mine will be next because it is obvious it is cheaper that way. A few months later, *House of Elise* is axed and replaced with the London network. The big boss comes up to tell me in person and when I leave the studio, I cry in an instant with tiny tears as I walk into Glen's office. He looks so sad for me. We've worked together on so many projects throughout more than a decade. The show is my dream, my vision and I deliver it a hundred percent full throttle every single show from 2003 to 2010. But it is cool with me and I still have my daytime show to smooth over the uneasiness of the big transition that is imminent.

The station listeners continually rise to somewhere around 400,000 to 450,000 and a fraction less over at Kiss 101 in the

West. I don't remember exactly as I've seen four sets a year for twelve years! But deep down I want out. I want to leave for a year or so but I have to be an idiot to jump ship from a well-paid, highly coveted role I truly love, plus my accountant is extremely busy. So, I wait, tick followed tock, tick followed tock. You can put in Leftfield vs. Fatboy Slim's 'Planet of the Phatbird', a perfect summer and firm favourite track of mine.

We all know that one day we'll be fully networked. It is just a matter of time. All the owners have to do is wait until eventually all the licensing laws are changed one by one so they can get what they want: total control with a full network as it costs less and equals more profit. I have been in the game a long time and seen enough law changes to allow or prevent station brand mergers and transmission areas. The big companies get richer and the industry throws people and jobs and whole stations out. Just like every other big business merger I guess, having never been in any other industry myself. It is all the same, just numbers and cost cutting! People down, profits up, cut out the middle people. It is restructuring.

Everyone will get cut except the lucky few who survive each time onto the new company. I know my show will be first as I'm networked myself having survived and replaced the former lunch show on KISS 101 (West). I welcome the chance to go first. I'm contracted and not employed so there is no redundancy for us. I get one month's salary and from there I set up my own business. The others all get chucked out about six months or so later when the East and West stations close permanently. A few move onto London including Michael, Sally and Kelly.

Everyone else loses their job. It is a shame really if you are passionate about radio like a lot of people are. All those jobs in sales, programming, presenting, productions, street team, promotions, office and so on. It is the listeners as well who are truly passionate about being seen working in the area as they are with us. We are connected with them personally and locally; we are real for them as if we are their friend next door. Anyway, there is a new presenter instead and their choice is carry on or stop listening. It is never personal radio anymore after that as there is none here. It is all from London.

I choose not to apply anywhere else. I crave change and independence. To work for myself, that is the new challenge and my ultimate goal. I've achieved well over a decade in radio presenting and DJing, and I carve out my whole career from music. I play music for a living when I can't read a single note. I always think that is quite an achievement in itself. It feels such a glorious moment in my life. A wave of new discoveries appears on my horizon. Life feels new again. Plus, I am free at last from the building and its orange walls (although a few got splattered with mini KISS logos). I've dedicated twelve solid years almost day and night to that building, slept on sofas, gained tinnitus… I worked my way up learning everything to become a professional on air and on decks. I've had the honour of working with an incredible team and met some great friends along the way.

My new business model requires a major financial investment and more time sacrifice. It is a bold commitment. Setting up your own business is always tough through the first few years and I'm about to be very skint. But wait a moment, something far more magical is about to happen! I finally get a drum kit. I have a digital drum machine with Logic and when I build my music studio it fully comes to life with my huge Behringer monitor speakers. It is incredible. I have everything I've ever wanted at the tips of my fingers.

In September 2010 I leave KISS, quit radio, build my own studio and fall out of a tree!

# CHAPTER 9

# THE 10S: MUSIC PRODUCER, VOICEOVERS AND BREAKING SOMETHING ELSE

In 2009/2010 just before I leave radio, KISS appears in CoolBrands UK and I feature alongside the London team. Probably because I am the only networked regional show and as I am female, it better represents balance. The year's presenter line-up is heavily male skewed, like much of the radio industry, which is typical of this time. In this edition we stand alongside powerful brands like Alexander McQueen, Harley Davidson, Orange, Ray-Ban, Russian Standard Vodka and Virgin Atlantic. (I kept my hardback book copy. It's a visual banquet of big sexy brands and striking photography. It's like a book of artwork.)

At home it is time for a new desk! I'm fitting out my room with my own full production studio with the help of a few producers. Andrew and Momo offer advice and help me set up and plug in some of the multi-function production suite and fix bits when I cannot. They help me in the first initial weeks until I'm self-sufficient.

I hire Sally part time as my personal assistant because she is so brilliant to work with and funny, plus always leaves lipstick on my mugs. It is like her little trademark signature, a nice neat reminder. She helps me with anything that needs doing and setting up DJ booking contracts and whatever is happening that week.

Cost (I don't use the word 'cost' often) is scary. When I think of cost it is more emotionally weighted for me. Money is pouring through my fingertips. I use the word investment. It's a far more powerful and constructive word and ultimately sensibly decision based. The total investment is £8,000, and I can hook up, connect myself, to any other studio internationally. I take a big salary hit whilst training for music production... (investment). These are the foundations and turning points in my exciting new life. A fully self-employed new project that I'm creating alone.

On my focus board, I write down changes so I can concentrate on the new plan. I split my business into four key areas (excluding the rental business):

- music production
- voiceover
- DJ
- iTunes podcast (this is just for profile and branding, not revenue)

My new working day starts with prioritising exercise, walking four and a half miles either outside or hitting my treadmill. Then I get to work building a vast array of new contacts in all areas:

- meetings with voiceover clients, reading and producing scripts
- promotions and pitching to new clubs and places for to DJ
- searching for new music and uploading to my library for the nightclubs
- iTunes podcast, produce and present monthly show
- learn Logic, study music production and produce tracks

## I HAVE A LITTLE ACCIDENT!

All right, it is quite substantial as I'm reduced to walking, damn it! Unfortunately, for the next four plus months my body is too broken for running because I fall out of a tree... in the dark. Yes, climbing in the dark! I am *VERY* STUPID, a little drunk and completely smash my body to bits! Oh dear.

This is a pretty bad start to my new excellent life. I'm fucked. I can't walk. Realistically though, in a lifetime of climbing trees since I was about six, this is the only time I've ever fallen… I decide one fall of this magnitude is enough. One can learn!

I say to my friends, 'I don't want to go out walking. It's too late. It's a bad idea. I'll get hurt.'

So, overruled, we go out. We often walk late at night as it's magical, isn't it? Being out in the silent darkness of the open countryside, looking at the moon and the stars. It heightens the senses bringing things into a different mood. I love it.

I say, 'Do not let me climb any trees. It's not a good idea.'

Walking for a few miles I resist many hundreds of trees, hedgerows, woods and small forests all very well. Not mostly because it is fucking dark at 11 p.m. but mainly because I've drunk several glasses of wine. Then I see the most magnificent tree. It is like a natural ladder. It may as well have had a halo shining on it! All the branches are so perfectly aligned that my brain has no time to contemplate why not.

With a small pocket torch between my teeth, it is just enough to my route. I climb easily and fast, grabbing branch after branch reaching higher up the ladder. Then I hear 'CRAAACK'. The branch in my right hand snaps clean off with my fingers griping it tightly. As I fall, slipping down the truck at first, I scrabble frantically trying to grab anything. I wonder where all the branches are now when I so desperately need them. Then there is nothing at all, just me freefalling silently though open air.

I can gauge the depth of the fall only by how long it takes me to fall. As a DJ my entire life work in seconds and split seconds, matching beats and mixing tunes. I am somewhere between the first and second floor. As my body weight pulls me backwards, I free fall for at least two seconds. It is a clear count of one, two, SMAAAACK. After two and a bit ahead of the three. I lie still flat on my back in a dry ditch. I lie silently only because I'm winded so hard I can't speak a word. I take in tiny gasps of air as my lungs have been squashed so hard.

My friends are worried as one of them sees me fall out of the tree and is shouting for the guys, but I can't talk. I want to but it is impossible to get enough air in to speak. If I'd climbed any higher I would have spun further round and landed on my head. From this height the fall rotation set me off leaning backwards and slightly at an angle, landing a fraction more on the right side of my body. I look in my hand. It is ivy. The huge thick branch I grabbed in the dark was in fact ivy, not a branch at all. That is what snapped as it is still in my hand. That's why you don't climb in the dark. They look the same.

I eventually catch my breath after a few minutes to speak. 'I'm ok,' I say as I try to stand. I stand up, half carried, and limp a few metres back onto the farm track. I try to walk and scream out in pain. Not a noise I've ever heard from myself before, more like a shrieking badly injured animal. My friend panics a fraction at this point. I can hear it in his voice. 'Do we need an ambulance?' They won't find us anyway as we're into the woods.

'Look at my leg, look at my leg!' I am almost frantic with pain, insistent. 'Look at my thigh. Look, there. There's a stick in my leg. It feels like a knife. It's like a knife in my leg. Is it bleeding?'

Response: 'No, there's nothing there.'

'What? Nothing? It feels like a knife. It's in my thigh. Maybe a stick, a branch in my leg? It's agony. There's nothing there? Are you sure?' I put an arm over each of their shoulders and support my weight. I slowly begin to limp the painful mile or so home.

The next day my whole body ceases up. It just locks up with bruising and swelling complete with black and blueish patches up and down my legs. I'm a freaking mess. My legs are black and blue in patches. I can't walk down the corridor to the bathroom without holding the walls. I can barely walk at all due to taking such a hit on my left knee and my right hip. The two damaged locations on either side firmly put me out of action. I have ten days where I can't leave the house. I limp myself to the car eventually and take myself to A&E.

The doctor runs some tests including one I'm not very keen on. She tells me she needs to place her hand up my butt or at least a finger to check for internal damage! What the hell? It is my legs that are the problem! Rephrased to, 'Are you sure you need to do that?' I'd rather not as I know my butt is working just fine. It's my legs that are not cooperating! Nevertheless, she thinks it very important so I don't slowly die from any missed internal damage. Oh boy, that is so embarrassing. However, it is a productive result as we can both now confirm my butt is working. Phew!

She runs a skin sensitivity test... I don't know exactly what it's called. They swap between a thin object, like a pin or needle, and their finger on my skin in various places. I can tell zero difference which confirms I've broken my nerve endings. It takes three months to grow the nerves back or however they fix themselves. It is my first insight into nerve pain and I gain some understanding of nerve damage that Mum always talks of with MS. Across my knicker line all on my right side feels like burning just from wearing them as I sit working at my studio desk. (Being honest I've never climbed since. Well, only trees. I still love a bit of bouldering or *daylight* climbing with a *harness* on a specially constructed *wall*!)

When I say to people I fell out of a tree, most people smile and laugh or try not to laugh. Oddly the words 'falling from a tree' are deemed less dangerous in their mind. It genuinely sounds laughable, sort of funny and it is, I suppose as I'm not enduring lifelong injuries with a broken head or spine.

If I switch it around and say to people that I fell off a roof, there is a look of immediate horror about them. Instantly recognisable is the danger to the human body of falling from the roof! So bizarre, isn't it? It's just a word or two words! Tree... Roof. The consequences of the impact are both the same. Minus the concrete or tarmac (hard mud is better). Thus, I have learnt from this event that falling from a tree is acceptable, falling from a roof is not!

I continue to work in my studio with burning nerve pain periodically every day and always when the cat rubs itself against me on my right side it hurts. Some brutal lessons learnt. Luckily, I haven't booked any gigs until the new year as I'm still setting up my business.

## GROWING THE BUSINESS

I build up a stack of private gigs and clubs. Sally and I produce contracts to standardise bookings so in 2011 I take on a lot of new clubs. In my second and third years I focus more on specific club nights with residencies.

My contacts in the music industry are extensive but for voiceover work I start from scratch. Guy the voiceover guy helps me with advice and some contacts and sets up my voiceover business. The ISDN line fitted connects to other studios anywhere in the world for scripts. As a voiceover artist one of my first jobs is an advert for swimming pools. It is largely voicing for radio adverts, some live sessions with producers at the other end, and others I just read, record and send audio. I work for Choice FM, KISS Network, Magic, local and digital stations with clients like Bovis Homes and in-store campaigns with JJB Sports.

I spend a year solid training myself with my head wedged in the book reading and learning Logic inside and out until I can produce my own records. YouTube is also a pretty useful tool. I never ever sit idle; I never watch films or waste any time. I just graft morning till dusk, happy living in my studio dream. More training but no certificate!

## FIRST TRACK WITH A PRODUCER

The first track I make is with my friend and producer, Tony from The BeatThiefs. I commission him to produce a track with me so I can learn from him and maybe get some tracks out. First comes a slightly odd track from me, in that I'm not really ticking any genres with it. It is an enormous learning curve. (I had completely forgotten I made it until I saw it online a couple of months ago!) I hook up with MC Fizzy who supplies the rap for it.

The next we build together is funky house, with a more electro edge called 'I Hate Disco'. This is so much more me! I supply a deliberately short angry vocal with just a few words. I have an offer almost immediately from a record label to get this signed but being new to the game I don't run with it and ultimately miss out. Valuable lesson learnt. I'm learning fast and achieving goals; it is all going to plan nicely.

I build my own fully licenced PRS (legally correct) podcast. I want to try this new platform on iTunes as it's something different. I even bag Sidney Samson for an interview. His 'Riverside' track is a huge tune in the clubs and on loop in my car. I mainly produce the show on Logic as my ears are taking heavy damage during this time, so I try to limit my DJ mixing where possible. Recording the shows audio on Logic means it can be produced at a lower noise level. That is the only reason: damage limitation. I produce a monthly episode of *House of Elise* over two years and when I'm satisfied I've ticked that box, I end on episode 20.

In 2011 when I'm eventually able to run again after my vicious tree incident, I work out routinely four to five times a week. I've been able to exercise fully again for a while, so I run, I cycle, I play badminton and tennis, and I love to swim. I like to rotate my sports a bit. I like my stepper for a sort of improvised boxercise. Listening to hardcore beats at 150 beats per minute is quite a furious workout! I'm still heavy though and it feels unfair given the amount of exercise I do. If you're content in your body, that's great but I'm not. I feel something is wrong.

## DJ DIARY 2011–2013

There are some multiples as I was a resident DJ at places like Karma, Buddies, Liquid, Loft, etc. There may have been a couple of pubs and weddings too. The locations are: Buddies

Bar in Cromer, Loft NR1 in Norwich, The Garden House in Fakenham, Kafe Karma in Norwich, Club Brazilia in Bury St Edmunds, Innocence in Newmarket. Boardwalk Bar in Clacton, Judge & Jury in Essex, Liquid and Envy in Peterborough, Liquid in Colchester, Easterns in Sudbury, The Gym in Bury St Edmunds, and maybe Heights in King's Lynn.

Over these two years I average around sixty DJ sets per year.

## ALL NIGHT LONG

In terms of time and construction of sets, I've always been a sprint DJ and a bloody good one, playing for one and mostly two hours and sometimes three. Usually, the resident guy or girl warms up and, if needed, finishes off the night. Over at The Loft I have to master whole nights of four to five hours and occasionally six! Another new challenge: pace the music, pace yourself. Pacing my body on a full night shift means necking even more Red Bull. (Right at the end of my career after fourteen years, I was taking Pro Plus instead to lessen the cans and sugar content.)

I work out sugar in any form is causing night sweats and adding to my poor quality of sleep. I'm pumping myself full of caffeine between 11 p.m. and 5 a.m. but there is no other way for me to cope with shift work. For me it is brutal. I have friends who are nurses and carers and they survive by coffee and just keep going. They're the true heroes. Plus, it's not easy to get coffee in a nightclub! I do try bringing tea with me to get away from Red Bull or Monster (I really did). I smuggle in a small flask of tea, but it is so hot in the club! Tea is a crap DJ drink! Noted.

Sugar is the problem. I can hear you thinking it! Even I know that number of energy drinks can't be good for me. I guess as an average I'm on two to four cans a set, so is it any wonder I can't touch the stuff now? I'm borderline practically allergic to it. REALLY! I wonder why…

I always promise myself I'll never play drunk and become reliant on alcohol to play. I substitute that for energy drinks. It is only later on that I begin trying to restrict my intake. I quite often scoff four without even noticing, if I get particularly excited! It is on my booking forms, a sort of Ryder if you like: water and energy drinks.

I have a very, very low caffeine intake these days. In fact, I gave it up a few times too but I decided in small quantities it's ok. Seriously, you try living without tea or coffee. That's probably the hardest thing I ever gave up for a while. I reconciled myself with the fact there are worst vices in life than three cups of green tea! Yeah, I'm so badass these days!

For the record, I estimate that I've played in the region of 700 DJ performances.

## NEW REVENUE STREAM

Towards the end of 2011, I'm expectedly skint! I'm not making enough money yet, as it takes years to grow a new business.

I'm investing so much time in training and all profit is being ploughed into music production. I start doing extra work outside of media and I drop back in on building to fund my 'habit' of music production.

One of my DJ and music producers is doing the same with renovating property so we have a lot in common both in and out the studio. It is a sensible combination of DJ at the weekends, build houses and produce house music in the week. We can literally be productive all the time!

I work in the family business as a labourer and this time it is mostly interiors. Previously I had more knowledge of external building. My first job is a huge bathroom and goes something like this. Strip out, prepare, assist, install, tile, grout, clean, painting preparation, filling, painting and snagging. To my surprise I quite like this mix of work now. I welcome the more normal hours and I'm really happy to be back on site again. I love a good bit of ripping out work. It's so satisfying, hammering and bolstering, smashing tiles to pieces. I find even with this I can build a rhythm and be fast. Bringing skill to a job brings pride. It is fun.

After being my heaviest to date even with working out five times a week just from sitting at a desk for a year, I'm terrified of the scales. Finally with this immensely active hard work 8 a.m. till 4.30 p.m. my body comes back to what is a sensible weight for me. I get building site fit again. I'd like a bit more or… well, technically less, but I'm grown up enough to accept we can't all be Kate Moss sized for a multitude of different reasons. A sensible balance of what is achievable is a better acceptance at this point.

## EAR PAIN

On 27 November 2011 I'm doing general building work at a large house in Thetford. There are several teams of builders, electricians and decorators all together on a full house total renovation. I'm working upstairs. The window fitters are working in the lounge taking out windows in the empty echoey building site room. I walk through the dust and get caught in the noise blast of the pneumatic drill and my ears physically hurt. I don't know what happens but something really hurts inside my ear. I stick my fingers in looking for blood, the telltale sign of a perforated ear drum. There is no fluid or blood but I can feel pain and I can hear ok. I've never experienced anything like that before. That is not good.

I'm off work the next day and again lying down to keep exceptionally still with severe vertigo almost immediately afterwards for several days. But something else has happened. I'm left with pain, noise induced pain, and I have to wear ear plugs from then on, and it's never gone.

I'm due to DJ at The Loft two weeks after this rather hideous occurrence. I have to play with a foam ear plug in my left ear to stop the sound. I try many types of ear plug but I never get on with the DJ ones as I find they stick out of my ear and scratch on my headphones with a very annoying sensation when you're moving them on and off your ears continually during the whole set.

Foam is better for me and when pushed right in, they stay in place more or less. Eventually I cut the left headphone wire which is a very disappointing experience for any DJ. Like cutting up a piece of your car or something of great personal value to you. So, I cut out the wire on my old faithful Technics that I've had from day one. Then use it as an ear defender over the top of my left damaged ear including wearing an ear plug. I have to swap ears, now switching to my right ear that is still working to beat match. So that side is coming on and off for listening to the external club monitor speakers. I've always been a left until now. Hence the left ear died first I suppose.

It is a pretty bad time as I have no other way of making enough money to pay the house bills and so I continue with both jobs as no one really knows what the heck is going on. I have problems with visual motion as the inside of my head swims around if I move my head too fast. For the next few years I cannot look at moving things, for example, as it makes me really dizzy.

I can recall very clearly that it takes seven months to become normal, such is the extent of the damage. I know this as throughout the whole thing it has pixelated my vision a fraction. Not enough to stop me doing anything but all my vision is around five percent ever so slightly pixelated.

Just like if you put a pixel filter over an image. Hence the ear damage must be linked to the eyes or nerves somehow. I'm working, but it is just a bit wrong, a fraction pixilated, and this is everything I look at. My whole field of vision, every day. Then after seven months it is normal again. It just goes away. Weird.

Later I'll refer to my hospital notes to remember the details, but this is the basics at this point. Noise now hurts! Noise? How? Loud noise really, *really* hurts. What the hell was going on? I'd never known anything about this scenario I was now living with. The pain was two parts on encountering too much noise: one, a burning sensation and needle-like pain in my left ear and two, physical pain creating neckache and headaches afterwards that tended to appear consistently three days later.

I am a DJ for fuck's sake!

I adjust somehow and carry on.

In other news around this time, my first official track fully produced by me has returned from mastering and is released on MMC via Spotify, Apple, Deezer and so on.

Released in October 2011: Nikki Elise's 'Pretty Lights'. MMC Recordings (part of Massai Music) is proud to present the debut release from the artist Nikki Elise.

Not as proud as I am!

# CHAPTER 10

# BREAKING MY EARS AND BUILDING A HOUSE

n 2012, having intentionally pitched for regional club work, working locally for the time being means travelling within two to three hours tops per night. It is a sensible and maintainable workload considering nearly a full day a week is spent searching and downloading new music to the library ready for the weekends' nightclubs. I don't want to lose time driving from place to place as I'm working my time efficiently. Music production is the number one aim and booking gigs further afield requires a huge amount of time lost traveling all over the place.

I've produced some funky house tracks and a dance track. These are different genres as the speed of the music, the beats per minute, are different. Once I have taught myself the basic skills in production where I'm right on target, I set aside around a year to train myself studying Logic and music production. Then armed with my knowledge I'd be back in the studio more with producers to learn to fine tune things and speed up the output of tracks.

Once I've constructed several tunes, I'll produce some in hard dance and hard house in my more typical *House of Elise* style. I'm looking to release through record labels like Tidy and Nukleuz. I know them from my vast list of record contacts (these types of styles and labels anyway) then I can look to build my club profile through bigger and wider event bookings. A little chain reaction of work. There are whispers of potential work in Dubai thanks to my iTunes podcast showcasing my genre.

Currently I'm DJing from Cromer to Essex and across Peterborough, Norfolk and Suffolk and I'm back home in Norwich. Norwich has felt like my home city ever since my Squares days and I love hanging out there... when I have time. I frequent Tombland with Lotty and the VIP in Mercy on occasion sometimes with Suz. Towards the end of the year, I start a residency in Loft NR1 (I still call it The Loft) in Norwich up to three times a month. I prefer the stability of fixed nightclub points for now. Regular work is more like being at home. Plus it is more efficient; less time is spent looking for work.

I also release some more tracks:

Nikki Elise's 'Raver', Inspirato. September 2012 available via Beatport, Spotify, Juno Download.
Nikki Elise's 'Brassic', Truespin Records. October 2012 available via Beatport, Spotify, Tidal.

I make a few other tracks that don't get signed and that shows it isn't guaranteed you'll get a label to invest in you. It isn't about the money at this stage, it's about profile. Raise your profile with records and raise your DJ profile with bookings. All the girls who were regular guests on my former show, Amber D, Anne Savage, Lisa Lashes and Lisa Pin-Up, they were all record producers and now I'm ticking that box too. My style is improving and it won't be long before I can look to the big labels and work on new tracks with DJ collaborations. That will bring more record sales, bigger venues and national and international bookings.

I also produce:

Nikki Elise's 'George'
Nikki Elise' 'Drumsun'. Although I wanted this laidback, it was mastered more driving. Not exactly what I was trying to achieve but it was all a learning process.

I also make an incredible remix (if I do say so myself) of Azealia Banks' 'Crump 212' (Elise) on my SoundCloud page.

My best ever remix by far, even if I ripped Harrison Crump straight of a twelve-inch record and due to that the pitch runs out a fraction. I just make it in a spare moment and hence I don't get a better copy to record and work on. I was just playing really. Technically it's not perfect but it's a monster track just for fun.

## MY EAR... WHAT THE HELL?

Sometime later this year, when my shit is really coming together, my ear busts again. It is almost an unbearable situation and now for a second time. No one said this was on the cards. It is not something I knew could even happen once, let alone twice. No doctor ever said there was a chance this could get worse so better change your whole life. I think it is viewed as a one-off unlucky accident and my ear drums are certified to be intact.

Tony and I are working in his studio mastering one of my tracks ready for release. Towards the end of our session, he turns a track up loud as it is nearly finished. You play it loud once or twice to feel it properly to emulate the club noise level. About halfway through, I feel immediate pain in my left ear again. It feels exactly like the pneumatic drill incident all over again. I don't say anything as I know it hurts but don't want to alarm anyone and there is nothing that can be done. I leave and go home. I'm devastated as I know what is coming this time.

With that, my left ear is broken again. It takes another 'exact seven months' to heal including the pixelated vision, ear pain and headaches. Following waiting on the NHS, finally I get to meet the ENT (ear, nose and throat) department and specialists.

## JULY: CONSULTANT ENT HEAD AND NECK SURGEON

Review required in the vertigo clinic. Intermittently dizzy for many years. Sensitivity to loud noise that brings on dizziness after two days. A pure-tone audiogram was symmetrical apart from a mild discrepancy in the highest frequencies. Requested CT scan looking for superior semi-circular canal dehiscence given the suggestion of Tullio phenomenon. This has been reported as normal. She struggles a lot with sensitivity to loud noise and vertigo secondary.

## AUGUST: OTONEUROLOGICAL AND SKULL-BASED SURGERY

Diagnosis: Hyperacusis. Motion provoked and visually evoked disequilibrium.

Plan: Vestibular assessment and rehabilitation.

Three to four bouts of severe rotary vertigo lasting three to four days before being resolved and well in the meantime. Music concert and pneumatic drill incidents – following this she was left with hyperacusis even to quieter sound.

Additionally on-going motion provoked and visually evoked disequilibrium.

Gradual improvement over the intervening months. Likewise, the disequilibrium shows a trend for improvement but has not fully resolved. There is bilateral tinnitus which is greater on the left and otherwise fit and well.

Both ear canals and tympanic membranes are healthy. Pure-tone audiometry demonstrates normal hearing. Vestibular function is unremarkable.

Past episode of vertigo would appear to be compatible with migrainous vertigo given its recurrent nature and duration. The most recent episode appears to be through acoustic trauma. Requested MRI of the head.

## WHAT IS HYPERACUSIS?

I've never heard of it. It's a type of reduced tolerance to sound where ordinary noises can cause pain.

From what I'm told at the time, hyperacusis is largely based on research from telephone call centres' workers' acoustic shock from malicious callers. You can't help but think mine may be slightly different as I have had constant loud noise exposure for a decade and a half. Who knows? I assume they have more knowledge now ten years later. One would hope anyway. My point is that although there are two trigger incidents (acoustic shock), it is by no means just those few individual scenarios I was exposed to, was it? I'm very sure the build-up led to those events.

## I GO FOR SCANS

One of the scans at the hospital is very unpleasant. (Probably the MRI but I don't recall which.) Mostly because you're strapped down on your back, your head locked in place and posted backwards into a large metal and plastic tube. It's uncomfortable to your senses as it's so small and claustrophobic and then they fire a very loud noise directly into your head. I'm in there for the pain in my head! I can feel the pressure inside my left ear. I can physically feel it struggling to deal with the process while stuff is continually fired at my brain. My left ear is actually heating up all the time. I can feel it, like hot and spongy. My right ear is ok.

For me, any noise will induce bad headaches and potential time off work to reduce my slightly panicky mounting stress as I have to endure this horrible situation. I've no idea how this heat sensation will affect me in the next few days. It could put me back in bed again. I spend many hours lying down to ease the pain in between working. To keep myself calm I call up my most loyal long departed tuxedo cat, Big Cat. I see him clearly and recall the smell of his paws, slightly aromatic (the only cat I ever had with a fraction of cheesy feet), his white and black legs and his loving face. He was always purring with dribble running everywhere, sometimes sitting on my head. Big Cat often pops up in my mind at times of great stress. Like a little and not forgotten furry helper.

After a while in my intolerable temporary tube situation, strapped down with loud noise, Suzie pops up out of the blue in my mind saying, 'It's ok, Nick, listen to the machine. It's like beats, init? Throw some shapes to the beats, Nick!' Which makes me laugh internally as externally I'm not supposed to move a fraction. I smile briefly hoping that doesn't bugger up the scan.

I'm finally at ease as the machine is making an enormous variety of crunching repetitive noise. It is house music's crude elements more or less. I'm lying in a rave tunnel with my broken ears feeling like half of my brain is being deliberately fried. My entire left ear is almost as if it is smouldering inside my head. I can feel it flexing a little under the pressure. Which I assume causes the heat inside my head. The noise vibrations cause movement for me and I assume the heat of movement shouldn't be happening! I get out ok and my head cools down quite quickly. I do not take any lasting pain from the rave tunnel, although my brain feels tired and my ears battered. I hope to never have to repeat that experience again.

## OCTOBER: CONSULTANT ENT HEAD AND NECK SURGEON

I'm pleased to tell you that the MRI scan didn't demonstrate any abnormalities. Will see in clinic in due course.

Then it goes quiet appointment-wise.

## GOING DIGITAL

In August 2012 I join Liquid in Colchester briefly. Bear in mind I've only got one useful ear now. I've no other way of earning money as this is all I know. I'm dyslexic and shocking with numbers so an office job is not ideal for me. House and houses, that is all I know. Plus, my symptoms do appear to steadily heal. Well, except for the hyperacusis bit, but it is manageable. I adjust.

For Liquid in Colchester, I need to learn digital. I test Traktor and I like it a lot but settle on Serato (I can't remember why). I invest in more studio kit buying the software and a powerful laptop and learn very quickly in a week and digitalise my music library whilst building a house.

Digitalising my multi-genre library takes a hideous amount of time. So, I do what styles I need immediately and slowly and continually add to it over the next year. So much time is spent searching for music outside of DJing, people don't realise the time that goes in behind the scenes. When you're up and running digitally after back recording everything you've ever owned for months and months on end then you can just add to it. Adding to it takes up a day a week. I never digitalise all my vinyl collection, because I'm not insane! (I had hundreds and hundreds of records in my collection. I guess maybe 300 to 500 at that time. I've slimmed it down a bit since.)

Following my intensive learning week or so, I can use Serato but I don't bond with it. I don't really like it in the beginning. I much prefer putting a CD in the decks. That is my specialist area. I assume like vinyl junkies like placing records on the deck. I'm very new to this equipment and I got by. I do the job and one night play a warm-up set for guest Nick Bright from 1Xtra.

## MEANWHILE... NICK IS BUSY BUILDING AGAIN

I hadn't really noticed but I'm focusing on specific work out on customers' building sites. I'm taking all the decorating work on. More and more painting comes up in between cutting and grouting tiles or fetching materials. To my surprise I find I'm good at this side and really enjoy it. I can labour on a site easily but I never have any firm attachment to the tasks; it is just something I can do. With decorating I begin to take real pride in my work and pay attention to all the preparation, tools, paint details and finishes. I begin seizing all the jobs that require painting but we are builders too so it isn't just painting. It is building, repairing, filling and sanding, and then finally painting. In between I'm attending a lot of hospital trips.

## DURING THE SUMMER I EMBARK
## ON PROJECT BUILD A HOUSE

I start the building work and I learn Serato at the same time. I want to make my own *Grand Designs* house crafted with my mind and hands from start to finish. I contemplate getting in touch with Kevin McCloud having watched him keenly for many years. I quickly summarise that it is likely I'll be largely grumpy due to the shift work and new enormously challenging build ahead, so it is probably not a good idea to add a film crew.

I learn quickly how to write and submit the full planning application throughout late 2011 and 2012. It is a lengthy process. It is quite a piece of research work and I thoroughly enjoy the totally new thing I'm dealing with. You know when you get a headache from learning? It is a lot like trying to learn to process from scratch alone. The researching, locating and drafting out all the detailed specific information that has to be incorporated into every aspect of the plan. It is an interesting challenge and I tick the box of planning and building a house.

I'm required to add in more information as months go by whenever the council requests it. Letters go back and forth, back and forth, and I thrash out ideas and plans for many months. The plans are drawn up and I bump heads (planning meeting) with the council until they eventually accept something I propose. There are all sorts of planning rules you have to abide by within your location. I settle on a massive renovation extending the house by around fifty percent including ripping off the back end of the roof and building out the side and rear of the property. Imagine two large rectangles that only just overlap in one corner.

I'm DJing, working on customers' renovations and building my first house. The first thing I attack is taking down the old garage and reclaiming all the bricks. That means chipping off the concrete and cleaning up maybe 500 plus bricks. It is tedious but doable. Reusing materials saves money.

I'm pretty decent on the mini digger although I can't pinpoint where I learnt this skill, just around as a teenager. My jobs are typical basic digger work such as levelling off all the site ground, having a word/breaking up the remaining concrete base of the brick garage and digging out the small trees and bushes, moving and replanting with an enormous mechanical arm and metal bucket (the only way to do gardening). It's a big job, site preparation. I have rotating rubbish skips on the drive for at least three years.

With my ears wearing standard foam ear plugs, I manage to carry out all this work wearing ear defenders over the top and it is sensible.

## SATURDAY 8 JUNE 2013

I average three to four gigs a month now having moved into my three Saturdays a month DJ residency at my new home in The Loft NR1. I really like being back in Norwich although this is the first time I ever have to learn to play some chart music as in 'pop'! There's always a new challenge waiting. I definitely am versatile!

In August of 2012 I end my iTunes *House of Elise* podcast on a nice round number, episode 20. I feel I've ticked that box and want more time back. I also decide to stop voiceover work as dedicating my mind and body to learning and building a house from scratch over the next two years takes everything I have left. I'm so physically tired it affects my voice tones and flow and therefore cannot compete at the highest level required for a professional voiceover artist.

To give you an idea of the tiredness through sheer exhaustion of doing all these jobs, at one point I develop a stutter briefly on and off for a couple of months. I assume it's just where my brain and body can no longer flow correctly with not enough power left in my circuit (me)! You see what I'm saying about voiceover work. It is tricky and my voice suffers routinely where it is deep with tiredness for weeks on end. Which gives a lovely tone but terrible for continuity! So, I make a choice and move forwards without it. Focus is really important. If you split into too many different things, you cannot carry them out to a high standard.

## AREAS OF BUSINESS

- DJ and music production
- labouring
- building a house… It is classed as an extension but it is as big as a new build.

These are my last two notes ever from DJing in 2013… I feel an ache in my stomach writing 'last two'.

Sat 8 Jun: Five-hour DJ set at The Loft NR1, Norwich
One-hour pre-recorded mix supplied free for 5–6 a.m.
DJ Nikki Elise set 12.00–5 a.m. Equipment: Used the club's PC and VirtualDJ with my hard drive of music. Back Up: CDJ-1000s. Music: Commercial/chart R&B, hip hop, D&B, dubstep, house and anthems.

For The Loft, I learn VirtualDJ software. It is a joy to work with and I love every aspect of it. It is so much fun to use and ideal for more radio edits and shorter tracks. I digitalise most of my twelve-year library for it. It takes months and months of work to get it onto my laptop.

VirtualDJ. Genuinely, it's not viewed as the best kit, probably more entry level gear. But hand on heart it's bloody brilliant. Genius modest little bit of kit. It feels more like radio playlist software. I master it quickly and I love it. It is especially useful as in this club I'm mainly playing radio edits and short tracks with a few longer mixes. Plus I'm getting to drop my own records too. It is a great last gig to see out my days. Thanks, guys, it was fun.

During the above set sometime, unknown to me, it would be my last ever professional DJ set.

## THE BEGINNING OF THE END

The next week I set out as usual driving to the city with my makeup on and high-heeled boots ready for business. It's a typical night. I start at midnight and around 1 a.m. I'm playing well with an ear plug in the left and fully covered up and beat matching with my right, the only good working ear. This has been working ok for a year or so fine. The first hour we play a bit quieter as the warm-up. The club is open really late so we have lots of time to build up the night. The pain comes again mid-set and it is immediate and immense. I can't get the mixer up full. I can't turn the volume up past about halfway. This is a total disaster. I can't play… I can't turn the volume up. The noise, the pain. It is unbearable.

I wonder what the hell I'm going to do. This has never happened before. The only choice I have is to leave before I do more damage. I think it is Steve and Craig who scramble to get a cover guy in for the night. I'm very grateful that they do. I go home with severe ear pain and physically in pieces. I only ever see the guys once more when I pop in to pick up that final payment, say thanks and sadly say goodbye. I think they thought I'd come back even if just for a guest set. I think they thought I'd be ok. No one has ever heard of this DJ damage scenario. It is so final it doesn't feel real. How can you break your ears?

## MY LAST EVER TIME IN A NIGHTCLUB

Sat 13 Jul: Two-hour DJ set at The Loft NR1, Norwich. One-hour pre-recorded mix supplied free for 5–6 a.m. DJ Nikki Elise set 12.00–2 a.m. Equipment: Used the club's PC and VirtualDJ with my hard drive of music. Back Up: CDJ-1000s. Music: Commercial. (Note: I only managed two hours.)

I don't think anyone could have predicted what would happen next.

My entire career is over. Everything I ever trained and studied for over fifteen years ended in that summer of 2013. Radio, all audio production and software editing, presenting, voiceovers, DJing and music production. All gone in a flash. I'll never play again. I'll never do anything ever again in the music industry. I can't put headphones on my ears. Not at all. Not even one sided.

My head is broken and my heart and my dreams are shattered across the board, and it is eminently clear through my constant pain. How can I have just invested all my money and time after waiting a decade to start my dream of becoming a music producer? How can my future and my life lie before me so broken? I look at my brand-new studio that I can't touch! I can't turn it on. My custom-built desk, monitors, mic, mixer, software, hardware, DJ kit and decks, all redundant. It is soul destroying.

There aren't really any words I can say or write that will serve to portray the loss to me. I feel empty trying to recall it. Like a part of me wants to vacate the feelings. I cannot fully recall it again; that's all I have. I can scratch the surface.

Eventually, after many months of waiting to see what would happen (would there be any change? Would I ever recover? Could I go back to media?), nothing happens. It is a permanent new level of damage to both ears.

Eventually I have to take apart and, one by one, unplug all of my equipment. I unplug leads with a bottle of wine sobbing my eyes out on the floor. Some leads into my studio desk mixer are still plugged in today. It was very hard to cut the cord. I kept all the equipment though and my records and CDs just like I've kept all my diaries. They still may serve a purpose and if so it will be different than before. Just a feeling I have.

## SOMETIME LATER, I TRY TO PLAY

After six months I'm asked to play a tiny bar gig for my sister-in-law's birthday, as a gift (and only as she is family). I think I'll try knowing that it will hurt, but not knowing how much. May be worth a shot but I doubt it. I manage a baby two-hour relatively quiet DJ set for my sister-in-law's fortieth as a birthday gift to her in December 2013 with about forty friends. It is her friend's baby Pioneer DJ set up in a local bar, so not like the noise of a big bar or club.

When I get home, I take a bucket of pain killers (so to speak) as the headache is too big. I never played again and never will. I knew it would hurt but she is family, and it was a very small low noise event so I thought it might be possible. I guess I wanted to try. It will never be possible again as it caused too much pain. I can't even get headphones on now. It's gone. It's over.

And I'm not trained in anything else except audio, sound and music. It was my whole life; it was all I knew. Music was my whole world. Music was my passion. Music was my love. Music was my job. Music paid the mortgage and put food on the table and it was over, FOREVER. A brutal lesson from life that I try to come to terms with, secondary to all the new pain, for nine months. Nine months of pain every single day.

I cry through the pain. I have to spend more time lying down in the mornings with both sides fully broken. I lie in agony for hours. I remember describing it like I've been shot through the back of my neck up into my head. I try ice packs day and night. I try heat packs too. Anything is worth a try. No one knows what to advise so I just try to live with something that no one has ever heard of, let alone can understand.

Mostly I take Nurofen constantly and co-codamol, and on bad days I drink a bottle of wine. (I am not advising that you do that ever. It's not safe, but that's how desperate I was not to constantly feel the pain in my head.) It always gets worse around midday onwards from less in the morning, like a ramp of pain. As the day progresses so does the pain.

Both ears are now gone. This time it takes nine months to heal but I never fully recover like before. I don't make a full recovery and my tolerance to noise levels is lowered further. What the hell am I supposed to do with my life now? I look at my focus list. I try to adjust my life. Areas of business: all audio, music, DJing, voiceovers, presenting, production skills, anything involving headphones and all my knowledge in these areas are gone. My ears, my music head, are rendered useless now by this spectacular arse kicking from life.

I decide to drift on life's tide, not thinking, not planning, not pushing. I have pushed so hard for so long and now with my record dreams shattered I adopt a different approach to my entire being. I want to become the opposite of everything I have been.

I take my foot off the gas, fully off, and I just drift. It is a very conscious decision to try to implement the reverse of everything I've worked so hard for since I was eighteen. I drift with life and I find it actually quite pleasant. I'm not looking, I'm not searching, I'm just working and living quietly. It is a whole new style for me. Life has changed significantly. I can no longer collect or listen to new music. I have to learn to adapt.

At the moment, with these limitations, what can I do now?

- labourer
- build a house…

I am satisfied this is enough of a project for now.

# CHAPTER 11

# HYPERACUSIS, BECOMING A DECORATOR, PRODUCING A BABY AND BREAKING A RIB

## MY HYPERACUSIS

Gradually I learn to adapt, working through the devastating and presumably lifelong effects of hyperacusis and all the restrictions I have to factor into daily life to prevent further damage. The limits it imposes on my body go from taut muscular pain across my upper back and shoulders to acute pain deep in my neck and head. The head pain is the roughest and comes last in a series of warning pains and it can be really intense at its worst. Once it arrives, it's too late; you can't stop it, you just have to go through it.

Currently this last couple of days at home, having endured a lot of screaming and a long meltdown, my head hurts at night as lying on a pillow squashes the already contracted muscles. The tiredness it causes too just drains me so much. The bigger the noise encounter, the worse the pain. At its worst it'll put me in bed for a few days until it eases off as I'm unable to function through it, but usually I can manage with medication and avoiding the worst noise situations. I can't avoid them all. That's just life.

From my amazing DJ career and love of music I ruptured my left ear twice and finally both ears once. I call it 'rupture' or 'break' as no one I've ever met has a better description and I know there was physical damage, I just don't know to exactly which sections within my ear. My prior normal life with a working body ceased to exist. I adapted to living with this condition.

I'm not special in any way. It's common for people to be injured through all walks of life. Sport, accidents, or work and with life-changing consequences it happens all the time. I'm no different except for one thing. It wasn't a condition I even knew existed. I did not know this could happen. No one ever said it could get worse than tinnitus. Most DJs tend to end up a bit deaf especially in your main headphone ear which is not ideal but can be assisted with hearing aids. A few DJs I used to work with have told me they use hearing aids now.

Would I have done something differently if I'd have known? Hell yes!

## REFLECTION

If I think about it now, what would I say to my younger self or anyone else getting into the music industry? I'd say just be sensible. It's not difficult and after all what happened to me is extremely rare. Everyone I worked with is still playing or producing music and doing just fine. I don't know if I was unlucky or inflicted it myself or the bouts of vertigo I experienced led to it. I don't know and it doesn't matter either way. It's happened and life moves on.

I would say to little Nick: don't put your bedroom music on as loud as possible; be rational about the volume. Don't crank the car stereo up so much, put it on medium. In all my time spent on 3,500 radio shows I would not have turned up my favourite tracks to near full with the enormous studio speakers. I would have worn ear plugs DJing and persisted until I found a pair that were actually comfortable enough for me to wear permanently during live performances.

There are many areas where we can choose sensibly given that now we know noise can do damage. I never knew it existed until it was too late. Ear plugs were just coming in when I was already playing professionally and yes, I should have worn them. It's about having a little respect for the one thing we love and cannot see: sound. So, perhaps it's helpful that I can share this advice. I think I felt music a little too much and also, I worked on many building sites. I see tradespeople or ground workers working and using power tools and engines and I think yeah, I'd be wearing ear defenders if I was going to do that all day. I wear them all the time now, much like most women carry handbags. I was never comfortable with those anyway! The on the shoulder position is ok, but what's with the weird bag hanging off your elbow with your hand stuck up in the air almost pointing at your face? I just don't get it. My hands like to be free not trapped by a bag and straps everywhere. I freak out thinking about it… much like all the skiing sticks! Nope!

No one wants to live with a condition that's half wrecked my life and steadily getting worse over time. Because on a planet where there is noise and air alike, you can't live without noise. I try to approach it sensibly in just the same way as if you might have a bad back from a work-related injury. You do your best not to make it flare up or, worse, cause further damage.

What I wouldn't give to be able to just watch a film on TV at home without getting a headache and I'm watching it at a really low sound level. To be able to cook in the kitchen without the kids talking and my head getting tired and ears sore from the noise. To take my kids to the cinema, something that's been out of the question for the last few years. Prior to that I could go once or twice a year wearing ear defenders. Cinemas are insanely loud so that's out now. It's a steady decline I face and I've got used to it.

I was offered white noise therapy which I tried for a week with intense pain. I've read an article from a music producer who stuck it out for six months and it adjusted his tolerance back down in the right direction so I believe it can work but not for me, which is bold to go against the specialist's opinion. And for a very good reason. I've always maintained it's a two-part problem. There is the nerve damage which is why everything appears too loud for me now, causing a nerve pain feeling, like an intense needle point of heat. The mixing desk or processor in my ears or brain is set at the wrong level.

I'm a hundred percent sure there has been physical damage too but likely no one knows exactly and to what areas. I can feel the difference in my head because if I'm sitting on my bed with the door closed and another door in the house shuts, I can feel my nerves flare up inside my head. It's almost like a light switching on, like a big rush of sensation in their response. The nerves jump up then go down in about a second, overreacting. This, I think, is what causes the tiredness as everything is working at the wrong setting. There is no big soundwave physically hitting me loudly as my door is already shut.

The opposite of this is if the bedroom door next to me where I'm sitting slams (which happens a lot with children). It's as if I've been physically hit round the head; if you hit me hard, it's the same thing. The pressure wave of the sound hurts so much. I stand dazed for a moment and gather my senses, like a boxer who has just taken a big punch. There is a physical reaction within my skin and bones. Something moves from the vibration and it hurts. The nerves do not hurt, that's separate, even if happening at the same time. Once a big metal petrol can fell onto the concrete floor in a small garage. The noise was so loud I had to stop work for an hour or so to get myself together. It was too painful as it was so close to landing near my feet. It was a TKO for me. I couldn't carry on that night. Certain materials or pitches and echoey places are the worst.

The best description I can give you is that the suspension is broken in both of my ears. Once, when it was working well, I could listen to all kinds of music, sounds and life's general hustle and bustle. Once the suspension is broken for good, you actually feel pain. My ear plugs are acting as my suspension. If the suspension worked, I wouldn't need them. I think some people focus just on the nerve pain and say, 'Oh, you shouldn't wear ear plugs.' Yes, that's fine, if the suspension wasn't broken as well.

The pain is nerve burning and then there's the physical vibrations; bits of me bang together inside my ears. I just don't know which bit is loose! All sound is vibration, either big or small. My suspension is gone. If you drove down a road with lots of tiny bumps you wouldn't notice to start with but after half an hour or a few hours you'd start to really notice, right? Maybe even feel dizzy or get a headache. And if you slammed into a massive pothole bursting your tyre and busting your wheel, you'd feel like you'd been hit as your head shakes in the car seat. It's exactly the same for me with sound. It's the vibration. It causes movement I can no longer soak up with my duff suspension. It would be great if I could get fitted with a suspension upgrade perhaps! Or a dampener of sorts! I can only dream.

If you factor in the exact same amount of healing time of precisely seven months, on both occasions for my left ear, the noise level tolerance dropped almost overnight but the physical pain to me indicates the damaged material, tissues, maybe cartilage (maybe cat food!). These were the bits of my ears that took a lengthy time to physically heal. The third break to both ears took exactly nine months to heal, to get pain free. It suggests that either the damage was worse, or my physical body could no longer recover in the same way or timeframe. Hence the recovery was not near as full as before, and I never recovered anywhere near as well this time. On the third break, it was game over.

It ended my entire career and all forms of income including laying waste to my newly built home studio and all my investment. I had to walk away from music and all of the media industry. I could still listen to some quiet tracks or low beats and bass DJ sets in the early days for a few years. But ultimately, I left it all behind, all the promoters, venues, records, my contacts, and, of course, all social media.

It was pretty freaking obvious life did not want me to be a music producer or presenter or voiceover artist in any way! So, what did you want of me, life? What was the point of this? These were the questions that rattled around in my mind. What would I do now? Would I ever find work I loved again?

I spoke with a couple of DJs afterwards who called me up for events or music production. I had to explain I'd never be able to play again and what had happened. I can hear the tone of their voice even now; it was almost as if a radio silence fell upon the phone call. A sort of disbelief, as in how does anyone handle that? You've lost everything. Was this the worst thing that could happen to a DJ, a producer and a broadcaster and no one had ever heard of it? Taking a DJ's ears must be somewhat like damaging a footballer's legs: cruel. Although I assume (as I'm not one) a footballer could still watch a game on TV or in a stadium. I will never walk around a festival or music concert again. I can't even go to a bar and enjoy the music and I'll never be able to put headphones on again. Noisy traffic is a problem. I drive with the car windows up ninety percent of the time as I have to reduce the noise.

## WHAT IS DANGEROUS FOR ME?

The hospital makes me aware of three specific areas in my new restricted world. Let's list them here. Situations that are dangerous and potentially causing more pain and even more damage:

1.  loud music
2.  machinery
3.  children

Marvellous! Well, that does not affect almost every area of my life, does it? At least I don't see any children really, so that's ok.

I continue to build the house wearing ear defenders for all jobs: hammering, drilling, sawing, cutting, cement mixing, dumper and digger driving. You name it I wear ear defenders, but I can still be on a building site whilst being sensible with my ears. I can do this and it is liberating to still have a big project on the go that I can learn from.

A self-employed schedule accommodates both jobs almost simultaneously. I'm earning enough money from building work to build my own house around that. Since I left college, I've always had two jobs so that's what I'm used to. The hours are, at times, hideously long but I'm not doing shift work for the first time ever. It is such a welcome relief. I don't feel I can ever go back to night work as it has taken a lot out of me and now it is time to move forward in a new direction. I have to adapt, learn and ultimately evolve.

## HAIR STORIES

All the money goes into building a house. It is the biggest investment so far and spread over many years. To save money

I cut my own hair for several years. I gain an unexpected fringe the first time around! I only screw up once in three years of self hair cutting so it isn't such bad odds really. Why does it feel like I'm cheating on my stylist if I go anywhere else? What is that kind of relationship built on? Hair trust? You don't realise you've entered into this kind of relationship until you're forced to cheat on them, by visiting, oh my God, a different salon! Only I'm too embarrassed to show my mistake. Never try to cut mid-length. It is a challenge too far and I know it. But the curiosity got the better of me that morning as I attempt the impossible mid-length cut!

I realise Toni & Guy have cut my hair for the entire contents of this book. My man at the salon is a cultured guy who's lived and worked abroad in some challenging jobs and eventful situations. Formerly he lived in the States working sometimes as a private investigator and as a district attorney assistant in criminal defence. We can share stories of our past working lives and now the work we love. We get stuck into some unconventional conversations together about our past experiences. He knows how to tell a story and can work my unruly enormous hair into a 'Rachel' although typically I want a new style on each visit. I've ranged from a bob to long for many years, probably as I was so restricted in my teenage long frizzy (witch's hair) years. I broke out of the hair mould.

He often says, 'You must have some stories…' and yes, there could have been so many scandalous encounters had

I have been married the whole time! I've had many forward suggestions from people and particularly women. From young women throwing flowers at me to the lady who gave me a tip, the only DJ tip I ever had (I think it's maybe just an American thing). I opted for sharing as I felt I was paid enough and gave it to one of our dancers.

There was one young woman who made me turn bright red, which takes some doing! Usually, my stage presence and my working poker face is pretty good, but not this time! She just walks right up to my DJ stand and says, 'Do you want to have sex with me?'

I'm familiar with the phrase, and I know it works well, but usually people start with 'hello', right? She catches me off guard a little and I'm thinking… *Hello! I'm working here… Ah crap, what to say?* I think for a brief moment and reply rather plainly: 'Errr, no.' Honestly that's all I have at that second! Ha-ha, it cracks me up thinking about that now. It was just so funny at the time. I was thinking, *I'm working here, I'm not on the menu!*

I'm pretty sure I have pulled guys before, judging by some rather intimate dancing but it isn't intentional and once a married couple ask me back! But I just like dancing and maybe I'm better at it then I ever realised! If the music is good, I like to dance and that's how it all starts. It is club land, so anything goes really. We're less bothered than the outside uptight world.

Just after I interview Ferry Corston when we both are playing Escape into the Park, he asks maybe indirectly (and also looking around at my production team), 'What are you guys doing later?'

I've done a hundred interviews and no one ever asked me that before. He is chatting about playing one of the big clubs in or around Wales that night, but alas I reply honestly with, 'We have to drive back home.' That is the most boring I've ever sounded! Just so boring (why did I have to go home?). I'm just a working machine, with this gig, that show, this travel time. I like to think he was asking me indirectly! Ok, he was probably married but come on, let a girl dream!

Fedde Le Grand gives a good solid regular interview. I hide well that I'm half melting. It's Fedde, come on! And when speaking with Sander van Doorn, he's just an icon of a producer to me. I love his music so much.

I am, of course, conducting my interview business professionally at all times! These are the things I'm thinking but don't say! I tell Mike afterwards!

Carl Cox is loads of fun to interview. He's a cool guy and so many more, so many fun memories. All the girls who are my heroes are now my colleagues at events or on the show. Many are listed in a little promo video I have made when I leave radio. It is a working description of who was on *House of Elise*. I spend more than two full weeks producing that one piece of audio. Possibly one of my finest productions I've ever made. The quality of my production work and investment of time around all my other work, I say it takes eighty to ninety hours to produce the perfect ten-minute audio. It's on YouTube as the finest showreel I ever made and Glen kindly supplied the video. It's a nod to the *House of Elise* music empire we built with national brand status.

During my decade and a half in the industry and looking at who was consistently in the top one hundred DJs during that timeframe, I interviewed eight out of ten of the world's top ten DJs.

## BUILDING A HOUSE

I sell my red BMW sports car in favour of a grey VW Golf Match because common sense demands change across the board. Horses for courses. Z3s are gorgeous and stupid on space as the only thing you can fit in the boot are golf clubs. Utterly useless. I've never even played golf! Anyway, this little Match carries tools on the back seat, lengths of pipe and timber on the passenger side, and happily transports piles of sand and cement in the boot. A Golf will get it done.

Living on a building site, I'm powering through. Jointly we put in the groundwork, the footings and the block work up to the damp course. I hire a team of builders being my family to brick up only the walls. Other than that, we do the rest of the jobs, inch by inch, everything except the roof trusses. It requires a team of people and a JCB from the kind farmer neighbour opposite. All five of us manoeuvre them all neatly into place without falling off the edge of the roof. Everything else I do. Well, except for the electrics even though I fit whatever cables I can in advance. It is back breaking work, alongside work, and hugely satisfying at the same time.

Anyone who's ever set about a project of this scale knows the personal sacrifices needed to get the job done. The vast extension is two storeys at the peak of the roof. I invest heavily in seriously long hours for years on end. When you're young, your body can take the pressure and recover well. My body walks continually around site all day and into the early evening and sometimes I just randomly vomit from exhaustion onto a big pile of rubble and I just keep on walking.

Sometimes friends visit and the roof will be hanging off, looking like organised chaos. It will be 10 a.m. on a Sunday morning and I roll out of bed, make a tea, immediately followed by coffee, and nip up onto the roof to stop the roofing underlay flapping loose in the wind to prevent an imminent flood.

I work twelve days in a row most of the time, which is obviously not normal, when you're talking about years, not even months. Twelve days a week it is. Then perhaps a day off might pop up. (It's a number I remember well because it is so obviously bloody stupid.)

At my worse, I am taking Nurofen and Red Bull for a couple of months solid just to get out of bed. I mean to drag my aching broken body out of bed. I tell Charly 2 and she says, 'Errrr yeah, I don't think that's normal.'

I say to my friends that it can't be right, but there seems no way out. A year or so after I'm into the build, a friend says, 'You'll burn out, Nikki.' I know she is right but there is nothing I can do with this part of my life. If there's commitment to a phase, you need to see it through. I mean on every level. I live there for one. It is taking all of my money and I can't afford to pay anyone else to do it. So, I grit my teeth and carry on. Blood, sweat and tears is an accurate summary.

During this phase of buckling muscular aches and pains and bulging biceps, I'm also the thinnest I've ever been since my twenties. If you work continually with no holidays and weekends for a year or two, it's a fairly stiff workout, so naturally you'll lose weight. To survive the constant pains, I adapt by drinking up to a whole bottle of Strongbow every other evening to numb my ragged-out breaking body. I wonder if this must have been what it was like in the Victorian period if you did a heavy manual labour job. Your body hurts so much of the time you're unable to ever recover properly as rest is not on the five sides of the A4 to do list. You probably live at the pub for medical reasons.

Suzie comes up from London some weekends. She brings a hob as there is no way of cooking anything with no kitchen although there is a microwave. I wash up in the bathroom sink for two months alone. That's definitely not hygienic.

I chop and chuck stuff into a slow cooker almost every day. Afterwards I cannot eat from any slow cooker again for three years. It makes me feel green just the thought of it.

But good old Suz, like a trooper, trips over a pile of wood, sweeps a section of bricks and screws to one side to reach the makeshift worktop. Undeterred by the chaos she gets cracking and makes something out of this world to eat. The flavours are such respite in the face of microwave jacket potato or hot pot slop again for the second year! It keeps me going. Mentally it helps so much having that something special and a friend around.

Her mum's house is a horrible atmosphere as she can be so vicious for no reason. Hence, she is at mine a lot when she lives at home. So much so that when we look at my house on the new Google Earth her car is parked out the front on my drive! This amazing determination to cook no matter what, with the living conditions she sees changing all the time, which are pretty diabolical, earns her the nickname from our neighbours of 'The Chef'.

'Oh, we saw The Chef's been round again,' they say through the hedge. She often send spares over each side of the fence. The Chef is popular with both the neighbours too.

Late evening and half-drunk, skip filling is an almost daily and necessary event. It is quite therapeutic in a way, like finally signalling the end of the day's tasks. Lugging massive heavy scrap objects around the site and hauling it up over the side.

Even if you think you've finished work for the day the slightly rusty, big yellow skip is always waiting for you! When I do finally clock off (no idea when… maybe around 6, 7 or 8 p.m. depending on the days to do list. It is mostly after the hot pot has been consumed), it is always, every night, back to the skip. Followed by my shower to cope. The shower signals the end of the day officially for me. Peeling off silicone from my hands and scrubbing the dust from my legs and face. I always work with a hat on and that stops the dust from clogging up my hair and pillow, keeping it away from my lungs as much as I can.

## ESCAPISM

My switch off and escape has become my bedroom as I have no lounge and no kitchen for a year or so. The entire house is basically destroyed for a long time during the creating process. The hallway is trashed right through with dust, plaster board and materials stacked up and you just sit in whatever is currently untouched. I do hoover some days even though friends ask what the point is. The point is, by the end of a week, shit will be piled so high across the walkways that it becomes a very dangerous surface to walk through and, don't forget, live in… I swap that for 'endure'! Spiritually I'm given the word 'temperance' around this point in my life. Wow, that is a tough cookie to master. I don't even know what it is.

In my respite bedroom, my sanctuary, I sit and watch the entire twenty plus series of *Time Team*. One after the other after the other. Tony Robinson, Phil someone and Helen Geake become my TV friends. This gives me total outage and much needed downtime form my gruelling world, month after month, year after year. I learn a bit about archaeology and firm my love for history.

Like Lisa Pin-Up has revealed on my show, she likes to relax by watching *Countryfile*, now apparently *Time Team* is my thing! It's a brutal period of my life, but big pains get big gains is the theory in general though, isn't it? I know how to fit, build and lay underfloor heating and pour and finish a polished concrete floor surface on top. Just in case you ever need one, I'm your woman! Ha-ha! I put some black, red and white marble in mine, a nice touch! It is a labour of love, and I will not do one ever again! Not ever! Seemed like a good idea at the time. It does turn out pretty spectacular given it is a first attempt.

There is no full heating for three years except a fire in the old lounge plus one small and one big electric heater. Ice forms on the inside of the old patio glass doors inside our lounge and one winter there is dripped ice the size of Calippo ice lollies. I sleep in all my clothes some winters to keep warm as I'm not great with the cold. I mean, inside cold. Outside is fine. Sometimes I just sit on the bathroom underfloor heating leaning on the bath as it is the only pleasant spot left. There is also nowhere else to sit really. I'm sharing this with the two cats who've moved into this room permanently. Cats are like a built-in weather report and the Cat-App will always tell you if the climate's good enough. The bathroom is very good; both cats winter there.

There is a year or two of non-stop working where I don't see many friends except going out a couple of times a year for a christening or the odd BBQ. There isn't much point going out as that wastes a day where stuff could have got done. Harsh choices are needed. Big dreams require a big sacrifice. Maybe too much sometimes.

Building control signs it off with a letter. I get a bloody certificate of sorts for this project! Well, it's a letter but it will do. The letter is a magnificent moment in time because it officially signals the end, *finally*, to one of the most gruelling, painful, educating, complex and most drawn-out projects I've ever attempted. Completion is important for me.

## MY NEXT BUSINESS

I start up a new business and become a decorator. Quite a change from all the media surface glamour, but remember I was a builder first. Criteria check: I work for myself, I'm self-employed, I love it, it is creative, I stay really fit and no more night shifts. It is absolutely perfect. The only downside is I can't do any of my beloved sports since my new career is very physical. My workout routines vanish because I get a massive workout at work each day of the seven in a week. I do miss it though, badly. There isn't enough energy left in the tank. Oh well, it isn't forever, and I'm still fit from work. I tell myself it is a small cost for now as sport is mostly removed from my life.

Most builders I've met hate decorating but I love it. Painting is really satisfying work and it is just a massive relief to discover I am in fact really good at something else! I like building things whether it's creating radio shows, DJ sets, houses or decorating. It is creative work. Every job is different. I repair and paint a lot on building sites, extensions, rebuilds and refits, and general decorating. Some buildings are dilapidated or pre-Victorian and the walls have holes through to the next room. When you walk onto a job the whole thing is a giant scruffy 3D canvas to work with and my job is to fix it.

From your basic needing a freshen-up coat to all the hardest jobs people can't do themselves. Like the hallway, stairwell and landing. Or the external render, windows and woodwork which require scaffolding or long ladders. Firstly, you assess the level of damage and repair accordingly, then work your way through the preparation stages. Until finally you can put some paint on right at the end.

I do small bits of carpentry, build furniture, change door handles, fit smoke alarms, silicone bathrooms and whatever is required. I am a pretty decent all-rounder now. I find it satisfying and I find something I can return to after I start a family. It feels so liberating to have discovered a new working way of life, learnt a new skill and to have a new income. I didn't think I would fall in love with work again after leaving the media, but I love painting.

I often think back to that school careers list and wonder if painter or artist was the number one spot that I've forgotten. I guess I'll never know.

## WHAT THE HELL IS THAT? <u>A BABY?</u>

Yeah, I think it's necessary to underline that.

When we get to a sensible level, nearly through the build project with maybe around a year's work left where the rest can be managed and completed by one person, my life moves on. Purposely I wait until I have secured my decorating business to return to after having a baby only because I would have shit myself far too much! I'm a planner; I need to plan to cope.

I put a baby on order and it promptly turns up via Amazon Prime in under a year. I have my first wobble around three months as I've never even seen a baby before really, like in my whole life! I don't really know what they are for as they don't have any fur like cats. Now I have one inside me making me vomit if I drink tea or coffee and making me retch so hard at the smell of lamb cooking that I don't eat lamb again for at least two years.

By the way… just to be clear, if I have not mentioned it so far. I *NEVER* WANTED KIDS! In fact, when someone asked me once, I burst into tears as I was never going to be able to do that. It was a no way. Not now, not ever!

But, and it's a big but, into my mid-thirties, those hormones finally say, 'Hey, how about fucking now then?' Oh God. This is the exact opposite of what my life is all about. I have to be growing up. Either that or I'm going nuts and I don't know for sure which one it is. Perhaps I am crazy! Lou has had kids and (I'm averaging here) in fact four out of five of my female friends do too, so I equate this may be normal, if not at all normal for me. I'm still mostly aligned with the sensible twenty percent of friends that don't!

So here I am somehow going to have a baby. Holy crap! I am assigned the most perfect midwife for me. A fraction older, all-knowing, calm, wise and confident woman. Exactly what I need. Pin me to the ground as life as I know it is floating off into space! Often she visits my house. Possibly because I spend so much time working up ladders and step ladders all day pregnant. I think it is because I have to rest my exhausted body and so do not drive out on my only downtime.

When I say rest, I'll be in bed for half the day as I'm too physically shattered to get up. Not because I don't want to get up. I have a million things I need to do especially as there is still no heating in our house. It is no way near finished and winter is coming. There is finally a very nice kitchen though and some bi-fold sliding back doors. Handy for keeping the cold out. Cardboard and plywood are terribly ineffective and completely unlockable! Another reason I do not go out previously as there were no back doors!

One time a cat dumps a by now magot-infested, fermenting rotting dead mole in what later becomes a lounge and we don't discover it for several weeks. Puke! I'm gagging when I remove it. It leaves an imprinted outline of mole on the floor. It is so gross! Describe the worst thing you've ever smelt in your life and that is it right there. Rotting mole. Far worse than anything else my senses have ever encountered. I'm literally turning green and gagging with a scarf wrapped around my face.

Anyway, back at it. Once, I have to meet the midwife at the library in town. I get there and sit outside in a circle of women with very small kids. These kids are categorised as babies or toddlers (a year or so later, I knew there was a difference. Go me!).

I go into her office and shakily point outside the door, blub my eyes out and I'm stuttering, 'There's kids out there.' It is nicely rounded off by sobbing ridiculously, 'KIDS I said!'

She knows immediately and picks up my distraught mass confusion. She just calmly looks at me and says reassuringly, 'Yes and you're pregnant.' She knows the whole thing has just become overwhelmingly real at that exact moment. That is going to have to be me in nine months sitting on the chair with kids all over the floor. Actual babies… oh crap.

## BEING PREGNANT: REALLY GREAT AND REALLY SHIT!

I take on painting a church at five months pregnant as you do when you're a professional decorator. It is roughly a three-week job in Ipswich up scaffolding and painting all the woodwork windows. A really nice bit of outdoor peaceful suntan work. Except quite tiring when you're up the duff. Working up scaffolding and woodwork always takes a lot of prep work.

When you're pregnant, your centre of gravity is thoroughly buggered as your weight is massively on the front so I'm totally off balance. Going up the ladder now, I have to doubly make sure I don't fall off by toppling over backwards. This is a very odd new sensation and quite a real threat. I fall asleep in the car every lunch break for thirty minutes or so on the back seat. Just passed out with tiredness. I manage to work a four-day week most weeks instead of five and I have to rest around that all the time at home, whilst still doing the general household whatever, shopping, cleaning and feeding people.

There is something up with my heart rate as after decorating at home it stays elevated for hours and hours ticking over around a hundred beats per minute lying down! Absolutely a dreadful scenario for aiding rest and recovery. I have my friend who is the midwife team leader at the hospital (who would later marry that guy as I predicted) come round as a friend and MOT me but my blood pressure is all ok. We listen with her stethoscope to the baby's heartbeat too. She reassures me that all my stats are ok. I feel so terrible after work, but why? It is odd.

It would be ten years before I realise something in me isn't quite working right. If I take on board a glass of salt water, it levels my heart rate out immediately. It is something to do with too much water diluting the body's electrolytes (I think, but don't quote me on it). Hence for me the extra salt fixes it. I'm not recommending that to anyone. I just know it works for me as something isn't working right. The things life will finally teach you in your forties. Like my lifelong headaches are just a back muscle spasm! Twenty years of pain. No doctor, physio or chiropractor has ever figured that one out. We might as well call this phase 'the fixing you forties' as you are so freaking busy fixing everyone else up until now!

I'm required to do extra building work at home on my days off sometimes or painting at home, but it has become increasingly difficult to do any more work. I have done extra work, smaller jobs like stacking out some blocks and fetching materials and tools for the swimming pool, whilst pregnant. But as you progress, getting bigger and heavier, the choices of painting the fence at home (which is about forty metres long) or going to work has to be made. Tough choices as life is changing. The dynamics of two people are becoming three. I can't see this clearly twenty-four-seven. I'm living with it and living with no coffee!

Interestingly I become completely unable to multitask! I mean it buggers off completely in the latter stages of pregnancy! I wonder how I become just so stupid! And so quickly (hormones I suspect). In a matter of months, I've gone from being able to run a broadcast from a full radio studio by myself (even though I wasn't in that line of work at that moment, I could do it easily if required) to having to talk myself through cooking two pans of vegetables on the hob! It is such a strange side effect! I am really stupid… briefly I hope!

My very last job is stripping the lounge wallpaper in a Victorian terrace for a sweet little older lady. Unfortunately, at seven months pregnant all the walls are a total nightmare underneath and cannot be fixed at all. Now I need several extra days to put up lining paper all over. My customer is fantastic about it, and I have to put on an extra few days and not through any fault of my own. It's just the circumstances. You just can't predict these things in the building trade. I've worked on many Victorian houses and properties; you strip a small area or two, assess it, then you just have to go for it.

I call in another pair of hands to help me for a day as by now I'm physically up shit creek without a paddle. We paddle out of the disappointment and bodily hardship I am struggling with. The disappointment to have to work longer and harder on my last job before signing off for my maternity leave. I started the job a bit late and it takes extra time. I start my maternity at seven and a half months pregnant, around two weeks late. It may not sound much but at that stage, anything extra is hard work.

Back in my own house the biggest project is finally finished: the vast kitchen, lounge, diner underfloor heated polished concrete floor, built all independently. I would have usually been drunk late into the night taking shift turns spending three weeks on the giant floor grinder and polishing machine but now I can't drink, so once I may have a half glass of cider but it is very rare now. I give up my pain-numbing cider as a necessary requirement of motherhood. Of which I don't realise you start becoming a mother as soon as you are pregnant. I thought it happens after something pops out! Another little lesson.

Fact! You can't sleep for shit in any position fully preggers. You're up about three times a night to go pee and you lose sight of your own feet several months in. I never bother buying any maternity clothes though. I don't need them, and I have no money as it is all being ploughed into the build. I don't order a single baby item, nothing, until I finish work as I don't have any time or energy to do any more. Friends keep asking what I've bought and I say, 'Nothing.'

They say, 'What? Nothing? You're having a baby, why not?'

'Because I don't have any time.' So very late in the last few weeks I bulk buy everything online for one baby, over about two days. I have been writing a list, planning.

I am determined to enjoy the few months of my maternity I have left before I pop. I am starving hungry and I do mean starving hungry. I eat every single three hours twenty-four-seven. It is a hunger nightmare. WTF is going on? I crave fruit and tuna but I can't eat fruit as I am intolerant to basically all fruit, and carbohydrates create too big a sugar spike then I get seriously sweaty and more insomnia. Nice! So, I eat a lot of protein. My midwife is happy with my diet although I have to cut back my enormous mugs of tea for a few normal ones.

I enjoy two weeks off work as welcome respite from the physical side of decorating. Well, as much as anyone can enjoy being the shape of a smart car, not sleeping, whilst being ravenously hungry all the time and not able to eat fruit I desperately crave. I search the cupboards at 5 a.m. (for the second time) for fruit juice as there is no fruit in the house. A packet of Capri Sun has to suffice. It seems to offer something to my intense need.

I get down hard with a heavy cold virus during my two weeks off, my luxury time! My lungs are filled with crap and they rattle and wheeze when I breathe. I spend a whole day stuck in bed coughing the entire time. I mean I cough for one whole day solid, like six hours of coughing with no medicine. Coughing like that is exhausting. I don't have cough meds. I'm possibly not supposed to take anything anyway heavily up the duff. I have no idea. My back is a mess due to this ridiculous (smart car) posture and those eye headaches I get. Plus, the weight I've put on... Two stone is not much really but it feels like a massive amount. One is mine, later I find out one is the baby, plus packaging, bubble wrap and string.

**POP!**

My back is hurting so bad that every time I cough, I have to sit up to cough straight. Otherwise, I feel like my muscles will snap. It is a pretty serious illness situation. I am roughing it out stuck in bed all day. The next day I break my rib. POP! The distinctive sound of my rib snapping just like a big stick.

Like I said, I am *TRYING* to enjoy my last month off work!

Not anymore! I am not enjoying anything right now. I can't sit on the sofa as it is so low it hurts. So, I have to sit on the dining chair, with backache, sick with continual coughing and now in absolute fucking literal screaming hell. I am lying on my side on the sofa, as I can't sit, with him having cracked a joke to try to cheer me up. I laugh which is followed by a cough and I can't sit up in time to level out the body muscles during the cough. Pop. An unmistakeable sound and the feeling of a loud pop inside my body. I am in agony. I roll off the low sofa onto all fours on the cold concrete floor as I can't stand. I am screaming my head off every minute or so. So much so I can barely speak sentences.

I call my off-duty midwife friend, screaming out in pain stuck on the floor unable to move. The pain is unreal. She assesses the pain and doesn't think I'm in labour but due to the severity of my pain I have to get to the hospital. No one here can drive. Great. I call the neighbour and Clare drives me to A&E and I apologise for saying fuck every time I scream out in pain. She is very accepting and forgiving thankfully. I am in agony. I am desperate. The pain is so bad, I can't think.

I sit awkwardly, waiting on the chairs with lots of people staring at the heavily pregnant woman screaming violently and randomly and wondering why she isn't being seen. Heavily pregnant women yelling wildly are an immediately uncomfortable situation for almost everyone. No one knows what shit's about to go down! Ambulance people don't much like all the mess that's inevitable. I've learnt this! I can't blame them. It's like a fountain of liquid eruptions. It's pretty gross if it's not your own liquid!

It doesn't take too long (possibly in case I died in the waiting room or more likely spewed baby fluids all over the floor). Finally, the A&E doctor sees me, a young woman, and she says, 'Can you do this?' Lift my arms or something.

'Yes.'

'Can you do this?' Move this way or something.

'Yes.'

'Well, it's not broken so just maybe a pulled muscle or something or backache. Take paracetamol, go home, take it easy.' Off you pop… so to speak.

I feel quite stunned that I've been seen and am out in about five minutes. I've been ticked off and chucked out. But I am very relieved it isn't broken but very confused about the level of pain. Excruciating. When asked in the waiting room for my pain level score out of ten, I immediately said nine. A ten would have been if I'd nearly snuffed it. I'd never got past a five before I reckon in my whole life. Even when I had my huge tonsils removed from my throat (maybe five or six but that's a very small area with localised pain) even though it bloody hurt every single time I swallowed my own saliva.

I head home swearing and don't sleep well on my left side. The painful side. That is only the beginning. The next day the pain is so severe I cannot eat as eating causes burping and that is like being punched from the inside. Mum happens to be there and just silently holds my hand. She knows I'm in a bad way. I cannot stand comfortably. I cannot move an inch. I cannot sit. I just stand holding the kitchen table with tears streaming down my face and I physically shake. There is no position that offers any respite from the pain for an hour or so at its most intense.

There is so much pain my body goes into tremors all over. I have never experienced shaking from pain before ever. Only trauma. On top of that day's occasional burping, the baby is kicking it from the inside. Excruciating is a justified word to write in here twice. EXCRUCIATING! The damaged area is repeatedly being kicked and poked by a mini me, and that second day is a living hell. I am in the worst pain I've ever known. I almost can't breathe through it.

My assigned midwife is away for around four days or so, just when I desperately need her. I do my best to get by until she shows up in my bedroom. I cannot lie down at all. I have to sleep sitting upright. I have to strap a belt to the side of the bed as I cannot sit on the bed and lie back to the pillow at the headboard. I use the belt to take my weight and lower me into a sitting position for the whole night, using the belt for the two or three times I have to get out of bed for the loo. I am forced to sleep upright for several nights until my midwife finally arrives. I call Suzie as I need help. She comes in as I can't even chop carrots for the pain. She helps me change the bed sheets and do all the stuff mates do for each other in times of a crisis.

I write my midwife a letter as I want her to know the level of pain I have endured as I can't articulate things very well and can't afford to miss anything. She calls the hospital immediately. They say they are full or something. I hear it. She says that isn't acceptable and she wants me booked in now. 'You make her a bed this afternoon.' She used to be a nurse so she knows what she is dealing with. Thank God someone does.

After a night in the ward, a female specialist comes by and feels my ribs and confirms I've cracked nine or ten on my left back. To be honest I know what a fracture is as I heard and felt the pop. That is a fucking enormous clue, isn't it? But pregnant women are kind of lumped together under back pain.

The ward doctor reads my notes and says, 'Hmmm, it seems a bit more than back pain, I think. I'll send someone to check you.'

'Yes, thank you,' I say unable to move.

When I see him again, I ask how I am going to give birth like this.

He calmly says, 'We have around six weeks left so it should be healed by then. The set of muscles used for birth are lower so it shouldn't affect it too much.' (That's positive thinking right there.)

No point saying anything to worsen my stress is there? I hope he is right. Hope is all I have left! My body is broken.

I am sent home with my broken ribs and nearly fully made baby. I am mostly pissed off because it turns out they could have given me something for the pain and I had nothing. I mean nothing during the worst thing I've ever felt in my entire life. The worst is over in a week but I don't function properly for weeks and weeks… my nice relaxing maternity leave! My midwife is quietly furious as had it have punctured my lung both of us would have been in big trouble. She says one of her other pregnant ladies has also broken one, so I'm not alone on her list.

## THE MORNING OF DELIVERY!

Exactly three weeks later after the rib thing, Suzie has broken up with yet another boyfriend which always goes well for me. I always get extra visits, extra love, extra time, extra dinner! She happens to be sleeping at my house when I stride into her room at 9 a.m. and say cheerily, 'Hey, mate, morning. I'm in labour.' My waters break around 7 a.m. and I wait patiently to get her up and get on with the very current job!

Calm fades fast and it quickly turns into chaos because the rib has only had three weeks to heal and it is bloody killing me. All I can feel is the pain in my ribs and then the pain of increasing contractions. One after the other switching from my back to my stomach. My back aches are becoming more severe. What if my back gives out and I am in agony from my buckled back? What if my rib snaps again? It is only half healed. I do sort of offer prayers to give birth in the daytime at least and this has been answered, albeit it is two weeks too early. I would have much preferred to have had the chance to heal my broken bones first. I mean priorities, really!

Panicked, we decide to call 999 for advice. We can't tell what is going on as I am in such continual pain flipping between contractions and backache. There is no escape from either pain, not in six hours at least. The operator quickly gets Suz pretty flustered and makes her check, with my consent, that the baby is not coming due to the level of shouting from me. I can see Suzie's face clear as day as I hear the operator in parts on speaker.

'Is she pushing?'

'I don't know… Nick, are you pushing?'

'I don't know.' We don't know because of the chaos.

I hear her say, 'What? Really…? Mate, they want me to check if the baby's coming!'

'JUST DO IT!' I order her immediately to carry out the job. Shouting instructions are paramount to committing her to the job. I have no idea what is happening down there; she needs to decide. Making sure my baby is safe is the only priority.

Her hands are literally shaking; I can see them trembling. After she's given them a quick wash (bless her heart) like a trooper she searches for a human head erupting from my cervix.

What are best friends for, honestly?

Ironically Lou is on my paperwork for baby delivery if required as she's had two. I figure she's better suited. But I am extremely grateful Suz is there when that morning unfolds. Clare next door has knocked out of the blue.

Suz says, 'Not now, Clare!'

I overrule her from my bed with, 'Let her in.'

My last memory of leaving the house as one person caught in physical hell is of being mentally taunted by wondering whether I will snap my rib again or if my back muscles will give out. Without a working back you cannot possibly give birth, can you? Somehow, I *do* give birth as that is the only option available. If I could have opted out, I bloody well would have jumped ship in any way I could.

Outside the house the drive has been almost completely ruined for weeks as it is a half-finished job. It is in part like giant sleeping policemen in shingle and mud all over the place and it is at least five cars long. Picture small sand dunes and you're along the right lines! The ambulance can only get two-thirds down it to my front door due to ludicrous parking conditions.

I get to the ambulance with some blankets wrapped round me. As it revs up loudly taking some power to lift off, up and over the bumping, it is swaying widely over the appallingly useless drive. It is like the perfect comedy sketch I swear. It can't have been any more uncomfortable if we'd had tried to make it so.

On arriving at the hospital flat out via swift trolley delivery, I am in constant pain close to agony and I cannot get in any position at all that is comfortable with my back under huge strain from the no way near healed rib and from the other end, contractions. Nice! I try the bed, but I can't lie back on it. I can't lie down, so I try the floor on my knees, but I can't get onto my knees and hold it. I try crawling onto the bed sort of on all fours, my least favourite suggestion from the several midwives in the room. I can't hold this or any fucking position at all. It is a nightmare for me. How the fucking hell am I going to get this person trying to bust through my insides out? My mind almost can't cope.

Eventually, feeling shattered and desperate, I sit on the toilet to pee with one young trainee midwife sitting right opposite me. That is in case if a baby flies out down the toilet, she is there ready to grab it. I can't even take a piss in private now. In childbirth, 'all dignity is left at the hospital door'. A well-known phrase and how true that is.

Having sat on the loo for a while as there is nowhere else I can actually sit down anyway, I realise the disabled or heavily pregnant handrails around me that I've propped myself up against (like braced myself against an incoming storm) are actually a tiny bit comfortable. With perspective it is just more comfortable than before! For the first time in four hours or more I sit with some relief, in between the continual pain of contractions obviously.

Amazing news, I can give birth on the toilet! The midwives are not at all happy with this idea even when it seems very sensible to me. I am not currently in hell, so that has to be good, right? Eventually I get myself off and they give me a pessary or something for mild pain relief for my backache and finally after six hours of living through the worst pain shitstorm ever, I am able to lie back on the bed to do the job.

Naturally I've ignored all birthing courses and have zero clue as to what I am supposed to be doing. I remember being in a daze with the gas and air and nothing happening but a lot of contractions pushing and screaming for a long time. Then in an instant there is a midwife shift change. I've been in hospital about five or six hours by now.

An Irish midwife appears by my face. She says to me very calmly and firmly, 'You're not pushing enough. You're pushing a bit then stopping. You must push all the way. If you don't push hard to get that baby out, we're going to be here all night.' (I remember thinking she had such a sexy accent! I love the Irish accent so much. It's the best on the planet.)

Either way she is a strong, firm woman who knows her business of firing out babies. Finally, the penny drops and I am on it, fully. I wonder if I'd had that advice sooner, would we have been a lot further on by now? I now know what to do.

Suzie pops back in and (apparently as I'd forgotten this bit) I say, 'That woman has told me to push harder and it funking hurts. Bitch!' But I am in business.

I stop yelling my head off in pain almost immediately and focus on the rhythm, notice the timing for the first time and I put the effort in fully. Annoyingly my team around me is still shouting for encouragement. I really want to say to them, 'Shut the fuck up!' I fall silent for hours so why can't they? It may cause an argument if I say that, so I keep quiet. No one has the energy to speak a word in labour, let alone get into a row. I assume they are doing their best to support me although I'd rather have the peace. I need to concentrate. Believe me, even the midwives think they are noisy; I can tell this is an unusual form of encouragement, more like a boxing crowd!

Anyway, after a very stiff twelve-hour lesson in how to give birth, finally the baby does get out of me. Six hours of build-up and six hours of pushing for anyone who likes to know their delivery details.

Poor Suz tells me afterwards that that day I covered her in every single bodily fluid imaginable. Way to go, Nick! As far as I know I didn't shit on her but basically may as well have! I do remember her catching my vomit as I throw up a Peperami all over the bed. She catches most of it in the first thing she can grab like the cardboard hats they have lying around! Maybe not hats.

Some Walker's Squares crisps are tolerated on my second attempt to eat after nearly the whole day without food. She does pop out to leave us alone while the actual baby emerges. But promptly returns in time to see piles of after birth all sitting in a large bowl at the bottom of the bed. It's the weirdest thing, isn't it? I have no care about anything right then. I can barely see from tiredness. It is a sort of shock and pure relief stage… it is all over.

I love how the midwives document this, filling in miles of paperwork as a normal birth! In their world, all this *is totally* normal. I can assure you it does not feel like that to me.

They say, 'Here you go. A lovely boy. Do you want to hold the baby?'

'No,' I say, 'Give it to him.'

I am broken end to end, ribs to crotch, completely wrecked my mind and I've sweated out my remaining whole body's fluids through all of my skin and the entire bed is soaked from being force fed Lucozade Sport (spiking sugar levels) and splattered with blood. It is quite a sight really. And all I want is a rest. I'm pretty sure I've earned a five-minute break.

After meeting my baby, next I get stitches which is just a perfect ending to a perfect day although I don't feel a thing.

I probably had something for the pain by then. A couple of stitches is fuck all compared to trying to shove out a human head. The midwives very kindly take baby for a bit so I can rest. They don't have many people in that night and have time to help me. I am extremely grateful for this gesture of kindness.

Battered, drained, bruised, back muscle ache, sore ribs, blood sugar sweats, ripped, stitched and tired… yep, I can't sleep due to the sugar causing the full body sweats and I know now preservatives in the sports drinks ('citric acid') are my worst enemy. Total exhaustion does not make a shit bit of difference for me. After wasting an hour of gently rustling around on my bed I know sleep isn't happening. I take a sleeping pill around 11 p.m. completely exhausted and I get about three hours of sleep, before I am woken up to feed a baby. Welcome to parenting!

I stare at him and cry.

# CHAPTER 12

# THE BUSINESS OF PARENTING

## THE HARDEST JOB I'VE EVER HAD

I'm very familiar with the phrase 'just because something's hard, doesn't mean it's not worth doing' but parenting is on another level. I was badly under prepared for this business which is also sometimes the best way to be. In my case I was stupidly naive! Ignorance has its uses!

The walls bend in front of my eyes from sheer tiredness. My eyes or brain or some part of shattered me just can't get a grip at all! Something I've never experienced before and now it is a regular thing for a few months. My baby isn't feeding enough and therefore is not sleeping more than one hour at a time! Yep, I get about a forty-five-minute or less nap in between him waking for five days. It is a devastating level of sleep deprivation that I've never known before.

Eventually I get help in the form of baby bottles and from then on things start to get rapidly better. I wish I'd have chosen both feeding options from day one but there are a butt ton of lessons all to be learnt and all at the speed of light with a new arrival sleeping on your chest. A lot of people are very, very keen for you to breast feed. Only when I realise it is not working properly does a bottle fix the disastrous consequences of malfunction.

No one ever says, 'Oh yeah, them boobs, they might not work.' Weird, huh? You just assume they'll work ok. It's part of the job, right? Nope, not really. It turns out mine are more just for show. Even though they are pregnancy huge and at one point actually turn square in a good demonstration of motherhood! I literally show Suzie a few weeks before. 'Look, mate, they are square.'

'Jesus, they are square!'

Well, truly I expected better from my assets! Sadly, it is not to be. Anyway, bottles are so much easier and quicker, however you arrive at a baby milk bottle sterilising kit.

In the two weeks that follow of screaming agony, having to always pee in the cool water of the shower using it like a fire extinguisher, I call my friend over (my off-duty midwife, not the NHS-assigned one). She confirms my stitches have come undone hence the intense burning and screaming agony during each toilet time. It is not a nice place to be in every few hours. And never sit on a hard chair!

Within about six weeks of my new family life, I know I'm not done and I need another one. Really? Are you kidding me? Nope, my deal is not done. I do not feel finished yet on this journey. I can't believe I'm even contemplating it. Who the hell would ever want to give birth, ever, and then actively decide to do it again? What is wrong with me? Clearly, I've gone insane.

Maybe I will adopt one as my mum was adopted as a baby. I always feel I may go this route one day. How has my life gone from zero kids ever until I'm about thirty-two to thinking, *Oh well, might as well fire another one out*. What is going on? I always knew from roughly the age of twenty-five that I would have a girl, but I'm looking at a little boy, puking all over my shoulder.

A boy is a complete surprise to me although two of my friends dreamt it, so they get a prize if I had one, which I don't. I don't even have a brain now. Mostly because I am functioning in a zombie state for several months trying to adapt to never ever sleeping in more than two-hour sections. I'll be in bed for around twelve hours trying to get enough sleep in shattered bits and pieces. Luckily the baby is also in bed about this much so it is doable. I can't imagine how women cope in countries where they don't get maternity leave. It's almost barbaric to force people back to work unless you're a lucky one who goes, 'Oh yes, my baby sleeps well!' There is none of that here, not for many, many months. What, like eighteen…

twenty-four months? They are really about four years old by the time teething and all else has fucked off and they may sleep.

I am oddly adjusting to my new family life, even for the cat it is doable. It has such a massive impact on every aspect of my life (which is basically never your own again). Having lost the older cat aged fifteen who was terrified of children in a very sad but also well-timed terminal illness, it is a very lucky escape for him. The one remaining cat is now a family cat. It is not just a cat. It's had an upgrade from a straightforward easy life to screaming and later on to be perpetually dragged around by one kid. It now has to deal with this new package as well. It can't now sleep in silence and cover in fur every single spot it chooses when it finds doors left open. One cot bed is totally off limits. This is just a fun challenge for a cat. I give up a few years later.

'No single event will ever change you as much as becoming a parent,' my uncle wisely once said to me. In another full three-sixty I feel I need this harsh and glorious learning. Being a parent is sort of like a trainee survival boot camp that doesn't end. Ha-ha! That's a great statement, admit it!

Military training is well known for incorporating this level of sleep deprivation and everyone wants to visit. Is my face sliding off? It sure feels like it is! I need to feel and endure the highs and lows of parenting. I need to walk this path in all its glory, sacrifice, humour, love and total exhaustion. My rib healed up ok if you're wondering. It was sore for around four days afterwards. There was so much soreness I barely noticed this bit gently aching all over again on my left side.

No one tells you this though: you're about to fall completely, astronomically head over heels in love again… with a baby. The overwhelming emotions of becoming a parent are insane. I'm asked a lot about the crying and don't understand. 'I'm not crying. I'm really, really happy. What are you on about?'

On day five I begin crying *literally* for about three days solid. It's like I sprung a leak! A relentless eruption of overwhelming emotion. We are all crying in a daze, even the cat is crying for different reasons. Its attention, stroking and peace have been acutely affected, and it is only getting fed if it makes an enormous effort shouting at us.

I now understand why people who have babies only appear to talk about babies for quite a while. Because they consume every inch of your life and there is zero time for anything else! I am always curious as to why this phenomenon happens when a new baby shows up. Because there's no freaking time left to do anything else!

Anyway, I enjoy my nine months of maternity leave as it is a wonderful time saturated in baby and family learning. It is such a long challenge starting with teaching a baby what daytime is and what nighttime is (ideally for sleeping). Nighttime used to be for sleeping anyway. They really don't give a toss. It's all about milk.

The day after the baby comes home, an engineer finally finishes off the heating system. First whole house heating in three years and well timed. I saved for two years with two years of saving my tiny personal income I had left. This money runs my car and I buy a staircase for the house. My personal spend is about £20 a month for several years. Any spare money still gets sucked into the house build.

## NURSERY

I still do what little jobs I can with the baby. The very first day I put him in a nursey is an eye opener. The nursery and staff are amazing, and I can't praise them enough. I spend the entire, full day working my arse off to paint his nursery room before I collect him in the early evening. It is very satisfying to get just one day to get some other work done and be alone. He looks completely bewildered and worn out when I get him but he is always really good with strangers, so I felt confident to put him in. On seeing him I realise a half day may have been better for him. Lessons learnt.

I pass him over the fence at two months and my wonderful neighbour Clare and her daughters take him sometime for two hours so I can get some sleep. My baby feeds every three hours twenty-four-seven. I get about one and a half hours sleep in between each feed. It is so hard, but so incredible as I stare down at him in the faint night light at midnight, 3 a.m.

and so on. He looks like a seal pup with such big eyes staring at me intently, in the faint night light.

The very next day he wakes up with conjunctivitis with his eyes glued with sticky puss. So much so that both eyelids are totally stuck down. I have to bathe them open with a cloth and warm water as when he is awake, he cannot see anything for twenty minutes and calmly takes this in his stride. A couple of days later follows severe D&V (diarrhoea and vomiting). I can get from my baseline seven loads of washing a week to fourteen loads in a week, easy. I am now a full-time laundrette, milkmaid, chef, cleaner and child minder. I am a house manager and I am a baby manager! I am desperate to get back to work. I need work, I love work (work loved me… which is bullshit), but that's how much I like work… I need work, *desperately*, for a break from my life!

The illness passes from nursery and schools and nicely (and astonishingly) onto me. I go virtually untouched my whole adult life then a baby infects me more often than if I deliberately keep mosquitos in my room forever. I am down with severe stomach pains, vomiting and the other! They are all different and this is one of the worst I've ever had. A twenty-four-hour thing. Twenty-four hours with eighteen hours of vomiting continually for me. I lie in bed and beg for it to stop. I cannot drink water for the pain.

I am unable to get out of bed. I limp to the bathroom, weak after another round of puking in the toilet to the pit of my stomach until bile is all that is left. I crawl out as I'm already on my knees. I don't remember for sure, but I know I cannot get the roughly seven metres to my bed. So, I go left and lie two metres away on the hallway floor trying to get my energy back. I literally lie down in front of the front door hall.

That is my first experience with my baby going to nursey for one day! Welcome to my new world of working parenting. It is brutal!

The rest of nursey is wonderful, and I need to balance this up here. It's important to be fair and give credit where credit is due. The nursery team itself becomes a stabilising factor in my new baby-filled life. They are helpful, friendly, funny and give respite from my new mum life. Put baby in here and go to work. God, I love going to work, possibly now more than ever! I go back after my nine months and break out of my baby bubble.

Obviously on many occasions I put my baby in screaming at full volume, kicking and hanging onto the door handle trying to get back out but that is normal for us. A constantly upsetting but factual way to start at least half of his days in nursery. I can assure you he is fine every time after that initial ten minutes. (I now know that this is a 'transition' for anyone autistic, hence the heartache of a near daily event.) It doesn't last too long once he is in behind the closed door. It is just getting him in. Often it is too much and I shed tears, then just get on at work. Such a depressing start to your day. Every day!

## ANOTHER BRUTAL LESSON

Many people still don't know but next I have a miscarriage. I was not able to talk about it, so I shut down. I'm ten days off telling people the exciting news that I'm pregnant at nearly three months. My midwife friend basically guesses it right but I put her off. Just. She's a clever woman. It's like she can suss you are pregnant by looking at you! You may not think it sounds a lot but for three months you've been carrying a little life inside you, looking after it, feeling and thinking all your hopes and dreams that will go along with it. Will it be a brother or a sister? There are one or two subtle differences with this pregnancy. I'm not puking up cups of tea by this point (and some other things that I've forgotten now).

One afternoon I begin to see a few drops of blood. Some hours later it is followed by stomach pain. This is bad news; I know this is not right. The midwife office is closed as it is too late at night. I dial my midwife friend in a blind panic, but I can't get her. It goes to answer machine. I leave a desperate message quietly crying down the phone, tears dripping down my cheeks. If I am dialling her number then I have a serious problem. The action of making the phone call is confirming in my mind my nightmare.

My pain is getting worse and I don't know what to do. Suddenly my phone rings and she has called me back. She is hiding from her family, out at a do, as no one knows I'm pregnant and it is confidential information. She does not yet know I'm pregnant until that moment. We determine that I am likely having a miscarriage, but it may not be a hundred percent, but it sounds like one. She tries to reassure me that I may not lose the baby; it doesn't always happen.

'Nick, you need to get yourself to hospital. Pack a bag. You're too far gone to stay at home. There will be a lot of blood loss. Get to hospital.'

I just got goosebumps and broke down in tears. I need to stop writing now. Even now eight years later, I'm crying. I need a minute please. I'm going to find the cat outside. I could use a hug.

It's ten minutes later. The cat's buggered off somewhere, not helping me, so I've watered some plants instead. I own three plants!

I will try to explain the horror of a miscarriage as much as I can, but a few details will likely go to the grave with me alone. I can still see the look of pain… (Hold on, the cat is now here, meowing its head off. Now you show up. Come here, furball. You could speculate me and the cat are linked… nope, it's lunchtime.)

When I was a younger adult, I spent much time talking with my grandma about many varied things. I loved her company. I can still see the look of pain etched on her face as she sat in her armchair in the lounge telling me she'd had several miscarriages and that was why she adopted my mum.

I remember thinking I knew nothing of the pain she felt and yet could see the hurt was clearly still there. She was desperate for a little girl, having had two boys and several or perhaps many miscarriages.

Now I also know the pain. I knew for many years I would have a miscarriage. My midwife friend said, 'That's impossible, Nick.' And yet I knew. Oddly I felt it whilst watching TV, Bruce Willis in *Looper*, in the small old lounge. I would say probably four years or more prior. I remember thinking, *What a random thought to have whilst relaxing into a really good film.* Why did I know such sad news? Why? What was the point? It was of no use and sad, so I never told anyone.

After I call my midwife friend, I have to 'get to hospital' but I can't. I can't physically move. I am losing so much blood I can't get out of the bathroom. I try to stem the flow of blood in and out of the shower. It is everywhere like a horror scene but no matter what I do it is dripping all over the floor, just everywhere. I need someone who can deal with blood and not everyone can. I need help.

Clare dutifully arrives again to rescue me. She is like a big sister really, on hand when I need back-up. We have the most difficult conversation you can ever have through a shut bathroom door. 'Clare, no one knows but I'm pregnant. I'm having a miscarriage and I need to get to the hospital, but there's so much blood.'

'Ok,' says Clare and we try to work through a variety of solutions to get me out of the bathroom including fetching more sanitary towels from her house but it is no use. There is too much blood and they are filled in a minute. I don't know what do. I go back in the shower.

The emotional turmoil inside my head as my world shatters is backed up physically by the raw sight of huge drops of blood spilling all over the pale stone tiled floor. It is such a sad thing to watch. The situation is hopeless. I can no longer sort myself out. It slowly dawns on me that I can't work out what I need to do. I can't fix it. I can't get out of this room.

In desperation I throw open the door standing broken in only my longish T-shirt with a line of blood streaming down my leg to the floor. I have no other options.

'Help me, Clare. JUST TELL ME WHAT TO DO!' I say desperately loudly. I beg her. I can no longer think for myself. I can't cope.

Her face drains in total shock at seeing the sight of me. (Fuck's sake, I'm crying again typing. Come on!)

'Oh God,' she says on seeing the damage, the unfolding mental and physical horror. I am losing my baby. 'Right. Put a towel between your legs.'

We get me into some trousers and finally get me into a vehicle. I get to hospital in fifteen minutes or so of silence. A porter comes out with a wheelchair and I go through to the A&E bed immediately this time.

Eventually I am transferred after a few hours onto the ward. I was in recently for a night just after my son arrived and I am back again and ever since pregnancy, the scans and my rib, it is starting to feel like I live at this place. During the night and day in losing my baby I am somehow ok about it. It is inevitable. It happens to a lot of women all the time. I trudge endlessly to the toilet back and forth, back and forth to my bed. It is an astonishing amount of blood even when you think you're done, you're not.

I talk to the women in the other beds and they are kind. One says, 'You're remarkably calm about this.'

I do shed a tear somewhere. I do not fully cry until my son is brought in the next day. He is wearing these little light blue denim sandals. He looks so sweet sitting on my bed with his seal pup eyes and at that point, I lose it and break down. I just lost a little him or her. All the other women on the ward beds quietly look away trying to give some privacy to my heartbreak that just shows up.

At home we have lost our baby even before it arrives. I mainly sit at the tiny outdoor table and stare into thin air for quite some time. I decide I will cope with this myself and I do not tell anyone. I mean anyone. Coping quietly is my way. My mum guesses at one point, and I actively put her off the trail, as I cannot discuss it.

Only Clare and my midwife know for many, many years. It's clear now that silence is how I operate for anguish, loss and sorrow. All of it. It is all I know. I have the choice not to tell people as no one knows yet and I decide to keep it that way. The hospital signs me off work for two weeks to recover. When alone, I sit and drink a glass of wine every day for seven days, trying to cope with the loss of life and loss of future that until yesterday I carried inside me. One day you're pregnant, the next day you're not. That simple sentence does not translate the effect on you.

## TRYING TO PRODUCE A FOLLOW UP

Making my first was easy. As easy as putting in an order through Just Eat. Making my next is exactly the opposite. It is so hard. Life is not content with me repeating what I know, what I've learnt. Oh no, no, no! (I'm starting to see a pattern here.) This time I am given the exact opposite situation. It's as if life teaches me the reverse in literally everything. I have to learn the lesson from both angles or, in this case, all angles, including the pain of a miscarriage. Really? Do I need to endure so much life training? I am quite keen for an easy life.

So now naturally, I can't get pregnant this time around. I start searching online and looking at fertility charts and cycles and anything else I have to do to get pregnant. I really didn't give a toss the first time! Looking back, it is probably my physical workload as decorating and having a baby are extremely physically demanding. My body is already using everything it has to run two lives. It can't give a piss about creating eggs on top. There is also a basic lack of time too with a toddler, bits of building a house and running a business.

Eventually after a year-ish, I secure another order. My mind is taunted a fraction by my miscarriage as all women (I presume) are wary after they've had one. There may be more. You try to put that to the back of your mind and look forwards as much as possible.

I miss my first scan on purpose as in I don't book one at all because I don't even call in the pregnancy. When I eventually call up the midwife team and break the news, they say, 'Why didn't you say sooner?' Then say immediately, 'Because you had a miscarriage and wanted to get past that date.'

'Yes, that's exactly why.' It is psychological. It is trying to protect myself from further damage.

After all this I want to protect my pregnancy as best I can. I stop taking on stupid jobs with extra risk, like massively high churches and long ladder work. I work two days with a break in the middle and then another two. They are only six-hour days. I still feel very tired as I have a toddler to look after now on all the days I am at home, not resting much at all as any parent will tell you. I paint woodwork in the summer sunshine at my brother's house for a month alongside their friend who is also a decorator and she kindly takes all the high stuff I need to decline.

My life is now well away from any stages, clubs, shows or media of any kind. I actively break up with all social media too. I don't like it much. I only have social media for work purposes. Nothing else. (Only surviving is my YouTube channel and I've not touched it since I left the music industry. It's sitting there waiting for when I need it.)

In this new life I can't go out as I've no time and if I do, I'll be hanging out at the local church with toddlers club on Tuesdays! I definitely have almost no time for all my beloved sports and only very occasionally can I squeeze in a short run. Oh, I do own a rowing machine but am usually too tired to get on it. Seven days a week is the relentless necessity and obvious part of parenting. About once a month I try to swim with Dad at 8 p.m. but I am so permanently exhausted by lack of rest that sometimes I cancel. Another time I try so hard to leave the house and get in his car and then break down crying and go back home to bed. There is nothing left to give.

I do get to spend some time outside at the children's park, perhaps four thousand times at delightful parks in two years at a guess! So, that's fun right? I go out all the time! As time goes on, I become sunlight deficient in winter, but I don't notice for several years! Fortunately, I can replace this simply by scoffing vitamin D. It's not the same as real sunlight and having my own life, but one tiny pill is doing a small and important function.

My rather adventurous life in all its former glorious tales of travelling the world DJing and presenting has firmly fucked off! I am trapped in my village a lot! A whole freaking lot and also the house where I work parenting twenty-four-seven. I take a lot of nice walks at least. Mostly with kids going bananas as they want to catch a passing duck and then having a meltdown when they can't! Defeated, I drag them home the quarter of a mile I may have managed!

In my head alone, I call this my dormant phase. I know I am waiting to get back to my own plans, my dreams and at very least a more normal life one day. (Initially I wrote 'exciting' and I removed that because clearly that's far too much. It's basically just fucking stupid! So, I've revised it to just a little life outside of parenting, the never finished house and Netflix.) I also bypass reading when the kids come as there is no brain space left for those little quiet pages. Not for years and years. I know other friends have said the same. Pick up a book? Are you mad? No chance, no energy! Reading returns one day. Well, one year, although not that often with the constant 'Mum, Mum, Mum' interruptions! That's not to say I resent it. I don't. I love being a parent, but it is fair to say it is challenging on an additional level. I can't just fuck off home after a really shit day! Parenting is the toughest job I've ever had and I'm only halfway in. The best is yet to come (unknown to me at this time).

## THE SPORTS WATCH... FOR PARENTS!

After my broadcasting days I took off my watch and don't wear one for about five years. Having lived my life down to the split second I want to be away from it all. Everyone has their phone in their pocket anyway, so that is enough. Eventually I buy a sports watch in the hope of tracking my fitness and progress. This turns out to be utter crap as the only thing you can really track is the blatant lack of sleep and constant exhaustion. I find it a useful purchase looking at body battery and rest and not so much exercise. I know I've had a workout, don't I? I just did it!

It turns out I am not heading towards mentally falling apart. I am just sleep deprived every single night for more than four years. In my parent life, it takes about seven years to get to normal nights again. When your head's killing you, all you do is glance at the watch stats and feel so relieved. 'Yep, another shocking night.' So, considering that, I am doing ok. There is even a TV ad now with a half dead zombie parent lying on the floor, rocking the cot. It is a whole marketing strategy. People know sports watches for parents tell you you're not nuts! It really does help me to see that on a graph clear as day. Life is tough. Some weeks I may add rowing or swimming but not often as there is never any energy left.

Another clear stat from my watch as a parent of two small things (maybe babies or toddlers) is I am walking 9,000 steps a day. Every single day as an average. Even I look at the results and am stunned by them. Some days I don't even leave the house and it'll still be 8,000. If I go out it can hit 10,000 or 12,000 or very rarely 15,000 steps. The new bigger house has a large downstairs but this just shows you the work going in as a parent that no one notices! Crazy! And there's no day off, basically not ever. Not even if you're ill. You just have to dig deeper into your low body battery so it is not surprising that swimming on top at 8 p.m. is managed about once a month on average.

I also learn with a watch that sleep does not cover rest! I think going to bed is rest enough. Turns out it is not enough at all. If you're working twelve-hour days continually and up for bits in the night, sleep is not enough in itself! This is news to me! Most insightful to see is that I need to aim towards a better balance even if I have to wait or barely survive for years. I'll be honest, it is bloody hard. I look like shit most days! I don't get days off. No time. (That was early on. As they grew it'd be fourteen-hour days and now I'm on fifteen as one of mine doesn't allow me rest! Brilliant!)

In my village I've seen a new woman walking up and down with a toddler. She seems friendly and we've bumped into each other outside my house. I've a huge bump as I am six months preggers. We agree that I may be able to see her after the baby comes as I have zero time to see or talk with any people ever with decorating and a toddler. I have no life of my own, only the parenting one. Many people will be familiar with this necessary total investment of yourself and your time.

Next new friend arriving soon though. Exciting!

## CARS

I also change the car when the Golf gearbox gives out. I buy a mid-range, big ass saloon mainly for the space. Horses for courses. And this vehicle has a family job to do. When Charly 2 arrives for our standard hook-up: a walk, talk and herbal tea, we discuss her current very similar ride, their new-ish sleek white Honda. It is much the same car really, just a different make. After her random flavour and my green tea criteria are met, we go outside and instead of comparing our usual two-litre engine size, BHP and full or part leather interior, we go straight to the back of the vehicle and get down to business.

I pop the button and up it goes with a gentle whoosh, and I proudly state, 'Look at the boot space on that!'

'Hmm, yes,' she nods and agrees. 'That's amazing. Much like mine. Do you remember when we used to stand and look at the front of the car first, like normal people?'

'Yeah, it feels like a long time ago, but hot dang, that's a hell of a parent's car right there. Look at the boot space.'

We laugh at how upside down our worlds have become.

Residing in the boot currently, I have two basketballs, two skateboards (one is mine!), two scooters and helmets, one bucket and spade set, one emergency bag of kids' clothes, one bag of car bits (like tyre pump and jump starter pack) and one standard medical kit.

And I can still get four bags of weekly food shopping in! Fucking incredible, isn't it?

What more can anyone possibly want from life!

## SOUND SYSTEM!

As a last car note, ironically my car has a mighty Bose sound system. It is by far the best and most powerful in-car music system I've ever had. It arrives in my life when my ears are already ruined and I've barely ever listened to it.

Awesome though… Probably!

Well, it is awesome till it malfunctions so badly I have to disconnect it completely. No real loss there.

# CHAPTER 13

# LEARNING ABOUT AUTISM AND FEELING GRATITUDE

## ASD

Since my son was born, I feel sure something is unusual about his moods. I ask my friend Patsy if he is autistic. But she doesn't know. Patsy and I are on a spiritual or social physical energy level like no other. We go to the same church sometimes but get into a fit of giggles (trying not to) but laughing hysterically like schoolgirls on the back row! It is really embarrassing as we genuinely can't stop! All very disrespectful when someone is giving a heartfelt speech at the front of the pews. I swear, it is not on purpose.

There is something up with our energies, like atoms colliding at the worst possible moment. Well, except for a funeral. That would have definitely been worse. We are like two batteries that push the current up. I apologise to my friend, the head of the church, profusely in case she noticed us discreetly pissing ourselves in the audience. She says, 'It's the energy,' and isn't bothered in the slightest.

Back to the point. The clue is in my son only has two settings: happy or seriously angry. There are no in between modes, not a whole range of emotions, big or small, like most people tend to have. The next massive clue something is unusual is swimming lessons. During my maternity leave time with him, I join up to swimming lessons, and it is so much fun. This is my best mum and baby time. By the second trip on the way to the pool, in the car park, he wants to touch every single car, which was probably fifty at a guess. Convinced this will make us late I try to go swimming, but apparently touching cars is way more important. He starts being totally manic (I now know it was a meltdown). I have to drag him screaming into and through reception many times.

We go to the pool and my toddler is the only one going berserk on the sidelines as we wait to start our class. I mean, I am trying to restrain him from getting into the pool, possibly drowning, howling, thrashing about, crying and yelling. All very peaceful parent and baby swimming times as you can see...

One time when we finally get into the class I break down and cry and say to the instructor (with my son having a meltdown in the pool), 'We'll leave.'

She says, 'Honestly, you do not have to. You can stay or do whatever you need to do. It's fine.'

We join in later on after swimming up and down a bit to get moving somewhere. Moving about helps. (This is distraction.) Sitting on the sideline waiting (queuing) is an absolute nightmare. Queuing? Nope, not possible!

I know (I strongly suspected) at eight months old my kid is autistic or ASD (autism spectrum disorder) but the trouble is I've never met anyone with it. I don't really know what it is other than a very basic understanding of something being very different. I have so much to learn and so very fast. The early days are incredibly hard. There is so much screaming. I say the early days and by this it is almost every single day, or at least every other, until about six... yes, six full years of screaming.

Meltdowns last exactly thirty minutes every single time. There is me walking around with my ear plugs in and ear defenders on. I have to keep a pair in each section of the house (otherwise I cannot protect myself from extremely loud, long high-pitch mega-decibels and further noise damage). I have to work out how to try to keep myself safe around this extreme noise. Sometimes, depending on the location of events, it is not possible to protect myself. My ears take a huge hit.

And so, I have to buy more pairs of defenders. One for work, one stays in the car, one pair attaches to the baby bag so I can see them at all times (as not to forget them), one by my bed, and one set in the kitchen/lounge. I need them ready for anytime, every day, when my ears are constantly under such extreme pressure, especially in the huge echoey lounge. Open plan living really is for before or after children! How many times I've thought that since. When it takes two adults to hold a screaming thrashing toddler down just to change a nappy, you know you have something big going on. It's hard. You'll cry.

It is a very dangerous noise level for me to be near and the pitch kids can get to is astonishing and it hurts a lot. It is really sad that because of my hyperacusis being around my own children is painful but I just get on with life as best I can. The trick is to mostly remember all the things you can still do and not worry about all the things that are now gone. I deal with it because I have to.

With ASD essentially everything in the early days is wrong. Every single thing you do or try to do, or don't do full stop! *Everything* is wrong! That is how it feels on an almost daily basis: that you are failing at life and life is falling apart. Stay in, get a meltdown. Go out, get a meltdown. Get in the car, get a meltdown. Sometimes I sit outside the front of the house on the grass, slumped against the cold brick wall with tears rolling down my face. That brick wall is at times the only thing holding me up!

Autism will beat you down hard repeatedly as you grapple to survive each twelve hours or so and try to learn what to do and more importantly what *not* to do!

Important note. Autism does not beat you, but it's the coping with it that can feel like that. Overwhelming, relentless, desperately trying to cope with each day plus any rough nights, whilst trying to understand it, manage it and build a better tomorrow for everyone.

Less screaming is the new goal over the next few years. That sounds simple. There is a bit less screaming by age five to six in the first child, not the second. Nothing is ever the same for me.

## DIAGNOSIS... WELL, MY FIRST EXPERIENCE OF DIAGNOSIS

We get our referral via the health team and start the long process of diagnosis at the age of two. I want to know everything I can to try to make our lives better because I can't even leave the house by myself, take a walk normally, or go out for the day. Nor attempt basic things like cutting fingernails or toenails, or cut hair without extreme lengthy crying and screaming at the end of it, middle or sometimes before I even start! It is so draining day in and day out. I mediate at lunchtimes or whenever possible as I have no evenings as a parent. If they are in bed at 9 p.m. then so am I, and I work flat out feeding, bathing, nappies, clearing up vomit, whatever. It is full on seven days a week. Boy can make an exceptional amount of vomit due to several health matters until he is about six.

Cutting two nails is so bad after not being comfortable with having to restrain him very carefully under my body and legs. Lastly from thought and desperation I resort to doing it whilst he sleeps. This is very effective and yet this does not work for hair! I have to strap him into a highchair with a bar of chocolate twice a year and use clippers to shave his head as fast as possible to reduce his stress to the bare minimum amount of time. He will be at least four before I can take him to a salon at all. A very proud day.

Two years later he is diagnosed as Asperger's, high functioning. (It may just be called ASD now.) Before he is one, he can count to ten even before he can barely speak all the words to count up to ten. I give him lots of fun and educational videos when he is younger as this helps keep him calm and hold his focus. There is a little one to twenty numbers video that has loud music and rolls across the numbers a bit like a dancing rolling pattern. It is very exciting and well produced. He knows his alphabet fully by the time he is two. YouTube is a lifesaver for me. It offers calm moments and it offers me help. He wouldn't have learnt his alphabet from me or from a book as he can't sit still enough, unless it is lining up cars in size and colour order.

His memory is excellent but his language is behind and he has echolalia. I have to teach him how to ask questions, a single question or any question throughout the day which is normally learnt automatically. If he wants milk or food, he can't ask the phrase or question, 'Please can I have milk?' Echolalia by definition means meaningless or unnecessary repetition of words spoken by someone else. So, when I speak to him, he often repeats back the whole sentence, at least for a few years anyway. Having read a book on speech years ago I understand how hard it is to create certain sounds and am able to assist by breaking letters, words and sentences down for him to pick up more easily. He walks at eleven months but doesn't ride a bike till four or five. He learns to swing back and forth on a swing aged seven. He is really frustrated by not being able to swing.

People often say what's the use of a diagnosis. Only with no understanding of the impact on all aspects in daily life can you think you're just ticking a box or it's just a label, what use is that. It unlocks support, guidance and understanding, training and help for playing, speaking, walking or just leaving the house! All the things that everyone else can do, like getting dressed or undressed! You can build coping strategies and help them understand what's going on and how to manage or even avert meltdowns. It's the same as every other thing on earth. Knowledge is power. You can grow from it. I'm sure some people manage without a diagnosis and if that works for you, that's great. I want all the knowledge I can access. I'm not afraid to ask for help when I feel I need it.

Life is so hard in the early days and I am about to have another baby. This birth is totally the opposite to the first, naturally. I don't want to get into huge detail about how traumatic it is, because one day my own daughter may read this book and I do not want to put her off. Plus, one graphic birth story is enough for this book anyway, isn't it?

I'll try to keep it brief or a bit shorter.

## DETERMINED TO ENJOY MY MATERNITY THIS TIME AROUND!

After packing up decorating around seven months pregnant, I book a massage on my first day off work, the very next day. It is one of the best massages I've ever had. It feels so great. What a treat! The next day I wake up with agonising pains in my hands (carpal tunnel). I didn't know it was this and wonder what the hell is going on. I can barely feel my hands. They aren't working properly. They are barely working at all.

I go to the doctor's a few days later as I can't sleep now from being heavily pregnant and the mild cramp-like aches from the carpal tunnel which kindly wake me up exactly every forty-five minutes right throughout the night. As soon as the pain builds up, I am awake.

'Doctor, I can't feel my hands. They are all numb and the aches and pain wake me at night constantly.'

'You've got carpal tunnel and it is likely because you're pregnant. It's quite common in pregnancy. There's more fluid inside during pregnancy and a build-up of pressure on the hand and wrists.'

I am a decorator. Might be that why? There is a lot of pressure on the wrists in the trade, isn't there? I was working just fine until the massage… to relax! But it may just be a coincidence.

The doctor gives me a splint and wants to send me off to another further away pharmacy to pick it up. Are you freaking kidding me? I sit looking at the doctor wondering why. Do you have any idea how difficult it is for me to drive here not feeling my own hands, at seven months pregnant and not having slept in days and I have a toddler? I neatly rephrase this to, 'But I can pick it up from the pharmacy right there in the corridor, can't I? Please? That would be helpful as it's quite hard to drive.'

I honestly wonder what she is trying to do to me. Please give me the splint now, so I can sod off home and not sleep *at all* until I give birth in, let's see, oh two months' time, with no working hands at all and not able to feel my own baby afterwards! Great… Possibly even perfect! The splint does lengthen my sleep from forty-five minutes to an hour or so.

At home I can't even hold my power tools properly. It is very disappointing. I can't use my battery screwdriver to move six small screws out then back in, once. I want to move up the front door chain lock to stop my toddler escaping. I can't even do that, the simplest of jobs. To explain how difficult it is, I spend time looking up carpal tunnel surgery online as I feel that desperate.

I am assured time and time again it will go away after I give birth and it is very likely as I've never had it before. Only sixty horrific nights of not sleeping and difficult days to endure then. Shaun, who I worked with at Vibe, spends a lot of time at ours and manages my IT and websites. He dutifully moves up the door lock for me one afternoon. He has a little baby now too and still manages to kindly visit with his partner Emma and help out. They are such a nice couple to be around.

This labour is, guess what? The exact opposite of course! I am in labour for three days. I go into hospital as requested by the midwives after my waters start to break. I am already pumped up to give birth like a pro. I am aiming for warp speed this time. I want a personal best. I've got my pushing sorted, my breathing right. I am going to take this birth down!

So, I am in hospital around 9 p.m. then everything just stops and eventually, the next day I get released back out. On the way home the next morning very minor contractions start up again. I just stay silent so I can go home for the day. Later on that night, I go back into the very late stages of labour for a second time. I literally feel like it is going to fall out in the passenger seat. The measurements back that up once at hospital.

Ok, so maybe *you* should have the choice here? If you don't want to know how bad things can go, skip straight to

'Full-Time Parent'. I might skip it myself actually, as near death is not a place my head likes to return to, ever.

## DAY THREE OF LABOUR: I'M DYING AND I KNOW IT

After things start to go seriously wrong, I know my baby is stuck but I feel no one is listening to me. I do not want to put in the finer details but this is what I can say. The basics are both my wrists and hands are numb and not working with carpal tunnel. I have canker sores all over my tongue and have binned my tongue stud as I've had enough of pain inside my mouth. My back has gone completely this time, the left middle muscle. Plus, I have bad sciatica for the first time ever that is shooting pain across my bum all the way down to my right knee. My body is a crumpled mess. I am in labour for three days where my waters should be breaking but are not properly and the very unusual stop-start contractions are all wrong. They are supposed to be continuous of course.

I cannot lie down for more than ten seconds because of the back pain in my middle-left side. That causes a huge problem as they can't get the baby's head monitor on properly as I can't lie down. People are getting stressed. No shit! Medically, legally, they have to monitor the baby's heartbeat at all times.

What is happening to me? No one has ever seen anything like it before (great)! It is only as my trainee midwife last time around (who is now qualified) says, 'If I'd not taken both measurements myself, I would not have believed it.' It is stop start, stop start, over and over for days and days. Any woman knows how you have to psyche yourself up for labour and mine keeps stopping and making me restart again.

It is devastating as my body giving birth is continually restarting me. I burst into tears and after that I wonder why the toilet outside the room is opposite the corridor in a place I clearly can't walk to. It is at least seven metres away. Last time there was an ensuite where I took the best shower I'd ever taken, once the job was done and I could stand again. Washing the blood, sweat and tears off felt incredible. Now, I can't even get to the toilet.

Now my head is splitting from lack of sleep and from my carpal tunnel, my hands and wrists are useless, my mid-left back muscles are gone, plus there is the sciatica pain to my leg. My mouth is sore from spots and I have a baby trying to burst its way out of me. And then I realise I can't push my baby out and it feels like an eternity of living hell from around 1 or 2 a.m. till 6 a.m. I become very aware in the screaming of labour and endless hours wasted that I am dying. With no one helping me. Remember, eventually I stopped screaming, pushing the first baby out eventually in silence with the pain score of ten. It is an utterly manageable rhythm after some practice.

My pain is now a clear twenty. This is not normal on a one-to-ten scale. (Now I will be careful how I put this as our midwives are highly trained and do their upmost to stop people from dying on their shift.) I know I will die in this living hell if I do not get help in the form of emergency surgery. But no one is talking about it. My midwife sits at her computer silently typing up notes with her back to me. I guess she thinks if she stops speaking to me for quite some time I may eventually get on with the job.

Make no mistake. I've been in labour for three days now and the baby is stuck and no one is listening to me. They just think I can't push it out. I feel like I am begging for my life, when I can't speak. I am too weak to manage the situation. My life is in their hands and hour by hour passes and nothing happens.

The screaming is so violent. Every breath I am screaming from the excruciating pains; the noise is unparalleled to anything I've ever heard. I am literally screaming for my life with each breath each time the pain comes, less than a minute apart. Even the midwife doesn't know why I am screaming. She says, 'Stop pushing for a bit.'

I say, 'I have stopped.' I stopped pushing hours ago because the muscles that push aren't responding.

'Why are you screaming then?'

'THE PAIN, THE PAIN!'

She says, 'There shouldn't be any pain if you're not pushing.'

I didn't know humans can make noise like that. I didn't know it was possible. I am breaking though nature's torture.

Nothing is right. I know if they do not choose to help me, I will die like this in the worst pain imaginable. It is the weakest position I've ever been in, in my whole life, and I am begging for help but am too broken to speak another breath and no one is listening, not for hour after hour.

Finally, another midwife or someone else comes in and looks and they have a bit of a discussion. She says there are two or three options. I know there is one option. I have to fight my corner in a state that in one to two days I will be dead. No joke. I am dying in labour. I say there is only one option: take her out of me.

They say again, 'You can push her out. You have a choice.'

'NO, I CAN'T! SHE'S STUCK! TAKE HER OUT OF ME!'

(I have a sort of detachment as I write this.) I have to wait for that scream round to finish to catch enough air to speak. I can only manage this one sentence. I grit my teeth, almost delirious and then shout as fast as I can the facts. 'I KNOW HOW TO DO IT... I'VE DONE IT BEFORE!'

They seem to think I'm not trying still. Still?

After, a second woman comes in and examines me. They talk amongst themselves and not to me and she goes off. I feel so alone. I feel it is hopeless. I can't sit, I can't lie down. I can only barely stand with just a shirt on with my body repeatedly contorting violently every minute with no respite and no pain relief except for gas and air which doesn't do jack shit for 'going to die in labour without immediate help'. It is nothing like the screaming of a typical labour. It is a completely different sound now. This woman comes back with a form. She says it is for an emergency C-section and if I choose that option, I'll have to sign it.

I am distraught in my basic need to live but I can't see the form. I have absolutely no clue what it says. I can see there is a lot of text and I can't talk. I hope desperately she is telling me the truth because I am so weak and so incapacitated now I have no idea what I am signing. I place all my trust in that stranger and hope she is telling the truth because I have no other option. If they are fobbing me off, if it is like a hoax signing the wrong form, I'll die. I think they have to be telling me the truth. I am in an NHS hospital but I have no idea what I am signing. I can barely hold the pen. I make an attempt at my signature on the page. It is just a line really.

After waiting trapped in agonising hell for five or six desperate hours suddenly everything happens at once. Maybe the bed is ready right outside the door and when I sign, it is just moments before they come so fast and grab me. It is like a whirlwind collection with so many people everywhere.

I know that finally after enduring this for so long, I now have a chance to live as I am taken away flat out on a bed screaming over and over. This will save us but I can't speak at all as I am whisked away immediately still with harrowing full volume screams rattling along the hospital corridors.

Eventually in theatre they get a needle in my spine after much time is spent feeling for the exact spot, and waiting in between my almost constant contractions and they have to work around the whole body twisting repeatedly, so precisely. After that needle goes in, finally the living hell I was caught in for so long ceases in a moment. The torture stops.

From that injection I sit still upright on the bed but calm and silent as my rapid breathing begins for the first time to return to normal. I think maybe God is with me in that moment when the pain stops. That is how desperate I feel. When you have nothing left. I am finally calm after the horror show I've endured for most of the early morning hours, tagged neatly onto the end of this three-day labour. I don't usually think about things like this. I feel sure I am not the only one who has pleaded with life in such desperate circumstances.

When I can think straight again, I am so aware that millions of women have died since the beginning of time, over tens of thousands of years, in this exact situation or similar circumstances. I am lucky to have been born at this point where the highly skilled and large team of people can fix this problem as routine. Presumably life wants me to live for a reason. It has just signed me off as 'Ok, you'll be fine now'.

## EMERGENCY SURGERY

Surgery is the most surreal thing and I'm not going to detail it all here but after a stop-start, on-off and several different failed attempts to remove the baby, one female voice says, 'The baby's head is sideways.'

There is total silence in the theatre room apart from that. No one speaks… except me. All I say quietly is, 'I told you she was stuck.' I am so grateful to be there getting help.

When they show me my baby, the woman who'd be talking closely to me right throughout the operation comes back and holds her tiny body freshly wrapped in a blanket right up to my face as I can't move much. I look at her tiny features and her closed eyes so close to my face. I break down.

*We are saved* is my only thought. The realisation of what I thought in that instant only then when she is out shows me how close we both came to not making it. I'm not being dramatic. It's just a fact of life. Giving birth is complicated. We live because it is 2016 and I am lucky I have an amazing team of skilled surgeons in our NHS who saved our lives in what for them is just a routine busy day at work. My midwife is at her desk filling in the forms quietly sitting with me in my recovery room. I thank her for saving our lives. It is all in a day's work for them. She doesn't say much. But I need to say that. It takes hours and hours for the movement to return to my legs from being numb.

Not so long ago, women and babies died like that and they still do in many countries, even here sometimes through complications. It is a very scary and very real situation. The gratitude I feel is enormous and is vividly with me every single day for several years.

I am in hospital for a couple of nights to recover in a surreal state of shock. That is trauma, but I don't realise for a while. I have lost a lot of blood which is normal in the operation I am told. I am just over normal at 1.2 litres, which is close to borderline. I am weak but I am alive. My vision is a little grey from low blood pressure. I can't feel my hands from the carpal tunnel but they do come back after about forty-eight hours or so. I can hold and feel the baby properly.

I cannot ever remember feeling such thankfulness and gratitude just to be alive before. Had I lived in a different time, I may have departed, even if they could have saved the baby. I would have ordered them or anyone to cut the baby out and forget about me. An exit point clearly showing up on my map. I've never encounter one before.

## PTSD

We are so lucky to be alive which makes the full-on constant highly graphic flashbacks from PTSD bearable. I have no depression though. I am buoyant after I physically recover from the C-section. This is what gratitude feels like and for the whole team from that night. The first anniversary is the hardest as all the trauma comes flooding back two months prior to her first birthday. I chew all my fingernails to shreds. But after that it starts to disappear completely and is gone within the second or third year. Like I said, we are the lucky ones.

I book an appointment at the library or somewhere in a group to discuss what happens… Absolutely no way. I am not going anywhere to talk with anyone. I manage to tell my mum the full story, as well as Lou and Suzie, then never really speak about it again.

Discussing that night (experiencing what very close to dying feels like) is not a good one for me. I call the midwives and they send the head midwife out to talk with me in person at my house. She assures me that everything that could be done was. Sometimes rare situations pop up like mine and they can't always be accounted for. Something similar had happened with measurements on one of her births once before but she tells me that lady did get the baby out. So, I calculate with my rubbish maths that in at least 3,000, maybe 4,000, births probably attended by the three or four midwives I've met personally, that something similar was seen only once by one other, the head midwife.

Her words and knowledge are sensible and calm in our home meeting. She says, 'Mother nature is cruel,' and that is very true, as I now know firsthand.

When I am chatting with my midwife friend afterwards, who is assigned to me briefly on home visits, she points out that at no point would the midwives let me die.

'I know,' I say, 'I know that. It's the NHS. They are bloody good at what they do.'

She says, 'The difference is you knew without their help you would die; you knew you were dying.'

I say, 'Yes.'

I have PTSD and flashbacks with it for a full year alongside being truly happy.

I deliberately opted for a hospital birth as I knew I needed to be there. I'd felt confident I could fire this baby out in a flash as I'd had a practice run! My midwife friend remembered I'd told her that I felt it might be a C-section a month before but at the time there was no cause for one. I felt it was on the cards for me. I think I feel too much. I've learnt about both types of childbirth now, normal and emergency, and I'm alive and I am extremely grateful.

It turns out I've experienced far more PTSD than I ever realised in my life although I will not elaborate. Life moves on. But with this event, this was the only time I was aware it was happening. The constant flashbacks made it so obvious. I just got on with it and presumably people can experience it far worse than I did. It was a manageable level. I've read recently it has a name. It's called birth trauma.

## NOTE: I AM DONE HAVING BABIES!

I don't know if you remember but there was an old TV advert for the awareness of drinking too much. It said something like, 'Alcohol, know your limits,' and Harry Enfield's comedy sketch came soon after… 'Women, know your limits.' Anyway…

I feel exactly like that with children! 'Children, know your limits.' I know my child limit is two! You may be able to cope with more or less than this number but I have most certainly reached my max load already. For real... I'm done!

Full stop. Underlined.

## FULL-TIME PARENT

I did not realise this would happen and I literally had no idea. Why did no one flag this up? I doubt it would have changed anything. Oh well, in for a penny, in for a pound! I am running my one toddler alongside my own life really well. Then another baby comes along and the whole world stops, as Lou once neatly described it to me. This is a bit of a shock not being able to manage absolutely fucking everything, all the time. And after struggling with... well everything, my body has finally reached its limit. This is new to me. I can't go on... I have to reassess. My body is giving out on me.

It takes a huge number of long hours to run a small business and a lot of strength if you're in a physical role like mine. It simultaneously takes a huge number of long hours to run two small children. I can't decorate and raise two children with hardly any rest as basically rest appears very infrequently with my current family life and kids. Zero days off neatly summarises it. I only count time off in blocks of four hours now. I rarely ever get any more.

First baby is in nursery for a few hours here and there and that is my rest until the second comes along. I get little rest anyway (if they take a nap, I nap). It is clear the only way to survive such long demanding hours every single day (as often I am the only one here) is to stop my small business for now. A shift in work, business income and homelife dynamics has to happen.

I try a couple of paint jobs here and there but it is just an impossibly physical workload. My body can't do that at the moment while they are young. There is no working childcare funding hours for both of them for some years as yet. It isn't what I wanted or ever expected but there has to be change right now so I may as well get on with it and enjoy my new role as much as possible.

Just to clarify, giving up work to work twelve-hour days with kids, every day, is very much *not* giving up work at all! It is just giving up being free, independent, being me and my adult lovely former life!

Let's have a look at all the luxuries that work delivers me and now doesn't:

- not leaving the bloody house to go to work
- not looking at scenery on the way to work
- not driving my lovely car further than the supermarket and the local park
- not enjoying a quiet half-hour lunchbreak

- not listening to the radio (albeit only twice a week for one or two hours on minimal volume with mostly Radio 4 so as to not get any further noise pain)
- not staying fit in a super fit work way
- not enjoying adult conversations, speaking with new customers, other tradespeople and not buying paint!
- not seeing enough freaking daylight for year after year, until I grow limp from sunlight deficiency!
- swapping cleaning up my car and tools for cleaning up butts and exploded nappies
- not going out or into the office to work. Not working, workey, work-work. Did I mention that? I think that means not earning enough money, but I almost forgot to write that

My grown-up independent life is eradicated. I am not the only one who feels they give up a lot to parent full time but that is what needs to happen. Life's choices are thrust upon you and driven by change whether you know it's coming or not. Plus, here in the UK we have one of the highest childcare costs of where? Oh yeah, anywhere in the world, so Google says! And probably on other planets and solar systems as any non-humans would have this way more sorted out than us! So, while they are young, I can go out to work at this point in my life because after deducting childcare and the running costs of the business, I can earn around… minus £20 a day!

Perfect! Yes, MINUS TWENTY POUNDS! Excellent. Plus, I'll be so exhausted from room decorating and dealing with two small kids that within a week I won't be able to stand up.

The new reality is I need to make this work and find joyful moments in multiple arguments for ice cream and catching bolted children chasing after crows. Plus, what? Five or six meltdowns a week? Lucky it is just one repeatedly screaming his head off anyway. That is enough. Just one.

On balance let's take the positives. There are some incredible moments parenting, even around all the meltdowns and crying (that's me crying)! I meet with Katya the new neighbour down the road with her toddler in tow. We have temporarily both swapped our work for this new trade and so we can share this unrelenting day and night child-raising challenge together. I'll text her at 7 p.m. and then walk up the road knocking on her door. 'Can you lend me some Calpol please?' That is our evening conversation. Riveting, isn't it?

## WHAT IS LEFT FOR ME?

The best any parent can really ask for is a bath. That's about all you have left. I quit taking a bath for around four years after the second arrives due to the level of interruptions and screaming outside in the hallway. Even if I try to barricade myself in with the laundry basket wedged against the door and ear defenders on. Yes, in the bath! Somehow a bath is just not working for me anymore. I quit baths and opt for my shower where sometimes I can hit a full five minutes without anyone walking in and yelling for crisps or with arms bleeding from a personally provoked cat attack.

## A PARENT FRIEND TO HELP ME THROUGH

I love how life keeps giving you new friends; it's possibly the best part, isn't it? I wonder a lot about what this exciting new friend will deliver into my life. Exciting, isn't it? I stand with my new baby strapped to the front of my swollen freshly glued up tummy just opposite the front of my house. It is the furthest I can walk two weeks following major surgery. It is a great venture outdoors; I may pass a wildebeest in at least fifty metres or so.

'What do you do?' I ask my new friend.

'I'm a PT.'

'A what?' I'm not sure what PT stands for currently.

'I'm a personal trainer.'

'Oh, ok. I thought you looked fit.'

I wander off home after ten minutes of pleasantries are exchanged. That is basically how long I can stand for at that moment. I wonder why life has done that to me. Delivered me a beautiful, clever, double language speaking (triple actually), fit personal trainer, very neatly packaged as my new friend. I have severe PTSD and am still a post-baby stone overweight (and I mean over my own extra weight) and I haven't left East Anglia in basically forever… well, since 2009 and that was unequivocally forever. My former glorious days of flying around the world for business or pleasure have firmly fucked off!

I ponder it for some time. I don't need a PT although the knowledge will be useful. I never lacked motivation. Motivation is not missing from me, is it? I wonder what else it is because it will be something for sure. People usually arrive to me for a reason. I wait and, as with the rest of life, it will become clear in time. She is funny and cool and has children of the same age; she dresses well as I want her jeans and jacket for that matter! I've never met anyone who's wardrobe I would steal. I even buy her a shirt one year as I know she'll like it.

We meet out in curiously non-wild village locations like a lane with stinging nettles and a patch of trees to have some kind of normal adult conversation. Discussing our love of London and all the former ridiculous things that randomly naked gym people do in the changing rooms! Pool testing and floaters! So gross! I'm not even saying it anymore! Also, her advancing pregnancy during work (which is not tolerated too well by gym goers) and having to tidy up and lift back all the weights while seven months pregnant. Then there is her background in marketing, my presenting and DJ work, all the countries we've visited, places she's lived and life *outside* of the village! Even if I can't get outside of the village mostly *ever* for basically another decade.

It is enough just to have a relatable good conversation about something else and often films. After Sandra Bullock's

*Bird Box* drops, we just start copying her character's kids' names and referencing my two with the same Boy and Girl. It is way cooler obviously! She texts me asking, 'How are Boy and Girl doing today?'

'Yeah, we're great thanks. They've got the pox! Boy looks like zombie a-pox-calypse with a drained white and blotchy red face with sunken eyes. Chicken pox. I've ticked it off our to do list!'

## EIGHT YEARS OF ILL

All this time, I am ill, compared to never having a cold as an adult. My only ever twice a year spring and summer laryngitis (KISS Weekender time of the year) seem a distant memory. That utter shitstorm… I'll say sixty percent of the colds are sinus type ones that for me create severe asthma, and that lasts for eight years!!!! Have a few more exclamation marks!!!!! Eight freaking years! That alone should make you want to eat all the contraception in the entire country. Who knew that could happen? No one, and there is nothing that can be done, so onwards I go with what is left of me. I suppose in all fairness, chronic stress, parenting and life exhaustion play a major part of it as I'm doing a lot better now. I've been ill four times this year almost like a normal person!

In the chaos of never-ending house building and two kids, I also forget to take my steroids. I think I am ok as the nurse has fixed me up pretty good, so I am ok now (huge mistake).

I am away alone looking after a toddler and a baby with a vomiting bug, literally sitting on my mum's kitchen floor having given up on life with exhaustion and quietly crying. With puke all over us, everything from my neck down is splattered in vomit, and I am trying to peel off my soaked stinking T-shirt from my torso without catching it on my face myself. Up day and night in a vomit storm. Then I return straight home having to paint the new-ish master bedroom. Rest is what is fucking needed! Not on my watch… which is basically every day!

My virus turns to a chest infection and spreads quietly unnoticed although a loud rattling in my lungs is ever present when I lie down. It has become normal to me during so many colds. And so here we are again, totally wrecked! Without the dedicated, hardworking staff in my local hospital I would have snuffed it again here. Just around eighteen months from when I last nearly snuffed it! Great!

I only joke because it is ludicrously serious! I could not have pulled myself out of that one. Nope, my body is failing again. My heart rate is stuck high in overdrive, like being out on a treadmill till you die. I can't get my pulse below a hundred so I can't sleep that night without a sleeping tablet. It's the fever that will take you. It's just the same as a car engine running out of coolant. It overheats and boom… eventually it's gone. I've never felt anything like it and there is severe pain in my right back (turns out my lung). I shiver all over like I've been thrown out naked onto the Arctic ice. Then boiling hot after two hours of warming up from freezing cold, back to overheat and then freeze again. A bizarre night before I am admitted to hospital.

After the ambulance crew visited the night before, in the morning, I can hear my mum in the kitchen chatting away. I recruit her to drive me to the doctors who send me straight for an X-ray with suspected pneumonia. I am desperately ill and fighting hard alone in my bedroom to pack a simple overnight bag. Then I limp to the car, shivering in three layers with my hoody up tight around my face with the heating on full.

## EXIT POINT NUMBER TWO

I wind up in hospital again with, and to quote the doctor on the ward, 'A bad pneumonia.'

My reply is, 'Is there such a thing as a good one?' as I lie stretched out on the hospital bed again. I am wheezing through my oxygen mask with half a lung frozen solid and severe asthma restricting the rest. Lou and my goddaughter Zoe, and separately Suzie, look terrified when they video call me. They speak mostly instead as I am too tired and short on breath with my oxygen mask aiding me.

When your lungs shut down there's not much time. It's crystal clear the importance of them functioning. Crystal! Nothing else matters. I am just trying to breathe. I am asked on entry if I want to be resuscitated if I stop breathing.

'Yes,' I reply through my oxygen mask.

She writes something down on her pad.

'Yes!' I say again, 'I want to live!'

'Sorry,' she says, 'It's just we have to ask that question.'

I don't mind her asking the question. I am just a hundred percent making sure she heard my answer. If she writes down 'No', I could be accidently dead the next day. The two small words of yes and no have never had a more important moment, have they? I need to clarify that is what is being written down as I can't see.

My lungs are adequately damaged by asthma and can only have a peak flow or function of around sixty percent naturally. That is without steroids. With a virus or a cold, I am basically moving around on one lung, dropping to around forty percent or more recently thirty-five percent. That's a pretty frightening tightening.

It has become completely normal for me to feel terrible for year after year that I just don't even notice I am moving around with a dangerous virus! Until I physically can no longer stand up. I literally had one drink the day before with Lotty on a rare visit to mine as I felt so dreadful. I thought it may numb my hurt.

After four nights away I am let out and that is in a wheelchair as I cannot walk further than the bathroom. Dad rescues a half dead version of me. He kindly wheels me out slowly with his one fully working leg! Good old Dad. I can't return home on no sleep. I make him take me to his house and sleep for four hours until I am ready to return to my family. Everyone knows you get barely any sleep on a noisy hospital ward and then there are two young children who haven't seen Mum in five days.

## RESPITE

Facing another full six-week recovery with no working body, Clare has to rescue me again and get wood in from the log shed so I can have heating. She lights the fire the first few days and then I continue myself as I don't feel I can keep asking her. I hate the cold and the pain of lifting the logs into the fire all day in winter. It is forty-five minutes a day to run a fire like that. Heating with only a wood burning stove powering radiators is a pain in the ass with serious illness or major surgery. I seem to be making life hard for myself! Stop getting ill for fuck's sake! I miss the former heating button so much.

It is eight weeks before I am fully healed. Until then, I had no clue as to what serious illness was. I was blissfully unaware! After a couple of weeks, I describe my recovery just off the cuff one day. 'It's like if I've been smashed on the rocks.' Immediately it comes flooding back. A clear vision from a year ago. Wow… as soon as I say it, I realise what I've seen. The image is like a photo. I see my body lying stretched out on a huge rock way down on a beach shore.

I start back with yoga as it is gentle and has been on my to do list for about ten years. It just takes me a while. I don't really enjoy it until later. (Recently it does seem to make my aching stiff middle-aged body move much better. I own a blue yoga mat so this is a very serious life commitment, isn't it? Turn on YouTube or Pinterest. I get to lie on the floor a whole too, so it's appealing!)

Around baby time, I get into *Vikings* on Prime. Lou and Katya are on board too. I watch it when I have time (not much). Half an hour about twice a week maybe really late at night like at least 8 p.m.! I love where it is filmed mostly in the Irish mountains and valleys and the greenery. Escape, escape, escape! Boy really likes it too and often comes in and watches the calmer bits and falls asleep on me. It shows how well it is produced if a toddler enjoys the peace and serenity. I love it so much that I have watched it, in full seasons one to four, *four* complete times! Yep. It hits the spot. The latter ones (five and six) are not quite as awe-inspiring. It's all about revenge by then. I have seen them only three times now!

## I LEARN ABOUT AUTISM FOR GIRLS. THE UNFAIRNESS OF IT

Whilst parenting I take just two holidays at Center Parcs from 2009 to the end of 2019 and to Shaun and Emma's exquisite wedding in a castle (it looked like one), the most beautiful French chateau. There I am child free for three days. That is the best weekend ever! Adulting! I survive on three spa days and two overnight spa stays for well over a decade.

I take one more Center Parcs break in 2023 only because I am homeless for a short period and that fills the gap easily and meets everyone's needs plus, I am never very far from my villa. It's hard and sometimes potentially dangerous to travel with two kids who often need more help as ideally you need one adult per child. Hence we always visit the same places and stick to the routine. It only incurs two full meltdowns! That's the extent of my travels in fifteen years. I'm just doing my bit for the planet really and thus concludes my holidays for a decade. It's a very short paragraph.

In brief baby news, my little girl is the exact opposite of my boy. She is a dream baby. She sleeps three hours more or less in between feeds and has four separate noises. One for happy, one for nappy, one for milk and one for boredom. It is amazing. *I got a regular one here*, I think. With varying moods and subtle tones, it is wonderful just to have that calm that I never experienced before. So much so that I say at eighteen months I don't need the two-year health check-up. So confident am I… I *was*!

## MY SECOND EXPERIENCE OF DIAGNOSIS!

When she turns two, my world is shaken so violently like I've been put through a juicer. Now I have two kids screaming their heads off with lengthy meltdowns! It is a perfect scene of bliss in my house!

I keep a diary, as requested by various NHS child health areas, with notes and videos for years until it just becomes a normal process. I spend four years banging on every door, writing to everyone, asking for help and no one listens. (I was up to five and a half now.) I ask for help on and off the whole time and get almost none!

A little after two years, with me scrambling for an appointment at the last minute, the health advisor picks up immediately that Girl is missing some communication, lining up puzzles and eye contact and refers us to the children's department again. They are not interested for the next… well, forever. They are just not interested. I know plain and simple she is on the spectrum but as she does not tick enough of the boy-based criteria boxes, she is just missed by the system. I know, because the NHS taught me what autism is! I can't pretend to know everything as each case is different, but I have learnt a great deal in this area. So why is no one listening?

**REPETITION!**

She continually draws which is acceptable although in the correct places would be best! Cutting is a favourite: pictures, envelopes, bed sheets, blankets, pillowcases, toys and hair. The number of wonky fringes that people presume I cut! Nope, not me! Clothes… actually she's been good at fashion modifications since she was around aged four. So much practice in snipping may have paid off a bit here. (Even just today she pointed out that two ears have been cut off two teddies and Barbie, who survived two weeks, now has a one-sided bob.) Her favourite soft toy goes on holiday to visit our tailor, where she has to sew on four new paws. 'I think someone has been cutting' is the verdict. I am told convincingly the paws had come undone with age! It costs. It costs to fix all the cutting! I give up! Fortunately, so far, the cat has not been sighted as a contender. (In the months that I've been editing this book, the cat's fur has been snipped. A sort of wedge shape had been removed.)

Let's not forget about the cost of pouring every household bottled liquid, shampoo, soap or gel out all over the place. The Sudocrem-covered wall and door take the longest to remove through my exhausted tears although pen does not come off matt emulsion at all.

Every single wall in the house has been drawn on I would say. We are probably at fifty plus pen incidents. Including fresh canvas, and now new bedroom walls topping twelve pen incidents in one year already. Interestingly these do not count as repetitive behaviours! We are talking hundreds of times! Yep, not repetitive at all apparently.

*Apparently*, this is just fine and totally normal! Not to mention £5 homeopathic (tiny tube) of kids gritless, soft toothpaste, the only thing that might get in her mouth as a toddler with sensory issues. The whole tube will be all over the sink, every time within in a couple of weeks. Teeth brushings are not easy at all half the time as a younger kid it was missed for the gagging. There are other social restrictions too, such as panicking as there are three other kids on a trampoline (friends of hers) so she can't possibly get on, at a younger age. Wearing ear defenders at the fireworks and the church for weddings. Freaking out when people look at her. There are a multitude of other things but it's very personal behaviour and I'll keep them private.

## RAGE

You hear the word meltdown a lot these days but let me tell you when a full one erupts it's violent, dangerous at times, and measurable by the time length. Girl's are consistently twenty-five minutes each time when a full one gets underway and still, apparently all that is not enough. Plus, because she does not feel safe to do it in front of others (masking) and therefore stops like a stunned rabbit unable to speak if other people or teachers approach in the school car park (which has happened a few times), it *does not* count! Also note here that Boy has never had a meltdown in school either, and only one on the playing field next door. That's all.

Here's a neat example. Her first day at a new preschool goes perfectly, all six hours, and then we have to stand outside of the car for twenty minutes with her kicking the seat in, crying and screaming her head off. I check with a couple of other parents and no one else has this. For balance I do not survey every single parent! All her group of friends cope just fine with the change of setting. End of rage! There are a lot of diagnoses in her family. Except her, of course. Ridiculous inequality.

## MASKING!

Why does it take me so many attempts to get Girl support? There are big questions we should be asking. Why does no one, until now, even look at *one* single video displaying her typical 'behaviour'? Why does that not count? Unless you meet her in her own environment where she feels safe and she is not masking, at least with my girl, you're not going to see the real deal. Which I think is half the problem.

Unless we do something to change the process and maybe the science behind it many more girls will not get the support they deserve. This is what some girls do better. They *cope*! They cover it up, blend in and cope for just long enough until they retreat to safety. You want to see the explosion then. It's spectacular and frequent.

I've invested a small fortune to get her the extra support she's due through her school years to be able to cope. Boy's diagnosis was, of course, *typical* and therefore free. Is that because Boy ticks all the boy-based boxes? Is this another reason why girls are so disproportionately diagnosed as it's so hard to get the freaking diagnosis? We are emotionally exhausted and half bankrupt and so eventually can't carry on. I have friends who've been missed altogether and mothers who spend twenty years trying to seek help.

I will state that since last year when I was told about 'right to choose', the new NHS free diagnosis, I am reluctant to take it as I've been down a similar road before. I choose a different route.

## BOY-BASED STUDIES AND DOUBLE STANDARDS

Is there enough science based on girls to make the assessments current enough and proportionately equal? Are they fifty percent girl-based and fifty percent boy-based studies? Not from what I've read. Although I'm not an expert, so hopefully I'm wrong and it is in fact perfectly balanced!

Having been asked if I want to train in ASD strategies and understanding by the NHS for years and subsequent local council recommending webinars and meetings, I find it so bizarre that nothing I've learnt counts either! At times, whilst searching for help and support, I've even taken the blame for this behaviour but *only* since I've been separated, of course! Before that I am told I am doing a good job at planning for Boy's needs. What a great job of adapting and strategising.

For Girl my multiple inquiries are just crushed year after year, two or three referral requests in total (I've forgotten exactly). I know I've made at least four separate attempts to seek help in a variety of different ways! So, all in all my quest to seek the strategy support we desperately need as a family, all of a sudden, I'm just being over the top and dramatic! I see quite a double standard from society there. Pause for a moment and think about it. Exceptional, isn't it? Is this the world they will have to grow up in?

Surely it's time to get updating it… Many people are realising that girls are acting differently. It feels like unless Girl is more autistic than Boy, I can't get anywhere and I can't get any help. Trust me, I've tried. The current system will slam doors in your face over and over and over.

What's needed is more studies specifically on girls. I have a girl with five years of notes who can be studied! If she so wishes to get involved. I've fought so hard for her and not been able to give her the support she needs. Whereas Boy has everything, Girl has nothing. Welcome to what having ASD is like for boys and for (not all but many) girls and women. I know we are not alone in this struggle. This is my experience as I cannot speak for every case, but I know other people will read this and go, 'Yes, my girl is ignored too.' Some of them will say this repeatedly. Others will have run out of money and energy to fight on. It's so draining.

It carries on all sorts of implications when truly she can't control some of her behaviours. My friends and family are astonished as they can clearly tell Girl looks more obviously different than Boy! Boy is getting older and blending into life much better. The lack of support and the unfairness is unbelievable. The divide is disgraceful.

Honestly, my friends are completely stunned that we can't get anywhere because they witness the daily and weekly turbulent effect on our lives. Crazy but true. They see all the tears, frustration and upset and all this turbulence has an effect on Boy too. He's trying to live in this house filled repeatedly with total chaos. God knows what my neighbours think! Fortunately, they have all been very understanding so far.

I get so fed up with the NHS dismissing it and only noting 'extreme behaviour' that I take a private assessment where she meets every single criterion for the assessment but not enough in the end. So, in essence I can now, following this report, say factually that she clearly has autistic traits, sensory issues, one-third speech and language, has quite hidden delays and personal skills, and emotional regulation difficulties. The ADOS-2, a specific part of the diagnosis test, clearly states moderate autism and *still* does not meet criteria in a couple of areas mainly social interaction and restrictive behaviour.

This is another arse kicking from life where I get to experience it from both sides. All the help in the world and then repeatedly nothing. And this is just a brief description of only a few areas. The more personal stuff I would not want to add into a book. I've proofread this with both of my kids to make sure they are happy with what I'm sharing. Sharing being the basis of helping. Maybe the start of a conversation for change will be the best possible outcome.

**NEVER GIVE UP**

Anyway, since writing this chapter, I've found fresh hope in the form of searching for a new company and a doctor psychiatrist specialising in ADHD and autism *and* the overlap in between. It takes me months of searching to find someone so perfectly knowledgeable in both areas. I can't fail again but of course I might. But I'll only truly fail when I give up trying and guess what? This doctor entirely agrees with everything I am saying about Girl and the challenges she faces including social problems, stress and behaviour regulation. Is it enough though, because of her clever mind and masking all day at school?

Now perhaps she was better able to blend in when younger, but now as she's growing, age is highlighting her personal struggles. I really thought I'd exhausted all possibilities after five years but there is a couple more ways to try, so I'm looking at these now. I will not give up on getting the help she deserves, so she does not have to go through life punishing herself for her extreme behaviour when she can't cope. Boy has all the support and, rightfully, so should she. Therefore, I will not drop it until I have tried everything. When I hear no again, this time, I may drop it. It's so draining that for me this is my last attempt.

## ASD INFORMAL TRAINING

I train in person with NHS child health specialists in autism understanding and strategies sometimes biweekly, but on average monthly, for two or three years.

I discuss and take advice from the NHS and the School Nursing Team (separate from the school) for two years. Quarterly conversations on average.

Via Sendiass online I take part in two courses with webinars over a six-month period: the Girl With the Curly Hair Project and Comic Strip Awareness. Discussions, ideas and strategies.

I've also taken a couple of parenting courses and webinars online. I'm no way a perfect parent. In fact, half the time I feel useless and fairly frequently I'm broken by it. When no matter what strategy I try fails and we go through the full force of ASD at its most powerful, it hurts and I cry. Sometimes I reconcile that I've done everything possible so I can't blame myself for the outcome. Other times it just bounces off me like it's just another typical rough day. We have them all the time! Like just the other night in the vets which ends in total carnage. I have to go back in and apologise to the receptionist! Several people pass by our car still in the car park twenty minutes later, looking briefly to see if the children are being abducted. There is an astronomical amount of screaming!

Ultimately, I've gained some valuable information and a little more progress each time, although I feel it's not enough. Not yet. Either way when I've exhausted all possibilities, and only then, I will know I have done enough.

Effort in, yes! Despite there being no result out for Girl… so far. (None that I will accept.)

# CHAPTER 14

# THE 20S: FIXING BURNOUT, RESTARTING MY LIFE AND WRITING A BOOK

## FOOD REVOLUTION

During my home parent phase I find the time to invest in my health and a full food revolution occurs! I cut out yeast (following the YorkTest results) for a year and it is the best stomach health I've physically reached so far. It is almost working normally. Well, apart from the fact I still can't eat too many carbs for the pain in my upper ribs, or any fruit or starchy veg without spiking sugar, and the night sweats causing sleepless night. Fed up with eating only one piece of fruit and basically green vegetables for years on end, I take on board my newly trained nutritionist, my oldest mate

Kate. She's called KT now but to me she'll always be Kate in much the same way she calls me Nick! Anyway, delivered over nine months, in stages, we rebuild my completely knackered, burnt-out body from the inside out. I own gut bacteria! Possibly for the first time!

That's a joke obviously but at some point, they must have buggered off. At my worst I own only roughly a handful of functioning different types of gut bacteria. The other rather useful ones are dead or vacationing in the Maldives. Hence, I can't eat because I can't process the sugars in carbs, fruits and essentially *any* sweet vegetables like carrots and parsnips. It all has to be heavily restricted to limit my night sweats. Before this I ate mainly butternut squash, brown rice and green veg for eighteen months solid with no potatoes or anything different carb-wise and there is only so long you can do that for! After that my body literally goes, 'I can't eat that orange squash again.' It point blank refuses! The conclusion is I lack diversity in my gut so it can't break down foods adequately, along with some markers suggesting inflammation. The tests confirm Kate's hypothesis which is great. We have much work to do.

## FIXING BURNOUT

I've been living in burnout for so many years that I can't say exactly how long but I think at least a few years. It feels almost eternal, a disastrous fatigued state of lowness and now, eventually, I am trying to salvage my body back from the brink. We test my adrenals to discover I've been living with adrenal fatigue and conclude that I am making steady progress at pulling out of this phase. We take small steps to address this, and repair and rebuild with probiotics, prebiotics, targeted vitamins, minerals and some other stuff I've forgotten. I put my entire old life in the bin as it is adding to the problem, if not the main cause. Drastic measures are needed.

With my nutritional revolution, I learn about healthy eating and what the body really needs to repair. When I start to dip, become emotionally or physically stressed and nudging into burnout again, I am consequently ill and the night sweats start to creep back in. Now I understand what is happening, it is easy to manage, having gained the knowledge to correct it myself. Eliminating as much stress as possible also stops it before it begins. At last, I can eat fresh fruit of any colour that I choose and it is amazing. I can eat fruit every day now. It is just such a simple job to be able to eat what I couldn't eat for a decade.

I learn about the point of fresh vegetables and become some use in a kitchen. I work out how to produce average and decent meals precisely cooked in the right way, but most importantly I learn what a vegetable is! I mean a nice tasting vegetable and how to cook them all differently. Thank you, Suz. I also use the internet and buy books, but books and I just don't work out well in the kitchen. My accidental teachings from The Chef pay off and now I eat any vegetables I like.

My last kitchen weapon is a notebook. As I can't remember anything, I keep my thirty-ish recipes that I like in the notebook. All spaced out in my usual bullet point directions so I can read fast and easily. I realise you need an excellent memory for lots of recipes and I don't have one at all; it's missing completely! The notebook stores it all, where my brain won't. It's so simple and it works.

I have currently quit cooking for years in favour of writing a book, which I much prefer! Well, I cook all the time for the kids. That's enough, isn't it? Cooking is just not my thing and don't even think about baking!

## ABSTINENCE

Having preciously quit loads of things including foods, smoking, partying, milk and listening to music (although sadly not by choice), I feel I have a good chance of quitting alcohol.

I quit alcohol in my longest personal challenge ever starting around 2018 and then into the next few years and even when my life is utterly falling apart. I take this on and I win. I smash my goal. I like the challenge of abstinence because I feel in control of something. That I don't need to rely on stuff to prop me up although I'm human, of course, and I do sometimes. Also, I like it as it drives change moving forwards with habits, not back. It is important to me to succeed at something whist I have practically no time to achieve anything else. I guess I function better with a project!

I achieve a full two years of being teetotal in the year before and during the breakdown and collapse of my relationship and through the following years of separating two lives conjoined like a marriage in the divorce-like process. I have found one drink I can now have that is sort of, or mostly, safe for my body! I drink the odd whiskey rarely as I don't have the time or much call for it, but on occasion it makes a pleasant change.

## LOCKDOWN

Everything I'd built to balance my noise exposure and stress in my life is taken from me in those three months. Psychologically, I lose all my external child support from nursery, school, parents, friends, parks, walks, swimming, meditation, a massage at the salon and all those kinds of things, like everyone does. The only good thing is the weather as it is unusually sunny with clear blue skies for months on end. I'm grateful we have the garden as I know millions around the world don't.

I resort to taking two showers a day as it is all I have left to be still and alone in the water for ten minutes. I find it hell, just relentless. I try to deal with one day at a time. No past, no future, no hope, none of my family around anymore to offer time or conversation. No friends, just today 7 a.m. to 9 p.m. every day. Just get through. The kids ask constantly when they can go to soft play. They ask nearly every day that I remember. It is heartbreaking to watch their little faces sink when I have to continually say, 'Not today, not this week,' over and over.

Around week six or so something amazing happens that I never heard on BBC News (which is on for hours and hours each day in the lounge). It's possible I just missed it as I don't 'watch' any news except obviously some brief bits that are needed during the pandemic to work out what I'm legally allowed to do in a society with our known world crumbling. The very basics are: can I go food shopping or not today?

From around the age of twenty, ever since I started in broadcasting, I read the studio newspapers daily. As an older adult I get fed up with generic TV news with no fair, interesting or decent global content. After trying some different news feeds, I settle on one news app. After some years with this in my life I realise I'm in some kind of important relationship with it! They have become my window to the world, my interesting friends, people on the pulse with a huge variety of news and culture. And not just local stories confined to this tiny island that I live on. I love how they don't hold back and tell it like it is. Real reporting, real news although we're currently on a break. I must delete it so I can focus more time on writing this book! No offence, guys. You rock. I'll be back.

I find this article, about ten days old by now, on my news app towards the end of April and it just changes my life and our lives. At some point around week six of the first lockdown it is decided that people with learning disabilities and autism can go out. Not that it 'appears' to be reported on the TV news in the lounge that only features coronavirus news continually as all other news has apparently disappeared from the entire planet. Now I can take my kids to the local park or a short distance in the car to the fields or paths. It is like a miracle; I've been thrown a lifeline to leave the house.

I hate not being able to go outside. It's like a nightmare to withstand and I'm sure many feel the same. It is genuinely making Boy's symptoms worse as if he's in too much it becomes the norm then trying to leave the house again becomes a massive issue. A reduced minuscule world of just a one-house world is unchallenging and so simplistically easy. Going out is vital to a normal routine. It's the coping mechanism, just to be able to leave the house, and these are all the bits that other people don't see.

## FURTHER DAMAGE

Physically for me there is the continual additional noise. I get through six weeks of the first lockdown without any pain then it is too much. I live in an incredibly noisy, echoey house filled with everyone for fifteen hours a day. I can no longer cope with the pain and start taking pain relief once a day and that lasts around ten months. Sometimes, I can go every two days. It causes headaches from new things like phone calls and friends talking, just normal everyday stuff. It is a new level for the next ten months. Thank you, lockdown, and I mean, in all fairness, I've got two kids who scream a whole lot of the time (even to this day) and two ears that can't deal with that. Another of life's ironic games aligns nicely there via lockdown and hyperacusis, sort of like a double attack!

It's eased a little now by adding in a balance of quiet time but mostly I have to use subtitles now and ride the volume between four and six, sometimes ten if it's a quiet scene. I can't watch a film normally with my family. It's not possible anymore. Mostly I don't take anything for it now. Maybe a couple of days a month depending on what happens. Mostly it's all the screaming I endure that's the worst cause of pain now. I try a pantomime at The Junction in Cambridge. I manage half of it before walking out and have a headache that lasts for three days. Sometimes you just want to try to do normal things, like go out, even when you know you can't! It's important to try sometimes.

## I AM AUTONOMOUS

How did I get there? On a more serious note, a few short years after both children arrive, my relationship (that I refer to as a marriage) is broken beyond repair. It has been crumbling for quite some time. That's a terrible place to reside. It is failing me and this situation has to be accepted, but I can no longer accept it. Change is necessary. I do not live, I only exist. When the lows outweigh the highs, it's over. I beg life to help me and not to have to make this decision, but nothing changes, so ultimately, I have to do it. I do it all alone. I tell no one to minimise the fallout and stop any potential damage to others. I dig so deep, to the deepest depths of courage that I've ever had to find, to walk out on my life. It is necessary and deeply upsetting to rip apart our family for good.

I can write a million things here, but I won't because I've got young children.

'Autonomous' is another word given to me spiritually to understand by living through the experience. Now that's just a word, isn't it? Autonomous? But there are implications of being and functioning at such a basic level. You're in a family and yet you're separated from life, from living. Being separate comes at a huge cost to both your mental and physical wellbeing. It's a downwards spiral of living but not really speaking, going through the motions, year after year. It's just an existence. How has my life arrived at this?

Professionally speaking this mode is called 'survival'. At this time, I do not know it exists. I know nothing about the human mind. I have much to learn the hard way. It is a bad time. A very bad time that over many years has sadly become normal. A normal state does not mean acceptable.

When I realise the extent of what I need to do to fix my life, I carry the overwhelming burden of breaking up our family for so long. My mother left when I was eight and although she is still around, I feel immense pressure and burdened with how to try to get it right for my kids.

The first lockdown nearly finishes me off. It is a living hell and so I go before the second one comes. It serves to shine a spotlight on all the cracks. It is brutally honest. If you don't face any problems perhaps you had a great time in isolation, but that is not the case for many. It is one of the worst years of my life. I operate mostly in silence except when I call The Samaritans four times that year. They are great listeners and very enlightening I learn. It is probably the most valuable set of phone calls I ever make when I choose to go it alone.

When there's nothing left to fix, it's time to go. Eventually, I leave.

## I QUIT MY OLD LIFE IN LATE 2019

I leave for the only place I can afford to go: my old rental house, having not been able to work full time since the first child arrived. I think deeply about all the women and men who would not have this back-up. It is ironic really as I tried to sell it ten years prior to invest in the home extension, but it just didn't sell after five months on the market, so I kept it. That's just pure luck or fate, or I prefer the word life. It is just life.

I guess no one ever thinks they will arrive at a low and I have been there for a long time. I take a Tim Han masterclass online. He's like a life coach of sorts. He does not suggest this exactly, but from this session I rate my life. I give it a two out of ten. I only rate it that because of my two kids. I use it like a starting point and over the following years the number slowly and steadily grows. I clearly remember reaching a five and thinking that is good progress, until I come right back up again to where I need to be in my flow.

In my second week, I set about the long road to rebuilding my mind and my health with counselling. I have never experienced it before. It is amazing. Everyone should try it if you reach a point where you need resolution. Go for it. Find a good one and stick with them. I find a new way to process and talk about emotions! I've hidden so many, for so long that there is a great deal of hurt to be undone. I even deliberately make myself cry now if I feel the emotional pressure is too high (if I'm starting to act too weird)! I learn to manage stress better, not always easily but better. I find that a simple release of built-up tension is really effective. Not just if I'm out filling the car with diesel or something, but at the right time and place obviously! Crying is useful and I never really viewed it like that before. I give it a bit of respect for it doing some chemical balancing.

I know all too well how this level of stress can show up in any number of health issues as time goes by. I want my energy back, the life force that has drained out of me. It is another understanding and a new teaching from life and how to heal from almost completely broken low energy. Reiki is a huge help to me here. It helps me balance my body systems better through energy flow by releasing my stress. I highly recommend it for energy balancing and stress relief. It serves me well. Who doesn't like getting to lie down peacefully on a bed for forty-five minutes with nothing to do and no interruptions? Come on, what's not to like?

I sell my quad bike, leave my partner, my home, the family business where I have a small admin job, even my cat. I leave the cat to minimise damage and to be kind although I want my cat desperately. I've never left a cat before. It is a kind of lasting empty. Every week I walk past the cat food shelf in the supermarket, always looking out of habit but walking past without picking something up. We are separated for a year before she almost magically appears one day with her worldly goods. A box of Felix, a bag of biscuits and two food bowls. We spend what precious time she has left together. Life sorts it out for us. Although she does nearly eat one of the hamsters. Never stop to send a text when cleaning them out!

## PERSONAL MISSION: SLEEPING

It's 2023 and ever since I left KISS in September 2010 I've made it my life mission to learn why I do not sleep well. I learn over the next decade it is linked to many different things. One by one I eliminate 'all' the things that keep me awake. I'm still not great at sleeping but much better than before and that's progress. If I work out or just physically move around a lot, I sleep better. Sitting at a desk is bad for me! I use my Shakti mat a lot, the miniature bed of plastic nails. It helps me drop into the rest state that I can't reach well without it. It's like a setting for sleep that I don't have naturally. I probably have it somewhere; I just can't bloody find it! Sleep is a work in progress.

## WHAT I BIN...

- Shift work. This screws me up badly. I'm just not tough enough for it!
- Energy drinks. How bad are they? I know, I took them for fifteen years or so.
- Food reactions from acidic things like lemon and citric acid, my kryptonite. It's in so much food.
- Takeaways are very limited as you don't always know what you're eating unless you can be arsed to read the entire nutritional content online for three dishes.
- Sulphites are terrible for asthma and sleeping.
- Even my asthma steroids keep me awake FFS! I literally must choose between bloody breathing and sleeping, every day! It's utterly stupid!
- Low balance of gut bacteria (sounds riveting!), causing night sweats.

- Workouts too late at night or too little!
- Staying up late. My body decides it's doing a night shift and then can't sleep at all! It's years of programming!
- Hormones. Fluctuating little tossers!
- Alcohol will always screw up your sleep.

A huge list and there's more, but I can't be arsed to write them all. It's not that interesting.

During this quest, I also gain a lot of insight into my blood sugars which is my other personal mission!

## PERSONAL MISSION: REACTIVE HYPOGLYCAEMIA

I don't want to manage it. I want it to fuck off! I've always remained committed very long term to my aim of finding a way to be free of the hideous reactive hypoglycaemia that's ruined half of my life and ruined most of my body externally. My main organs are holding up well despite the decade or more where it forces me to eat. I call it 'chained to the fridge'. It is so bad that if I don't eat, I feel sick, then I get shaky and hungry, followed by buckling over with stomach cramps and then vomiting at the end from hunger all in three to six hours of not eating in the daytime. At night I may make eight hours sometimes. It ruins my life to a certain extent. I hate it.

At home I have a few times been so ill from not eating (when I didn't know I had it) I can barely walk and I am hunched over in pain. But the worst one was at Global Gathering when

I became almost unable to speak, couldn't walk and nearly blacked out shortly before I arrived on a medical bed. In part it destroys my normal life. I can only speak for my own experience with this condition, not for anyone else.

I've had to force feed myself daily for about the last nine years to get the around 2,000 calories I'm burning each day. My body will not burn fat stored, only new calorie intake. It's a living nightmare. It's hell every day and incredibly expensive as everything I eat is designed to be slow digesting to stop me from having to eat more, like steaks, green veg and brown rice. Never white, it's useless for hypo. And gluten and yeast free. I track this exactly with calories uploaded on MyFitnessPal. I am accurate within fifty calories every single day, so I know these stats are true.

Life hilariously makes me intolerant to half the food available and then gives me a medical condition whereby I have to eat all the time. Plus, it's taken me my *whole* adult life so far to figure this out! That's a very funny joke, life! Only if you've lived this day and night (full night sweats) for twenty bloody years, can you laugh at the irony and cruelty of the two conflicting situations. Thanks, you total asshole! Who planned my life? Was it a joke that I was not in on? Anyway, if you're spiritual you might assume I planned it all a long time ago. If so, that was a foolishly stupid idea, wasn't it?

Anyway, funny aside, the doctor once says to me, 'You've described that with a simply brilliant analogy.' I use car fuels as my description. My body will only burn dirty diesel fuel (food). It will not access any of the electric battery (fat stored). Whatever calories are burnt, the fuel gauge then reads empty, which equals hungry! It uses even more calories in (food) if I decorate and burn 3,000 calories a day but I still must eat 3,000 calories a day to stop sickness, vomiting and insomnia because it refuses to select the right fuel source. It will not alternate between diesel or electric. A situation from which there's no escape!

My fuel switch is broken. The fuel programme is faulty and it's a viciously cruel perpetual cycle. For example, if I'm really ill with say asthma or Covid, I still have to feed myself the probably 1,800 baseline calories or I'm sick from reactive hypoglycaemia on top. It is a horrible condition to live with. When I am pregnant, I am forced by chronic hunger in the third trimester to eat every three hours for twenty-four hours each day for around three months. I only put on a stone in body fat, the other stone was baby and packaging. Baby comes out so thin he is only a fraction over the safe level where they then keep the baby in hospital. I get to four hours on baby two, maybe as I can eat some more fruit that time.

It's important for you to note that I can only share my own personal situation. I do not pretend to know how it affect others. I've only ever met one other person who has it. All I can do is to never give up trying to find the answer. Never give up no matter how many things I read, therapies I try or money I invest in looking for the switch to break in my defective programming. I am stuck with this for two decades.

It's taken me twenty years of searching, trial and effort. Now cure is a strong word so I don't use the word 'cure' yet as I have to go the rest of my life without it emerging again and my body could switch back onto that faulty setting at any moment. For now, I can say I'm in remission from it. I wonder whether to use that word or not, remission, but it really has tried to kill me a few times. I just only wrote about the worst ones.

If I don't eat within twenty-four hours, I'll be unconscious. One day I'll be a hundred percent fine and the next my speech becomes slurred, my body shuts down and I'm close to slipping into unconsciousness from dangerously low blood sugars. It's not pleasant and it's physically painful. At times my body has tried almost eating itself from the inside out when no new food comes in. I've had trouble standing from severe hunger when everyone else is just normal. I just thought I was a lightweight. I didn't know it was a medical thing in my twenties. It's a pretty serious situation I've endured several times. It hurts.

Every single thing you do at home or outside you have to factor in your next snack or meal to balance the blood sugars. Make sure the freezer and the fridge has enough stock. It's a bit like when everyone panic buys for Covid in the early days, except that's my normal week. Every day, every car journey, every trip or holiday, every friend's house, every A&E waiting room visit.

Whatever I'm doing I need, ideally, food that's slow releasing low glycaemic index. Ideally high protein and fats are best for me. I don't eat sugar unless it's in fruit plus ideally wheat free, gluten free, yeast free and sulphite free because of asthma. It's an almost impossible list to juggle. Although if desperate I will eat literally anything that's available. *Anything*. Survive first, worry about the sandwich later. Honestly, it's a total pain in the ass and continues through each day and night, year after year. It's a food and blood sugar trap that you can't escape.

## CURRENTLY, I DO NOT HAVE REACTIVE HYPOGLYCAEMIA!

Since September 2023 I'm free. That's big news!

## FACTS

I was not born like this. I did not inherit genes as no one in my family has this. I did not contract it from someone else. All of which leads me to believe that my body caused this. But how? Why? Spiritually and in a more Eastern approach to thinking about health issues, did I cause this situation or did external events happen to me? Was this illness made as a reaction to events I experienced? Again, I can only speak of my own accounts and not on behalf of others.

## WHERE IS THE ROOT CAUSE?

Is the illness connected to my stomach or my brain or both? Where does it start in me? These are the areas I have specifically concentrated on by reading dozens of books on personal healing in many forms. I've taken many forms of non-medical treatments. Remember there is no cure, not according to Google, only foods to manage it.

Only *manage* it? Jesus, I don't want to manage this for the rest of my days, forcing myself to eat calories, thousands and thousands of them, that I don't want. I get fatter and fatter every day as a result. I want to stop eating so much protein, so many animals. I want it to stop! That is my goal. If I can fix me, can others be fixed? Online I've never seen the word cure. Maybe you have but I haven't. So, if there is one, it must be rare as it's not at the top of Google.

## TURNING HYPOGLYCAEMIA OFF!

Throughout my twenty years I am shown glimpses of hope that keep me going and forge my curiosity. Glimpses of it switching itself off for short periods. Ranging from twelve hours to two weeks but it always snaps back on right into full-on reactive hypoglycaemia. It is devastating every time.

The freedom of not having to eat continually, to wake up not starving hungry every single morning (if I even make it through the night without hunger). Not buying the entire supermarket every seven days. I watch the scales go down immediately, then it splutters. My stomach engine stops working like a normal person and switches back again to faulty. Decorating is the only thing that brings me into some sort of normal weight range.

My normal setting is reactive hypo. In my normal setting of faulty and with chronic hunger again, I gain weight constantly and permanently every day with no end. I have to keep two different wardrobe sizes to allow for this over the last twenty years. That's due to the physical work. If I'm at desk, I'll gain weight no matter how hard I exercise but if I'm decorating it gives me a chance and I lose weight. Essentially, I must exercise a phenomenal amount to get near to regular! Decorating is my only way at the moment.

It's interesting that my hospital tests show I'm 'not' hypoglycaemic as when taking the glucose blood tests I am 0.1 over or under the threshold. The hospital man is extremely unhelpful with no advice whatsoever. He says only one thing to me: 'You're not, so goodbye.' Helpful I know! Next my GP takes a look at the results and says, 'Wow, 0.1, so basically you are, aren't you? Given you suffer all the reactions from it, you really are close enough.' It's good to get clarity on it. One test result, two very different answers!

## GLIMPSES OF NORMAL

I have been free from hypoglycaemia on these specific occasions. First one is spiritual healing at my church. I have been involved in perhaps forty or so energy healing sessions while I study energy flow. Only once my teacher Carol gives me healing and something else happens other than relaxing and possibly healing. There is a huge shift, a let go of tension, in my head, neck and shoulders. My shoulders feel like they drop two inches and I feel a huge sense of calm and know the universe will look after me.

I walk out of there and feel physically taller, more upright, more confident, as I walk over to my car. I know something big has happened. I feel different. I am not hungry for five days. It is so incredible to be free from food. Free from the fridge. One night I literally eat half a sandwich at a family party and go home and sleep easily with no food in me at all. It is like a miracle. Something I thought impossible has just happened. Only devastation follows as the hunger kicks back in on day five. I go to probably six or seven healings again after that desperately trying to hit that spot again. I cannot.

But it teaches me the most *vital* lesson. It can be switched off; it is not permanent damage. If it's not permanent physical damage, then it must be something like chemical or hormonal, muscular or tension, emotional or psychological or perhaps the vagus nerve and gut programming? I need more knowledge to understand it better.

## FOOD POISONING WORKS (ONLY ONE IN TEN TIMES THOUGH!)

Even through vomiting and food poisoning I still need food with my faulty setting. I only ever have two where I don't feel hunger. Yep, all the rest I have to endure cramps, vomiting, probably the other too and still bloody eat. Otherwise, within a few hours my blood sugars fail and then I am ill with that as well! Once, this happens and I reset to normal briefly and I lose half a stone in two weeks (remember to cook pork properly). It does not last, so why not?

I hate food. It's pretty clear it's ruined my life. I do not eat for any physiological reason. It's purely chemical. You can't outrun chronic hunger because it will try to kill you. So, should I repeatedly give myself food poisoning? I consider it seriously. I don't think this is a viable option to controlling it, plus I could die... probably not ideal. Also, with eighty percent of food poisonings, I still feel bloody hungry!

Is it an energy block? Is it a broken connection in my stomach? I don't know. I'm looking for the specific body part that's broken or blocked. I've been through a course of reiki and acupuncture and a truck load of counselling, but this does not cure my hypo state. It is utterly fantastic for stress relief, and I highly recommend all of it.

I once have a counselling session and following that I walk for a few hours by a river, meditate by the lake and snap. I am free for twelve hours. No dinner that night! Amazing news! But it does not last! *But*, a big but, I'm on the right track somewhere. Therapy just nearly works. That is a breakthrough in a new way. Plus, I'm not puking anything up. It is better.

Once, using meditation after practising Wim Hof's breathwork techniques (The Iceman), I physically open the tightness in the top my head and it lasts for twelve hours where I feel no hunger. My head feels completely empty for that one night. It almost feels like I'm walking on air! More progress but temporary and it causes a severe headache which is quite an unpleasant side effect. I've tried twenty times since, but do you think I can reach that state again? Nope! Still disappointing. All good research though.

But after ten years of experimenting, I'm starting to believe the blockage, the root cause, is my head not my stomach. Brief unblocks are coming from healing, counselling, hypnosis, food poisoning and breathwork. How can I get it to last?

I want a permanent solution. I want a cure.

## HYPNOSIS

Once, I hypnotise myself with Paul McKenna's hypno gastric band. It works the first time only. Believe me I've tried more than thirty times since over seven years or so and it refuses to work again! But another glimpse of reactive hypoglycaemia being turned off. With that I lose half a stone in two weeks. Piece of cake. Well, I don't eat cake but you know what I mean. Peace of steak is more like it.

So, is the problem in my stomach? I previously saw a hypnotist for weight and she was no use at all, so I gave that up. I don't like food so thinking myself thin is not the answer here. Will power is not the issue. After many years I take on board a second hypnotist and although we do some good sessions it does not get me the result I am searching for. We do bump into a fun regression though! I show up as a boy on a boat which I know already is pretty accurate. Still no progress though.

I start with a third hypnotist. I do not give up! Have you noticed? And I get a hypno gastric band. It lasts ten days and I lose three pounds. Tosser! Not the hypnotist, she is great… Tosser reactive hypoglycaemia. A gastric hypno band should stay in place! What the hell? Not for me as it is twice now that they have stopped working. I reassure her it isn't the first time one has fallen off and one day I will come back to her. In the meantime, I have to finish with my nutritionist to be sure that is all fixed.

FFS… what do I have to do to beat this? I'm running out of ideas.

## STOMACH SURGERY

I've looked at surgery three times over the last five years and it ranges from around £4,000 plus. I look at a gastric band, which I'm not quite heavy enough for. The problem with surgery is there are risks of complications and (rarely) also death and I have children so that's out then!

I also call and investigate the relatively new gastric balloon pill thing. But we (the consulting doctor and I) can't be a hundred percent sure if, when restricting my food with a virtual huge balloon in my stomach, this will in fact set off my reactive hypoglycaemia, meaning in less than twenty-four hours I'll be rushed to hospital dying from my own surgery with dangerously low blood sugar and needing surgery to remove it!

If there's even a chance my body knows that the balloon is not real food, I could die as I then can't access the near 2,000 calories a day I need currently. Great… Bollocks. Life is unfair.

I read a great deal on self-healing and energy flow. Donna Eden has a book titled, *The Healing Power of EFT and Energy Psychology*. Donna is a world leader and teacher in energy healing. She cured herself from fast approaching death from MS. Like many other books I've always been fascinated by how to gain these skills for myself. Is it possible that I can learn or master the power of total self-wellness like Wim Hof has?

All the indicators are if I can locate the switch in me that's faulty, if I can then isolate the root cause and fix that, I can be fixed. I will try till the day I die to figure this shit out. I want my body back. Desperately. Let's remember I can work out five times a week or decorate for twenty-five to forty-five hours or be on a building site twelve hours a day and still be heavy! What gives? Nothing by the looks of it.

## THE THRIVE PROGRAMME

Taking the Thrive Programme is incredible and it helps me better align my thought process so much better. It improves my ability to think clearly without crowded emotions taking over. I need to reprogramme myself and I take on a personal coach Kate to get me through. I know this requires total investment from me and with her on my team I know I can do it. I have so many external problems it takes me four years to finish the course (it's an eight-week course!). Then you fly a couple of months solo after the initial training.

Life, well, *my* life anyway, is so hard for me in those last five years that my coach even retires, but graciously honours her commitment and gets me through, even after she finishes working with clients. I do not want to be the one that got away! She gets me through.

Thank you, Kate, for delivering and thank you, Rob, for writing the most powerful simple set of tools that I've ever seen. What's unusual about Rob's model for success is that you don't need to spend a grand on a coach unless you choose to. Rob's not in it for the money, or he could have said, 'Buy my course!' You can buy the book, complete the book and fix your mindset easily for about £40! He's giving you the chance to change your life at almost cost price. He'd rather you got better than he got rich! There's not a great deal of those qualities about. You have the option of the full coach course which I take as I know I need a firm boot up my ass to sort myself out.

I call it, 'Thrive: learn the language of thinking!' No one teaches you how to think in the best way that you're capable of thinking. With this book and/or course, now you can! I just want control of my thoughts and rid the negative thoughts and loops; it is like the M25 in there.

If I swim up and down the swimming pool, about five current problems just fill my head and swim up and down with me. I can no longer shut off thinking. It is out of control. Even with all my meditation skills my mind is draining me, draining my mind and therefore my body battery!

Thrive helps me to recognise and fix my thought patterns and that's the one thing I've never been able to master by myself. With all the stuff I can do, I simply can't manage my own head. It is just running on automatic all the time. It is such an annoying space in my head. I want me to be helping me, not wearing me out. I always wonder why I am shit at mindfulness and now I know why! There is no 'now', no 'peace', just worries from the past and future. It's overcrowding my mind.

It cannot give me the cure for my reactive hypoglycaemia, but it leads me there most definitely with the new thinking beliefs I create, and now have. I want to take control of my thoughts and get them to be positive and orderly. My head is now an orderly space again. I will never be able to thank those at Thrive enough! Thank you! I recommend it to anyone. It's incredible and simple to understand. Try it!

One interesting thing is where you may have had negative dreams. Like with me, it is always turning up for a radio show or DJ set with the wrong equipment in place. It's not being prepared, so what will I do? Even in your dreams you will become confident. I'm not a professional but I think it's your subconscious running your powerful new programming throughout. You'll become much more confident in the dream state which is often the reflection of your waking thoughts, your self-esteem. You can cope!

## TRY AGAIN

Still, with my condition, at times I think I'm crazy, bouncing from one type of therapy to the next with more and more healing sessions. I start balancing my own chakras in mediation too. Powerful, but does not cure me. I do not want to look backwards ever again after I complete Thrive but I know I have to resolve something deeper to stand a chance of losing my hideous blood sugar condition.

I start looking at how the body stores fear on the internet. Fear is the opposite to trust and it's corrosive. If you've had your trust shattered many times, you experience a lack of trust in life, in the process of life. Even if you don't know this yet. I begin to realise from Thrive that I can trust myself again. Trust is something you create. I need to adjust my perspective on trust. I oversee my thoughts and emotions and ultimately change my perspective. I own my 'trust'. I just realised this. It has been broken but it cannot be taken. I own it, I create it and I want it back.

I can see now, looking back, had I known counselling was available, I would have taken help at the time. It was never mentioned and so it wasn't an option for me as it didn't exist. Perhaps my silence signalled I was ok, I was coping, nothing was a problem. Everyone used to think that not talking was better, even me! It made you stronger. It couldn't be a more backwards way of dealing with things for me. That now feels like a very old-fashioned approach.

Many of the bad events I've experienced have done a lot of damage internally, even if outwardly you don't know. You just brush it off and carry on. Trauma means business throughout your whole system, mind and body. That's why it carries that heavy duty name. It's doing a thing all of its own without your knowledge or permission! Therapy was not really a thing a decade ago and I really didn't know anything about. I'd never had any. I never needed any, or so I thought. People are starting to realise that naming your emotions helps you order them, process and better let them go. Plus, I've done what I thought was enough, being that I have sought a lot of counselling in the last few years.

I grew up in a time that was 'least said sooner mended'. Don't talk about it and it will go away. I learnt to live not speaking fully and so not ever quite processing right, although I thought I had. I can only see this when it is pointed out to me by my counsellor M in situation after situation. Silence has been my usual strategy in every complicated event and sometimes sadly it is the only option. Sometimes silence is necessary.

## I RETURN TO HYPNOTHERAPY, BUT WITH POWERFUL INFORMATION

With my third hypnosis person, they give me results from a temporary hypno gastric band which are usually permanent for others (just not me, of course). Armed with my ten years of knowledge from trial and elimination and learning so much from counselling, can we crack this together? I feel I almost know what I am looking for now. And if I fail then please help me and slap a band on at the end as a last resort and maybe it'll last longer this time. My homework has been done.

We devise a plan A and a plan B. We discuss analytics as the way to help me process the pain and grief I carry. I understand what we are doing but I only discover how it works as we go through it together. I've never really gone this deep into me before.

## SWEEPING, PROCESSING, RELEASING

Don't underestimate how hard it's been for me to come through three years of counselling, as well as completing the

Thrive Programme and then go back deeper into my past than ever before, safely, in hypnotherapy. We agree the band will be a last resort if we cannot locate the problem in my subconscious that is affecting my body.

Remember my subconscious responds to the band but only for ten to fourteen days. So, can we build it a better platform to start from? She explains to me that there are two types: analytics and suggestion. I'm responding to suggestion (the band) but it does not hold. Why not? To find the answers we have to back-scroll though my subconscious for what's taken eight sessions so far. I know I need one or two more, but I must publish this book for now!

She gets me down and simply waits to see where I land at a point in time, a place, and lets me do the work at my own pace. She's very patient and it's astonishingly powerful and emotionally very painful. It becomes clear in session after session that I've experienced a lot of trauma and more PTSD that I didn't know I had. My watch tracks my stress at the same level as when I sit at my desk writing this book! I can see clearly on the stats. It's a safe way to look back at things that you don't ever want to look back at again.

My body can take this in its stride, under her guidance and skill. My heart's not elevated at all in this subconscious replay of multiple agonising situations. But my physical and emotional reactions are enormous: tears, crying and sobbing for the whole session. At times I'm hyperventilating and grabbing my own head in anguish. I think some of it must be incredibly hard for her to listen to although it's her job and she's trained for it.

After the first four sessions I have to put myself to bed for a few hours, such is the level of emotional pain that has erupted in my head. It is more of the splitting headache and wiped out feeling that I have with all my previous counselling. I google it to find out what it is I am feeling afterwards. Turns out it's got a name and everything: the therapy hangover. And I'm right back there again reliving the 'the hangover' again and it's exhausting. It takes me forty-eight hours to recover each time. It totally wipes me out of energy, but we get closer to cleaning it all out. Personally, I've named this process sweeping. We sweep through my memories, my pain, and let it go.

I would never have understood this concept had I not taken on board analytics myself. Another unexpected life lesson. These are all the reactions that I would have had at the time, had it been safe. But if you're not safe, you can only try to get through, to survive the moment. It's fight, flight, or freeze and sometimes silence. You do whatever you can to survive at the time. My body was completely unable to cope with various situations over several decades.

Eventually we reach a place where I can sift through memories, and they do not bring an enormous upsetting reactions. We can 'sweep' around my subconscious and I scroll through my life until I eventually begin to bring up happy times. If I process it now my subconscious has no need to hold it anymore, storing all that fear and pain that had no outlet previously. The wave of emotions and real physical pain is so intense. It's astonishing. Your mind knows all that detail even after so, so many years when you think you're fine! I've forgotten most of it, but my younger mind hasn't forgotten a single detail.

Only once a skilled physiotherapist asked me if my back knots were trauma related as they were quite unusual. I replied, 'My counsellor will say so.' So, there is for me a huge part that stores my excess emotion in the muscular tissue of my body. It's like my body offsets the damage any way it can cope. I assume others might become unwell in other ways perhaps. I've quite a few female friends now who have been diagnosed with fibromyalgia. Most of them appear to have this connection of not great events! One friend Laura, who's a new addition in my life through parenting, has mostly recovered. She says it only flares up rarely now when she is overly stressed.

Historically it's the more Eastern way of medicinal thinking that emotions can cause ripples throughout the material structure of the body, affecting energy flow and organs. Think tai chi, acupuncture, reflexology, the five elements, meridians and so on. I'm still at a fairly junior stage of my learning here, but I love it. A little interest of mine that I read about, if ever I have time to read!

## BREATHWORK

Even when I feel resolved in the actual last session, I still have reactive hypoglycaemia! Still! I feel frustrated as I feel in my soul that I am so close. We have a clean sweep and are onto good things in my memories. I feel it will be the week I will get my result and I am disappointed not to have it.

I begin using my watch for breathwork in my daily routine. I know Wim Hof is really onto something by getting back to basics. Breathing properly is missing from our modern way of life. Especially if you experience stress frequently. I even take a cold water challenge around June time. I sit silent and calm for twenty minutes on my first attempt letting go of everything. I have no need to shake from the cold. I turn that off recognising it as survival that I don't need. I sit dead calm and still I can feel my 'brick' in my central forehead. That's where my illness resides! I've known this for a while now.

I search online, letting go of fear. I use the second ten-minute meditation video on Google and work very physically hard on my breathwork as guided. It takes ten minutes and I feel the whole inside of my head like a muscular tension or block lift up and out. I can feel the movement and cracking of air or tissue moving like when you have a massage.

My blocked feeling, that I thought often was stress, moves fully. I push it upwards and out and release. The brick, the crushed tight feeling, just goes. So far, it's been gone since.

Following years in spiritual energy work and thinking, nutritional changes, counselling, Thrive, hypnosis analytics, finally, I am ready and it releases with one breathwork video on YouTube!

I have been free from reactive hypoglycaemia now since late September 2023. I am eating fifty percent less calories than before. My diet is perfectly balanced already from ten years of trying to get it right, combined with all my knowledge from my nutritionist. It's a dream come true.

Obviously, it could snap back on any day. I know that more than anyone because it's turned back on so many times before, but I just keep going, hoping I've done *all* the groundwork to release the physical tension in my head that caused the illness throughout my body and I hope it will stay away forever. It was so hard trying to manage the symptoms starting to show up during daytime every three to four hours or so. Maybe it would have gone with breathwork alone, but I'll never know the answer to that. Also, would it have been like the band and the other attempts before that lasted two weeks? Honestly, I'll never know. Perhaps someone else can figure that out?

## HOW DOES IT FEEL?

At times I thought I'd never achieve this. It's demoralising time after time when yet another trial course of action doesn't work, again and again for a decade. I've invested thousands and my hopes and dreams into beating it, just to feel free. I thought it might never happen but if I gave up searching for the root cause in me I knew it would definitely never go. I kept going year after year, decade after decade. I hope that by sharing this other people can take this information and it might help them seek a way out. How many people have it and then it stops? I have no idea.

I make it clear that this is only my resolve. I cannot speak for other people's situations. I hope that by sharing my story it will help others think about options and possibly be noticed by medical science. As Western medical science still has no answers, self-help was the route I took as there were no other routes available to conquer this condition. At least none I knew about. There may be some somewhere I've missed. Maybe I did it all wrong and I don't care. It has worked... for now anyway! It's still working six months later. I'm still well. Time will tell.

I can't even believe I get to write this. I lived with it for twenty years. We could locate almost the approximate start date along with my diary entries from being so ill at festivals when no one else was. I do not know if it was one singular time or multiple events across many years.

I still cannot believe the day has come where I can speak of a positive outcome. For so long it was just a dream. I've not told many people. I guess I'm still cautious as it's failed so many times before. But we think I'm really onto something this time. I've rebuilt my foundations (Thrive) inside and out and reprogrammed my subconscious thinking for the better.

For these results to be accepted officially, I have to take the blood glucose test again to prove it. I would be happy to do so if it's ever required. I can tell you that my personal fifty percent reduction in food costs and food shopping time and doubled time in between meals is proof enough for me. I can go all night from just a small dinner with no supper (supper was a constant requirement for thirteen years).

The best feeling is I don't even wake up and want breakfast. I'm not even hungry after twelve hours over night. It feels just so free lying there in bed in the morning, every morning, not hungry! I know I can pass that test easily now. When I took it in my mid to late twenties I had to ram myself full of food at 8 p.m. just so I wouldn't shake and vomit by breakfast time. I felt hungry and ill, trying to get to the hospital that morning.

And it's water too. I was drinking a third more than I needed to each day. I'm now at the normal fluid intake level. I think my internal organs must be delighted to only have to process a half load, a normal amount.

I can also say now that my difficulty sleeping is not linked to reactive hypoglycaemia. The process of elimination was helpful. They are separate things. Now I can look at just that. I've already resolved around eighty percent of it in those thirteen years of trying to work it all out.

Halting reactive hypo has increased the number of nights I sleep right through. I sleep right through about twice a week now. Previously I would not ever sleep a solid night. It would have been one solid night in every two years or more. So having stable blood sugars has helped enormously.

There's still a bit to work on. It's always good to have projects!

## TRYING TO WORK!

I moved house twice last year alone and I even sold my rental property, closing that business after twenty years so it was like starting from fresh. There is so much change, even I struggle to keep up. Naturally there are several new desks along the way. Some are crap (and you know I like a nice desk) but they work all the same.

I custom build my current contemporary wooden desk as by now I want something unique. I buy an old bland 1980s chunky turned leg, oak coffee table for £20. I strip it down, cut up the top to from square edges, fit industrial matt black metal legs and finish it with a waterproof varnish. It is such a transformation that it makes it onto our group chat. This will be my writing desk and, well, the everything else desk! I have been writing this book on and off for four years around working, helping alongside carers to look after my disabled mother and sometimes her house, and then my two kids with the amount of time that the on/off ASD assessments take.

Being honest I do find it incredibly frustrating that I just can't work as much as I want to! Parenting… I don't think I've properly adjusted to it yet! It's just everything you do takes so freaking long when you've got kids! Who knew they'd fill up your life so much… it wasn't in the manual! (If there was a manual, I didn't read it!) I'm not asking for days or weeks off or holidays (I barely saw my friends in the last year), I just want to work enough to keep me sane! I need one thing in my life for me! And so, I *will* finish this book… or die trying! It has been quite hard at times. I can feel my face half sliding off through tiredness some days. I work over Christmas this year to squeeze out a few more precious working hours.

## EAT, SLEEP, WRITE, REPEAT

Sometimes you have to make big sacrifices to complete your vision. I only take most of the day off if I'm too tired to stand up and that's every month or two. This is the commitment that I need for this writing project, writing a book. Which turns out to be mostly all about editing. That's where the time goes! So, I have found that out for myself. Edit, edit, edit. Edit some more, then again and more… Fall asleep making editorial changes in your head. Then jump out of bed to write it on the pad next to the bed. Done (I think)… Plus the list by the computer and on your phone! Plus, further editing! It's quite astonishing!

I do want to get that work–life balance back again. Not that I'm very good at that. I know I don't have the best track record! I feel a couple of days off is long overdue. At least abstinence makes the beach grow fonder!

## I HAVE TO QUIT MY JOB AGAIN!

On top of all the change, life has made me choose a new path. Again! I can decorate with rest, but my kids do not yet both understand the point of rest. So adequate rest is sketchy although so much better than my old life. The business of parenting with my current family situation and being on call for my mum ends my job almost overnight. I have to give up my much-loved decorating business and work out what to do next. It is chaos in my head while I think through my options factoring in my noise limitations. Life flips me upside down again and tips me out all over the floor. Great! I love decorating. It is a great job helping people with all their interior or exterior designs.

I was once family parenting, then co-parenting and now I'm single parenting. I've seen a few angles. Honestly, I had no idea how hard single parenting would be and they don't get enough credit for it. I don't mean me. I mean others who have done it for years, decades or possibly since birth, like Laura. It was the first time I could recognise just how hard it must have been for her. I only guessed at what I presumed before. It's not quite the same.

My kids have some additional needs and that requires more time. It impacts the basics in life with such difficult mornings and I'm often kept on my feet till 10 p.m. and sometimes much later. Often the basic things become very complicated and other times it might be fine. You never know quite what might happen. It also affects the type of childcare setting and amount of time off school and then there's doctor, dentist and hospital appointments and regular sickness and all that stuff. Plus, schools always wants to take half terms, end of terms, summer holidays and even Christmas! Then there's a million bank holidays a year where I used to work extra! Recently a lot of king and queen days and training days and strike action days that are needed so they're hardly ever in school at all!

When I was in school it felt like I was always in school. Perspective plays a role here! Honestly, I never fully noticed until I was operating as a lone parent. It's quite a shock.

By the way, why is it referred to as 'single parent' with some sort of medieval name tag attached to it? Is it single in terms of meaning one or not dating as I still haven't figured that out? No one cares if you're married or not, partnered or not, dating, Tindering, matching, whatever! Whose business is it if I'm a Mrs, a Ms, a Miss or just me? Even my bank card finally just says *my* name! About time.

All I know is that as one person still thinking I can take on as much work as I like, it's not working out the way I want it to. I'm killing myself here trying to work around not being able to freaking work! It drives me nuts. Everything I want to do, I can't do, like provide an income from work. Get up and go to work? Nope, someone's sick again, not today! Half the time it's me sick because they infected me! It's a perpetual parent nightmare.

I think it's also fair to assume that the ten or twenty years I just pushed through by taking more caffeine were not good. Now my body utterly refuses. It firmly puts me on my ass, unable to go on. It's like hitting the wall. Before, I just broke through that tiredness. Not doing so couldn't be an option. Since burnout or the children thing there's no more reserve left in the tank. I just lie face down on the bed for several hours. It's so boring but my body declares this is the only option left.

All of this leads me to believe that if I was employed I'm pretty sure (absolutely sure) I'd have been fired within three months, making it excruciatingly hard to hold down a real employed job! I'm grateful I'm self-employed as at least I don't have to worry about keeping my job. My adored, so rewarding, successful decorating business. Well, I didn't worry about keeping my decorating job right up until I lost it! I didn't see that coming!

Marvellous… so, I have to start over again taking all my knowledge and skills with me… growing! It's more like being snapped in half like a stretchy stress toy, but do note the word growing instead. It always sounds more positive.

## I'M A WRITER!

I also knew I would not decorate forever. It was just a feeling really. So, I'm so excited for the release of this book following years of learning this new skill called writing! (Something I always sucked at.) I think being somewhat dyslexic has shown up, not just in my hilarious spelling and inability to see mistakes. That's obviously going to happen. But mostly as I tend to write sentences within the paragraph all jumbled up. Just like reading words, typically I'll have the right start and finish, but the middle can be a bit of a free for all! Much time has been spent trying to work out the correct order of a paragraph… and each paragraph! Plus, editing, marketing, promotion and so on. This won't be the last thing I write either. I feel there's something else. I've learnt all these skills, so might as well make use of them.

Somewhere down the line I will test to see if my ears will hold up to the large amount of studio work required to voice this book. I'm not sure they can currently. At least I wrote it, so reading my own script should be easier on my eyes. I've seen each sentence fifty times by now.

## ART

I am venturing into new territory with artwork, which I've been thinking about for five years. I have colour now where I used to have music. Colour is the basis to my life now: colour and calm. I love it! I'm not interested in brushwork painting, I'm into fluid painting, resin art and 3D pictures. Plus, I still get to paint, just on a much smaller scale. Did all the chaos lead me discreetly to the canvas?

I've many other plans but usually I work quietly, without speaking, until the project is complete. Well, apart from a few friends who have had to suffer hearing about the book project for the whole four years! Good work, guys!

## DRAMA!

I apply to be an extra on *Vikings: Valhalla* as it is the perfect job for me filming in Ireland and it's somewhere I've always wanted to go. It's drama and drama that I can do because I don't have to read and remember loads of lines! I can finally work, travel and be on a film set. It is like a moment of clarity, something that I desire. I am so excited that day having read about the opportunity in the news. I get the form in my hand and know it is perfect for me. Then reality smashes me back down to earth hard for two reasons. I realise I can't go because of this parenting job. The kids don't travel well and what about that school thing? And there's my ears, which are broken, so I can't be around crowds of people let alone any noisy battle scenes. So, I shelve my idea. For now. But I assume one day I can be free, right? It's just another 'not for now' piece of work. I don't know about my ears though. They may never be free again.

## MY NEXT BUSINESS IS QUIET AND ALTERNATIVE

Following training I'm starting my next new business soon and at last, I will get a bloody certificate! It's a totally new line of work for me. It will be working with people and wellbeing in a field I've never professionally looked at before. I'm excited for this chapter.

Ultimately, one day I want to plant trees… hug the planet a little bit! That's how I want to be involved in the future when I can, when time permits me.

And perhaps I'll dip into property again but not right now.

I've a few other things in mind, but I only focus on one or two projects at once.

## A NEW PAIR OF EARS!

Here's some very interesting news. In the time I've written this book, there is now a treatment available for hyperacusis. It is overwhelming to read this completely out of the blue and to begin thinking there may be a chance for me. I was told there was no surgery available the last time I asked here in 2022. From nothing to some hope! I cry when I read this news online from America and I set my sights on getting there after contacting the company.

Specialising in hearing loss and hyperacusis, this surgeon has operated on around fifty people with a success rate of around seventy percent. Firstly, I found this in the USA but now there's also one chance I can get it right here in the UK. I found this news online in 2023.

I am in the initial stages of talking with my potential surgeon. We do not know yet if I will be a suitable candidate and whether it will work or fail. I never think about what if it works, only that I must try. My only concern is if it makes the condition worse, then I won't be able to live normally. That, I cannot risk. It will cost a lot of money (investment). Paying privately appears to be the only option.

I'm happy to be a human Guinea pig, even if it fails for me, the surgeons will learn and it can go towards medical research trials and studying the condition and potentially help in other cases. Maybe one day it will be available on the NHS. I've read it affects around 1 in 50,000 people, so it's not really a priority.

## DO I MISS DJING?

People often ask me this question. I've been to enough concerts (the last one was Chase & Status at Newmarket Nights). I've bumped into Sam from Vibe Breakfast a few times recently as our paths crossed again. We both said, having left presenting and DJing, people still ask us if we miss it. Hell no, not for a second. Honestly, we did enough. I made enough shows and played enough nightclubs to last a lifetime and she feels the same. Plus, we both have a rattle in our ears and the same recurring dreams about going to a gig and not having the right records to play! Yep, I still have that dream but rarely now! (I literally had that dream again last month. Dang it!)

## DO I NEED MUSIC?

I'd certainly like to have the option to enjoy music again just normally, not loudly. I don't think much about what I can't do. There's no point. Concerts are a luxury I don't need as I've learnt to live with almost no music at all these past few years, so I'm used to it. I've had a lot of practice at living without music. It's just the opposite from my younger days.

It would be helpful (let alone incredible) to be able to watch a film normally with sound on the TV in the lounge with my children as I can't anymore. I mostly watch with subtitles and sound at level four to six. It's not very exciting! It's more the basic everyday things that would be useful. I'd like to be able to cook dinner when the kids are in the kitchen with a friend over without their chatting giving me a headache. I can get headaches just from people or kids being in the house if it's lengthy and in the same room.

The most basic need from music is to change your mood. I'd love to be able to work out with music or dance. I can't even imagine what it feels like to dance. Anyway, it's just a luxury I used to take for granted. And those days where you just go, 'Oh, not more flipping laundry to put away, I suck at it!' Here sometimes even I crack and put a track on as quietly as possible on my phone just to cover over four minutes or so of tedious tidying. Any more and I'll get a headache anyway. I pay a heavy price if I listen to three or four tracks. Self-harming with music is just silly really. Although I still do it, very occasionally, out of desperation! So yes, I do need music like everyone else. I just can't have it right now, if ever.

Rarely, me and Girl put a track on whilst I'm cooking. She likes this Ed Sheeran track and it's got no beats so that's more manageable for me. I can do that. Just to be able to listen to some music with her would be magic or in the car which is how I grew up. She likes playing the keyboard as well, so I would like to be able to listen to some of that for more than just a few minutes at a time. She's so helpful and plays with the volume low to help me.

I do feel that when Girl is sixteen there will be some kind of concert. Highly likely I presume for any growing kid. But I can't be there, not if she's watching her favourite band or performing music or dancing on stage. Obviously, it's very disappointing knowing I can't be with my kids for those big moments but that's how life is now. I will never attend a football match. Or any event with a large crowd. I'd like to just sit in a bar with music but that's just not possible.

I would love to able to run or kickbox for fun again but again it's not essential, is it? It's just something I used to like. The vibrations, the loose bits in my ears, mean big movements are all too painful. I can walk, I can march flat out, that's enough. I'm grateful. I still swim in a slightly adapted manner with virtually no splashing! It made me become a neat swimmer as half an hour with underwater bubbles is noisy. You'd never even think about that, would you…? It's very loud for me.

## LESSONS LEARNT

Dream, work, plan, achieve.
Survive, cry, adapt, evolve, eventually thrive!
Be kind. It costs nothing.

I also fractured my toe just a tiny bit! I didn't even notice for three months so it doesn't really warrant the ink used in this sentence. Who knew there could be a good type?

## COLLECT NEW FRIENDS!

They all have a little something to teach you or assist with in life. Call on them when you need them, and they will do the same. It's a happy flow of energy. Laugh with them, cry with them and love them all individually. Every one of you is freaking awesome! Thank you for gracing my life. I hope one day to have more time to spend with you. My life has been a little manic so far, hasn't it? I'm just landing back in my life, my time zone, again. I've rebuilt me with your help. Not all of you get a mention here but you know who you are.

I thank my family and my parents who have supported me throughout all. Never wavering, never judging and always there for me. I truly know how lucky I am that I was gifted with good parents. I would have made this chapter of my life without you, but it would have been so much harder for us. Dealing with and learning to manage chronic stress and beat it has been challenging. I never knew it could kick my ass so hard. I have learnt much. I thank you for helping me when I most needed it and in general all the other times you were there for me.

Thank you to my children who crack me up. We laugh so much. You hug me when I cry, and some days bring me peanut rice cakes for breakfast. You require me to dig deeper as a person to not give up and expand on what I thought I knew. I think they will be surprised and hopefully impressed when they find out I've written a whole book... a *big* book! I like to work quietly on projects... Surprise!

## TEAM

Keep your contacts and build a strong team around you. To delegate and appreciate others is important to me. I put these in a very rough timeline.

Lin, Mum number two, is assisting me with life and editing on this book.

J, accountant. I'm no use with numbers. He's my right hand in business and a mine of knowledge for more than twenty years. I thank you for your continual calm, helpful and friendly approach.

Sally, PA and friend. To quote her, 'God bless' Sal who's departed to a higher place. I love you, my friend. I hope you hear Wham in heaven. That would be great. Love to your family.

Emma, singing lessons. We had such a laugh and I learnt. That's the best way to learn, right?

Carol, spiritual teacher. I learnt to look at life in full. Thank you for giving your time.

Big Fish Photography. Credit where it's due. You're amazing. I love working with you.

M, artistic director, Toni & Guy. I enjoy our chats and your work, obviously!

KT, naturopathic nutritional therapist. Fixed my body from the inside; she rebuilt me! Oh, and for sorting out peri! Peri is a pain in the ass! Perimenopause is such a stupid word from the 1930s (I think) that I quit using it.

The Samaritans. Giving their time for free and for when you trained Mum. It takes a very special type of person to do that job.

M, counsellor. Knows more about me than anyone else and has not only rescued me from my lowest depths but taught me to self-notice the chemical imbalances and states that the human mind will place on the body to help you cope. It makes for better wellbeing, quicker insight, recovery, resolve and emotional wellness.

Kate, Thrive coach. Wonderful woman who supported me on and off for over four years of trying to achieve a two-month course, even after she retired! My freaking life was utterly ridic for a while with external events!

X, reiki and energy flow. So much healing capacity from your knowledge and skills.

R, acupuncture. Makes you feel more comfortable in your own skin. I'm learning from your book.

Publishing Push. Publishers helping me get my ten-year dream finished.

I would also like to thank the NHS and all the staff I've worked with and all those who saved my life twice. Although they'll say they're just doing their job, it's more than a job, isn't it? Fixing unfixable health situations?

Thank you. A *big* thank you.

## TIMING

This is what I can share for now. I've learnt most things are usually about timing. Work happens at the right time. Projects happen at the right time. People happen at the right time. Life orders time. It's called synchronicity (so Lin says)! Sometimes things happen at the wrong time! That's always a big lesson and you can't do anything about that. You'll learn at least, unless you want to keep repeating your mistakes!

I've been sky high, felt beaten down, been stretched and I grew. I'm older and I'm wiser. I have understood the teachings from situations. I might not have it perfect, but I get it!

Health is an important balance and if you're sporting cracks and breaks, when possible, invest in you.

Healing starts with time. For a long time, I had no time. Healing could only begin at the right time.

I am also keen to get in some of my downtime that's eluded me for nearly a decade, in much the same way as when I DJed for six years with barley any gaps! I even like the pub now! Having never mastered the pub in my twenties I get it now. I can do a pub! Well, if I have the time! I find myself almost hallucinating about sitting in a beer garden, chatting to friends on a warm summer's evening. Put in some hours of nothing much at the pub? It sounds so perfect now! Perspective!

Time for walking, cycling and getting back to my racket sports (without the tennis ball hitting the racket and causing minor ear pain) would be nice. Nice but again not necessary. I'm used to managing it.

A splash of swimming and rock climbing would be neat. And then the biggies: snowboarding and surfing. Following 2022 and a very near attempt at a holiday I even got my wetsuit ready (it's just quietly sitting in the wardrobe). I had to cancel three days before although I was kind of expecting it. I haven't had much luck with holidays lately. It's getting closer. That's the best way to view it… it's a work in progress.

Nikki Elise x

Evolve.

The end…

Only joking. This is just the beginning of the middle!

'Hey, kids. Who swiped all my paint?'

One last thing!

A month before this book was sent to the publishers, Girl finally received her diagnosis. We have it and we did it together.

Girl finally got a diagnosis of autism and ADHD. There's always something new for me to learn.

I strongly suspected ADHD for several years from the chaos that filled my house. Finally, it has brought clarity to us all and I can be sure of what we need to try to achieve to help. Well, sometimes it will help, other times nothing works but overall, I've a far better chance!

Girl can be sure too. The confusion for her and emotional damage has been hard to watch. She feels such relief at knowing she is a good kid and not the bad one she has felt all along, no matter what I said to try to reassure her. We're talking about self-esteem here and it's vitally important to health and wellbeing. We can learn to manage it better. So far, I only had the internet and my instincts!

We have a support plan. We can learn.

We're on it.